Macro-Economics
in Question

Macro-Economics in Question:
The Keynesian-monetarist orthodoxies and the Kaleckian alternative

Malcolm C. Sawyer

**READER IN ECONOMICS,
UNIVERSITY OF YORK**

M. E. SHARPE, INC., ARMONK, NEW YORK

Library of Congress Cataloging in Publication Data
Sawyer, Malcolm C.
   Macroeconomics in question.
   Bibliography: p.
   Includes index.
   1. Macroeconomics.   2. Keynesian
economics.   3. Kalecki, Michal.   I. Title.
HB172.5.S95   339   82-3221
ISBN 0-87332-218-5   AACR2
ISBN 0-87332-220-7 (pbk.)

Printed in Great Britain by
The Thetford Press Ltd, Thetford, Norfolk

Contents

List of Figures

List of Tables

List of Main Symbols Used*

B	Bonds
c	Cost of capital services
C	Consumption
d	Degree of monopoly
d_k	Demand (by one agent) for good k
D_k	Demand (by all agents) for good k
e	Elasticity (usually of demand)
e_c	Elasticity of costs with respect to output
e_m	Elasticity of mark-up with respect to output
f	Input prices
F	Fixed costs
g	Growth of output/productivity
G	Government expenditure
H	High-powered money
i	Rate of discount
I	Investment
IM	Imports
K	Capital equipment
L	Labour
m	Mark-up of price over costs
M	Money
n	Price of material inputs
N	Material inputs
p	Price (of output)
p^e	Expected price
P	Profit rate on sales
q	Cost of capital goods
q_i	Output of firm i
Q	Output (total)

*A symbol which is only used within a few pages is not listed.

r	Rate of interest (real)
R	Revenue of firms (net in Chapter 2; sales in Chapter 5)
s	Reserve ratio of banks
s_p	Propensity to save out of profits
s_w	Propensity to save out of wages/labour income
s_i	Share of output (of firm i) (Chapter 5)
s_k	Supply (by one agent) of good k (Chapter 3)
S	Savings
S_k	Supply (by all agents) of good k
t	Rate of taxation
T	Target real wage
TX	Taxation
U	Unemployment
U_N	'Natural' rate of unemployment
v	Capital-output ratio
V	Wealth
w	Nominal wage
W	Total wages/labour income
X	Exports
y	Real income/output
Y	Nominal income
δ	Rate of depreciation
ρ	Internal rate of return
π	Total profits
$\triangle x$	Change in variable x
$\dot{x}$	Proportionate rate of change of variable x

Preface

This book has two central purposes. The first is to present a rather more critical view of the Keynesian and monetarist approaches to macro-economics than is usually found in major macro-economics text-books. The second is to present an alternative approach to macro-economics, derived in the main from the work of Michal Kalecki. It will become apparent below that the major difference between the conventional approaches to macro-economics and the Kaleckian one arises from a basic difference over the nature of a modern capitalist economy. The conventional approaches rest on a perfectly competitive view of the world whilst the Kalecki approach draws on an oligopolistic view.

The book has been written to be accessible to undergraduate students of economics who have taken a basic second-year degree-level course in macro-economics (as represented by text-books such as Branson, 1979; Gordon, 1981). Particularly in Chapters 2–4 a knowledge of conventional macro-economics is required. References are provided in the text and in footnotes for those wishing to pursue particular topics further. However I hope that this book will contain much of interest for professional economists.

It is always difficult to isolate reasons for writing a book and for advocating a particular approach to economics. In the case of this book and its advocacy of the Kaleckian approach three influences were at work. The first one arose from my research on industrial economics (some of which was undertaken with Sam Aaronovitch and reported in Aaronovitch and Sawyer, 1975). From that research it was clear that industries and the economy were dominated by a few large firms, and we sought to explore some of the consequences of that domination. Within industrial economics research focuses on questions like how do more oligopolised industries compare with less oligopolised ones in respect of price, profits, technical innovation, etc. But there is also a need to explore the macro-economic consequences of an oligopolised economy. Indeed it may well be that the macro-effects of oligopoly are rather more important than the micro resource allocation effects.

The second influence arose from research work on the determinants of inflation (some of which was reported in Henry, Sawyer and Smith, 1976). This had the effect of emphasising to me that the conventional approach rested on perfectly competitive assumptions with the view that excess demand lies at the heart of inflation. Yet the conventional approach did not rest on secure empirical or theoretical foundations. But the expectations-augmented Phillips' curve often played a central role in macro-economic theory, and the related concept of the 'natural' rate of unemployment has been particularly influential in policy discussions. Further, whilst target real wage bargaining and cost-plus pricing received much empirical support, their theoretical base was underdeveloped and their consequences for macro-economic theory largely unexplored.

The third influence was the reaction to the state of macro-economics. When I first learnt macro-economics, optimism in Keynesian macro-economics and the power of Keynesian demand management policies to solve problems of unemployment and inflation was at its height. The strong impression was that appropriate adjustment of taxation and public expenditure would keep the economy on course, with changes in the exchange rate there to prevent balance of payments problems. In Britain, low growth and cost inflation were seen as yet unresolved problems but the use of informal planning and incomes policies appeared as likely solutions. In the light of experience this optimism gradually disappeared, leaving a disenchantment with Keynesian economics, and particularly its ability to deal with problems like inflation. Within macro-economics, the monetarist revival placed many question marks against the Keynesian analysis (beginning with the Phillips' curve), and emphasising the crucial role played in Keynesian economics by price rigidity. Yet whilst monetarism succeeded in undermining Keynesian economics, the monetarist alternative did not present a picture of the economy which I could recognise. Its assumptions of perfect competition did not accord with research findings in industrial economics, and its use of the expectations-augmented Phillips' curve did not accord with much research work on inflation. More strikingly as unemployment rose in Britain from the mid-'sixties onwards, from a base of around a quarter of a million to a level of three million, monetarism and its offshoots (particularly the 'rational' expectations school) produced more and more sophisticated models which appeared to deny the possibility of any substantial unemployment. Thus monetarism did not appear to match major aspects of the real world, despite frequent protestations of beliefs in positive economics.

The work of Michal Kalecki permitted these three influences to coalesce in terms of my own thinking. For his work included the major Keynesian ideas, such as the principle of effective demand, the importance of investment, etc. (which he had discovered independently of Keynes), and yet incorporated the notion that in capitalist economies industries were typically oligopolistic. Further, despite adherence to the ideas of effective demand, his work provided some explanation of failures to reach full employment.

In many respects this book is in the nature of an interim report. It seeks to outline an alternative framework for macro-economics, whilst recognising that many loose ends are left. Notably the foreign and financial sectors have been treated very summarily. There is also a need to extend the analysis in terms of its dynamics. In each of these cases the approach given here provides a starting point for further extensions.

Some of the ideas in this book were tried out on students taking a course on Macro-Economics Alternatives at the University of York in the summer of 1981, and I am grateful for comments received from those taking that course. I am particularly grateful to Sam Aaronovitch, David Currie and Bernard Stafford who read and commented on a first draft at short notice when they were all particularly busy. Needless to say they are not necessarily commited to anything said below. Thanks are also due to Chris Robinson, Audrey Hewlett and Julia Raine who typed the manuscript. Finally, this book would not have seen the light of day without the forebearance of my family over the time and energy devoted to its writing, and for this I am particularly grateful.

September 1981

1 The Nature of Macro-Economics

Introduction

The publication of Keynes' *General Theory* (Keynes, 1936) sig-
nalled the emergence of macro-economics as a distinct area of
economics, and for the first thirty or so years of its separate
existence macro-economics was largely dominated by the Keynesian approach. The last fifteen years have seen the challenge of the
monetarists to the Keynesian orthodoxy, as well as a questioning of
the correspondence between Keynesian economics and the economics in the *General Theory*.[1] The principle of effective demand,
which constituted a major part of the break-through by Keynes, was
discovered independently by Kalecki and published in 1934/5 in
Polish.[2] For numerous reasons, of which the language of origin was
one, it was the version of Keynes rather than that of Kalecki, which
was read, taught and applied. The approach of Kalecki differs from
that of Keynes in many important respects, and more sharply from
the approach of the monetarists. The major purpose of this book is
to argue that the approach of Kalecki provides a more fruitful and
realistic starting point for macro-economic analysis of a developed
capitalist economy. In the first part, we argue that although there
are some important differences between Keynesians and monetarists there are some basic similarities, and that many of the shared
features do not provide a useful or realistic macro-analysis. In the
second part we begin the development of an alternative macro-
economics which is inspired by the approach of Kalecki, though we
do not follow the writings of Kalecki slavishly. We use the terms
alternative macro-economics and Kaleckian approach synony-
mously below to indicate that approach.

The dominance of macro-economics by the Keynesian approach
in the period from the late-'thirties to the late-'sixties and the
subsequent largely successful challenge by the monetarists spilled
over into policy-making. Particularly in the nineteen-sixties, the
governments of Britain and the United States pursued policies of

seeking to control the level of employment and output by manipulation of public expenditure and taxation, with the government
budget geared towards the achievement of full employment and
other macro-economic objectives rather than balance of the government budget. These policies were often labelled Keynesian, and
indeed the first quarter of a century of the post-war world has been
labelled the Keynesian era.[3] However, so-called Keynesian policies
were often based on a simplistic version of the Keynesian model
which focused on the level of aggregate demand, with a tendency to
overlook the money supply implications of any government deficit
which resulted, and some would argue overlooking the balance of
payments consequences as well (Eltis, 1976). Consideration of
aggregate demand diverted attention from the ability and willingness of firms to produce output to meet demand, and the consequences which low levels of unemployment (particularly over a
sustained period) and relatively high levels of demand would have
for inflation. From the mid-'sixties onwards, Keynesian economics
came under increasing criticism, and the world-wide rise in the pace
of inflation contributed to the force of that criticism. Keynesian
economics had found inflation difficult to deal with adequately
(discussed below pp.69–75) and since sustained inflation requires
a comparable increase in the money supply, whether as a cause or a
consequence of inflation, this led to a concern over money. The rise
(or perhaps resurgence) of monetarism began with publications by
Friedman and associates (Friedman and Schwartz, 1963; Friedman
and Meiselman, 1963) which argued that the money supply was a
more potent factor than autonomous expenditure in determining
economic activity, and by implication monetary policy was a more
effective instrument for controlling the economy than fiscal policy.
However that debate could be contained within the *IS-LM*
framework which was used to characterise the Keynesian approach
(discussed below pp.45–54). But monetarists were soon arguing
that there was not a long-run trade-off between inflation and
unemployment which has been postulated by many Keynesians in
the form of the Phillips' curve (see Chapter 4), and that the
economy moved quickly to the 'natural' rate of unemployment
(Friedman, 1968). This, and later more sophisticated models, suggested that a private enterprise economy possessed strong stabilis-
ing properties if left to itself, and that governments were not
required to pursue stabilisation policies to maintain full
employment.[4]

During the 'seventies, governments often moved away from avowedly Keynesian policies to emphasising monetary, if not monetarist, policies.[5,6] Much of the debate in macro-economics was seen in terms of Keynesians versus monetarists, even though precise definitions of those terms proved difficult.[7] However, the ground for the debate has been increasingly dictated by the monetarists with emphasis placed on the role of money supply increases in determining the rate of inflation and on the importance of the supply side of the economy in determining the levels of employment and output. Indeed, it could be argued that these points have been largely conceded by Keynesians in the sense that *in the long run* they hold. The debate has focused on questions like how fast the economy moves to the supply-determined level of employment (i.e. the 'natural' rate of unemployment), or how quickly changes in the money supply affect the rate of inflation.

We do not attempt precise definitions of Keynesian and monetarist here. In Chapter 3 we implicitly define those terms by indicating the nature of the theories and positions which have been associated with each of those terms. Because of the dominance of the Keynesians and monetarists, there is a tendency to place any author or idea into one of those categories. However, we do not use the term Keynesian to include those who describe themselves as post-Keynesian (Eichner and Kregel, 1976; Eichner, 1979; and issues of the *Journal of Post-Keynesian Economics*) or those associated with the Cambridge (England) school (e.g. Nicholas Kaldor and Joan Robinson). Indeed, some of the propositions of those groups are used as critiques of the Keynesian and monetarist positions.

It will be argued below (especially in Chapter 3) that Keynesians and monetarists share a common 'vision' of the world (or more accurately the capitalist world). They differ over questions such as the interest-elasticity of the demand for money or the speed of adjustment of the economic system to the 'natural' rate of unemployment. Such questions are seen as resolvable by empirical observation and econometric estimation. In policy terms, these differences spill over into questions like the relative importance attached to fiscal and monetary policy, and whether governments should attempt to 'fine-tune' the economy. The outcome of these debates can be of considerable policy significance. A government which believed that the economy is strongly self-stabilising would forego increasing aggregate demand during a recession, whether by fiscal or monetary means, in the belief that such stimulation was unnecessary (and might well argue that it would have harmful inflationary consequences). If the belief in self-stabilisation were mistaken, then foregoing expansionary policies during a recession would inflict unnecessary misery in terms of unemployment and loss of output.

An important element of the common 'vision' of Keynesians and monetarists is the assumption that the supply-side of the economy is perfectly competitive.[8] The perfect competition approach suggests a harmonious equilibrium outcome in which the interests of various groups in society are reconciled. It also suggests that observed outcomes result from choices made by the people involved (as will be apparent in our discussion of unemployment below pp.162–166). The Kaleckian approach, in contrast, starts from an oligopolistic view of the world, which we argue in Chapter 5 provides a more realistic starting point for the analysis of a modern capitalist economy. The oligopolistic approach brings conflict between groups to the fore, particularly that between capital and labour. It will also be seen that many observed outcomes (particularly the level of unemployment and output) do not correspond to choices made by individuals, but rather are dictated by the over-all operation of the economy. Thus, in the case of unemployment, its level is not determined by workers choosing between employment and unemployment (as in the monetarist approach) but fluctuates around a level at which wage demands are restrained such that real wages grow in line with productivity.

In the monetarist view, unemployment hovers around the 'natural' rate of unemployment and is, in an important sense, voluntary. In the Keynesian view, unemployment arises from a malfunctioning of the system, mainly a lack of aggregate demand, which can be corrected by appropriate government action. In contrast, in the Kaleckian approach unemployment serves to rein back the demands of labour for higher real wages to a level which is compatible with the profit demands of oligopolists. Unemployment may also arise for reasons of deficiency of aggregate demand, which is inevitable in a capitalist economy which is inherently cyclical for reasons explored in Chapter 6.

It is significant that in the Keynesian/monetarist theories, the division of income between wages and profits is largely ignored.[9] The distribution of income is important in the alternative approach in a number of related ways. Savings by the private sector are influenced by the distribution of income between wages and profits, and the demand for investment influenced by profits and profitability. The distribution between wages and profits is strongly influenced by the real wage demands of labour and the profit objectives of firms. The reconciliation of those forces also influences the level of output and employment, with unemployment serving to rein back the effective demands of labour and excess capacity the demands of capital.

The argument that the underlying 'visions' of the world held by Keynesians and monetarists are basically similar can be met with the response that these common elements are correct and valid, and that the debate between the two schools of thought is concerned with tidying up a few loose ends. There are a number of points to be made on that response. We indicated above that the Keynesian/monetarist approach adopted an atomistic competition view of the world whilst the Kaleckian approach took an oligopolistic view. It could be objected that the evidence outlined in Chapter 5 supporting the oligopolistic view rather than the atomistic competitive one merely concerns the *assumptions* of the models whereas no attention need be paid to assumptions and the predictions should be tested directly (Friedman, 1953). We would argue that if, for example, one wished to predict the relative speeds of a stone and of a feather in air when released from a height and were provided with two alternative theories one of which was based on assumptions of a vacuum and the other on the presence of air, then one would tend to prefer the latter to the former. This does not mean that the latter theory is necessarily better since the former may have features which offset its less realistic assumptions. But it creates a presumption in favour of the latter. In the case of macro-economics, we know that very considerable research effort has failed to resolve the outstanding differences between Keynesians and monetarists. We would expect that research over many years would be required to dispose of a particular approach, and we have to make an initial judgement as to which approach is likely to be the more fruitful long before we can hope to have sufficient evidence on the accuracy or otherwise of the predictions of a particular approach.[10] It should be noted that the structure of the economy evolves over time, and the nature of the appropriate theory may change over time.[11]

Economic theories not only serve to help or hinder our understanding of the way in which the economy operates, but also condition the way in which people think and behave. The effect of Keynesian economics on public attitudes to the level of public expenditure and budget deficits in the post-war era is a good illustration of that point. An economic theory (such as monetarism) which strongly suggests that unemployment is largely voluntary and a theory (such as the one discussed below) which suggests that unemployment serves to discipline the workers clearly would have different impacts on the way in which unemployment and the economic system is regarded.

The dominance of the Keynesian/monetarist approach has meant that most empirical work published in the academic journals has been within that broad framework. Such work is often concerned with the estimation of relevant coefficients or with discriminating between alternative hypotheses within the broad common framework. Little attention has been given to empirically com-paring the Keynesian/monetarist approach with the Kaleckian approach (and indeed that is likely to be a huge task). Further, relatively little attention has been paid to the estimation of relevant coefficients within the Kaleckian approach. Empirical work on the consumption function provides an example. Much work has been undertaken on estimating the marginal propensity to consume out of income, and on testing the validity of alternative theories such as the Keynes' proposition, the life-cycle and the permanent income hypothesis (discussed on pp.18–23 below). There has been re-latively little work on the idea that the propensities to consume out of labour income and out of property income are (economically) significantly different.[12] However, when economists have been faced with problems such as explaining pricing behaviour or with preparing economic forecasts, then they have often used parts of the Kaleckian approach rather than the Keynesian/monetarist approach. For example, price changes are seen as determined mainly by cost changes rather than by excess demand, investment is related to changes in output rather than the rate of interest.

The notion that economic theories are discarded when they appear to be rejected by the weight of evidence seems to us to take an overly optimistic view of the way in which the economics profession operates.[13,14] The response to evidence contradicting an hypothesis is likely to consist of a mixture of casting doubt on the statistics or the econometric technique used and of modifying the hypothesis. The description of the fate of the Phillips' curve by Katouzian (1980) illustrates this when he writes that the Phillips relationship was originally not much more than a statistical generalisation from history. . . . Once it was presented it was not difficult to 'discover' some kind of theoretical basis for it. . . . One or two critical doubts about the basis of the relationship were cast, but they were simply ignored. Then, towards the end of the last decade massive *indirect* evidence —i.e. the concurrent increase in the rates of inflation and unemployment —began to shake up conviction in the Phillips relationship. Nonetheless a theoretical 'solution' to 'explain' even this massive 'anomaly' was soon discovered. . . . It was discovered that the Phillips Curve has been shifting 'outwards'. But the 'solution' is inherently untestable for it depends on a knowledge of the *expected* rate of inflation and the circular concept of 'the natural rate of unemployment'.[15]

There is a number of differences between the Keynesian, monetarist and Kaleckian approaches which are inherently untestable. The question of whether the relationship between labour and capital is essentially harmonious or in conflict would fall into this category. It is also difficult to test whether the appropriate set of aggregates has been selected for analysis. However, there are some areas where the Kaleckian approach can be compared on an empirical level with the Keynesian and monetarist approaches. In Chapter 7, we argue that there is empirical evidence which supports the Kaleckian approach, sufficient to make a *prima facie* case for paying serious attention to that approach.

The assumption of perfect competition is at the heart of most conventional economic theory, whether micro and macro. In those areas of economics which investigate markets and industries more closely, the assumption of perfect competition is often dropped. This is particularly so in industrial economics, where much discussion revolves around which variant of oligopoly theory is 'best' rather than over the use of perfect competition theory or of oligopoly theory. In labour economics, matters are not so clear-cut with many labour economists adhering to a neo-classical approach. Nevertheless there is a substantial body of opinion there which argues for a different approach stressing the role of trade unions, the effects of inter-group wage comparisons and the like. The alternative approach cannot incorporate all the complexities which industrial economists and labour economists would stress. However, we argue that relatively simple representations can be devised which incorporate many of the major determinants of prices and wages relevant for macro-economics which are stressed by industrial economists and by non-neo-classical labour economists.

The case against the Keynesian/monetarist orthodoxy and for the

Kaleckian alternative is argued on four broad criteria. First, we argue that the starting-point of the Kaleckian approach (the oligopolistic view of the world) is a more realistic one than that used by the Keynesians and monetarists (the atomistic view). For the reasons given above we feel that assumptions are of importance in the construction of a theory. Second, in Chapter 7 we outline the case that the predictions of the Kaleckian approach are supported by the evidence, whereas in many key areas (such as unemployment) the Keynesian and monetarist approaches are not. Third, we argue in Chapter 4 that in the key area of inflation theory the conventional approach has lacked consistency. Finally, the Kaleckian approach highlights certain key features, such as the division between labour income and property income, which are ignored in the conventional approaches.

The nature of macro-economics

Macro-economics is often seen as more relevant than micro-economics. In part, this reflects the origins of modern macro-economics in Keynes' response to the depression of the 'twenties and 'thirties. Macro-economics continues to deal with topics such as unemployment and inflation which are at the centre of public discussion of economic policy. In contrast, resource allocation, whilst central to micro-economics, is peripheral to most public discussion of economics. A major reason why macro-economics appears relevant is that the variables in the analysis are labelled with 'real world' names. Thus macro-economics deals with variables such as consumption, savings, investment, unemployment. These variables are measured, more or less accurately, in national income accounts and other government statistical sources, and appear to correspond to 'real world' magnitudes. In contrast, micro-economics typically deals with abstract goods, which are not intended to have real world counterparts. Thus, a consumer is often portrayed as maximising a utility function $U(x_1, x_2, . . ., x_n)$ subject to a budget constraint. But nothing further is said about the nature of good 1, good 2, . . ., good n. Labels may sometimes be attached to variables, but it is not intended that those labels have significance. For example, we may call good 1 apples, good 2 bananas, . . . but the analysis does not in any way rest on the properties of apples, bananas, etc. In contrast, in macro-economics when a variable is labelled, say, employment it is intended to have some of the properties of 'real world' employment.[16]

The measurement of some of the key variables of macro-economics cannot be determined from *a priori* theoretical reasoning but only in an empirical manner. For example, in the case of money '. . . in the context of this more general approach to the problem of the demand for money, the correct definition of money becomes an empirical matter' (Laidler, 1977). The way by which the 'correct' definition of money is determined empirically is by discovering which definition of money correlates most highly with variables like nominal income (which it is believed to influence) or which definition of money provides the econometrically preferred demand for money function. Similarly, Keynesian theory makes much of the distinction between autonomous expenditure and induced expenditure, and the division of expenditure into those two groups has to be made on grounds such as the degree of correlation between different types of expenditure and income (Ando and Modigliani, 1965).

The use of 'real-world' names for aggregates in macro-models gives rise to two related difficulties. First, the properties ascribed to a variable in an economic model may not be completely co-incident with the properties of the 'real-world' variable.[17] An example of this arises with the neo-classical investment model (based on Jorgenson, 1967, and discussed below pp.24–26). In that model there are two factors of production. Purchases of the services of factor 1 in one period do not carry any commitment to future purchase. In contrast, the services of factor 2 require that factor 2 is purchased, although it can be re-sold in subsequent periods. Factor 1 is labelled 'labour' and factor 2 is labelled 'capital'. In giving labels to these factors the immediate impression is created that the variables of the model correspond to variables in the real world with the same name. But in this case, it could be argued that 'real-world' labour shares some of the properties of the model-capital in the sense that employment of labour in one period often creates a presumption of future employment. Conversely some forms of 'real-world' capital share the property of model-labour when, for example, capital equipment is leased for a single period.

Second, the properties of a variable in one model may differ from the properties of a variable with the same name in another. The simplest example arises in the case of money. In some economic models, money is defined as a financial asset with a constant nominal price with a zero rate of interest, and in others as a financial asset with constant nominal price and a constant rate of interest. In some models, the key feature of money is that it is a non-interest bearing government debt, whereas in other models the main property of money is that it is a generally accepted medium of exchange. The discussion in Chapter 2 provides details of the way in which different authors have characterised money in their models. The dangers which arise here are those of confusion and of conducting inappropriate empirical tests.

Another major difference between micro-economics and macro-economics is that the latter deals with aggregates and relationships between aggregates. But the choice of aggregates may be crucial. Leijonhufvud (1968) in his discussion of Keynesian economics and the economics of Keynes argued that the two approaches differed in terms of the aggregates used. The details of that discussion do not directly concern us here but his remarks on aggregates are pertinent.[18] He argued that

the immediately antecedent stage [to making explicit assumptions about the relationships between the variables in the model] in model construction, i.e. the selection of aggregates, is often the stage where implicit theorizing enters in. . . . The first type of assumption [about a particular mode of aggregation] is often left implicit and particular aggregative structures are thus left to develop into undisputed conventions while at the same time controversies rage over the second type of assumption [on behavioural relationships between variables] (p.39).
Differences in aggregate structure means that one author has left in relationships which another has removed by aggregation and *vice versa*. This, in turn, implies some disagreement on what classes of events play the most significant role in determining the value of the variables in which the macrotheorist or policy-maker is ultimately concerned (p.40).

Another consequence of aggregation, as pointed out by Leijonhufvud, is that relationships between variables which are compressed into a single aggregate variable are automatically suppressed. For example, the use of an aggregate called consumption carries the implication that changes in the relative prices and quantities of different consumer goods are considered to be unimportant (for the analysis which uses that aggregate).

In conventional macro-economics, income is treated as an aggregate and thereby differences between wages and profits are ignored. Thus, conventional macro-economics theory can say nothing about the distribution of income between wages and profits and rules out for example any differences between the effect of wages and of profits on savings. In contrast, the Kaleckian approach places considerable emphasis on the roles of wages and profit.

Another dimension of aggregation is aggregation over economic agents. The most common aggregation here is over firms, households and government. There is a tendency to assume a common interest between members of the same group. In general, we maintain the conventional aggregation over economic agents.

A consequence of the ideas of Keynes has been a macro-economics with money and bonds as the main or only financial assets, and which portrays households as savers and firms as investors. Investment is financed by the issue of bonds, which are purchased with the savings of households. This particular characterisation arose from Keynes'

translation of the most important features of British economic history into economic theory. He managed to give theoretical clothes to all aspects of British economic life that mattered most. . . . Everything in the *Treatise* and the *General Theory* is derived from the British experience: the assumptions, the protagonists, the stage, the action. How else could we explain the peculiarly central role of money, and of fixed-interest securities, the peculiar absence of investment, of common shares, of anything relating to capital accumulation? How else could we explain the divorce between savers and investors, and the completely passive role labour plays in the action? (de Cecco, 1977, p.22)

In passages prior to the one just quoted, de Cecco describes what he believes were the key features of the economy of early twentieth-century Britain which formed the back-cloth of Keynes' experience and led him to the particular characterisation of the economy. The important point is that conventional macro-economics incorporates a particular characterisation.[19] Indeed any macro-economics will incorporate some characterisation. But the nature of the conventional characterisation is not usually made clear or even discussed. We argue that whether or not the characterisation of Keynes was relevant for the 'thirties in Britain, it is not relevant for advanced capitalist countries in the 'eighties. In particular four crucial features of developed capitalist economies are contradicted in the 'vision' of the world in Keynesian monetarist models. First, the importance of profits is neglected, particularly the influence of profits on savings and investment. Second, oligopoly rather than atomistic competition is the norm in product and capital markets. Third, labour is not a passive economic agent, but bargains with firms over real wages. Fourth, the money supply is not predetermined but can be varied by the banks over a considerable range at their discretion in response to the demand by the public for loans.

These four features lie at the heart of our discussion in Chapters 5 and 6. The work of Kalecki incorporates these features (particularly the first two and the fourth), which provides the justification for describing the approach as Kaleckian. These features can be clearly seen in the collection of some of his major papers (Kalecki, 1971).

These features arise from our characterisation of the important institutional features of advanced capitalist economies, and include the following. Large corporations are the main investors in capital equipment, the finance for which comes to a substantial extent from retained earnings. A substantial proportion of workers belongs to trade unions, who bargain with employers over wages and other conditions of employment. Money is largely credit money, part of which has been created by the government but most of which has been created by the private banking system. Whilst we cannot be sure what are the institutional assumptions made by the Keynesian/ monetarist orthodoxy since they are not spelt out, we would suggest that they are approximately as follows. Markets are approximately perfectly competitive, with households as net savers and firms as net dissavers. Finance for investment is largely raised by the issue of bonds and by indirect borrowing for households with banks acting as intermediaries. Money is exogenously determined or enters the system through government deficits.

The most that we would claim for our institutional assumptions is that they encapsulate important features of some advanced capitalist economies in their present phase.[20] Different institutional assumptions would be required for analysis of capitalist economies a century ago, and different ones will no doubt be required in the future. In general, we would expect that the institutional arrangements will affect how people behave, help determine the constraints on individuals and organisations, and thus strongly influence the course of events in an economy.[21]

What's to follow

The next three chapters are devoted to substantiating the arguments that the Keynesian and monetarist approaches to macro-economics are based on a shared 'vision' of the world, and that both approaches suffer from a number of serious shortcomings. In Chapter 2 some of the 'building blocks' of these orthodox approaches are examined, particularly the determinants of consumption, investment and the demand and supply of money. One purpose here is to expose the neo-classical origins of these building blocks, and to argue that some key features of the real world are neglected by these traditional building blocks.[22] Chapter 3 seeks to indicate that both the Keynesian and monetarist approaches considered as macro-models, are based on similar views of the underlying nature of the economy. In Chapter 4, we examine the orthodox theories of inflation—essentially the expectations-augmented Phillips' Curve. We argue that the Keynesian approach does not have a coherent theory of inflation, and that the monetarist approach has not been consistent. We also indicate how views about inflation fit into the general framework discussed in the previous chapter.

The remaining chapters are devoted to exploring the Kaleckian approach. In Chapter 5, we discuss the 'building blocks' of the Kaleckian approach, looking at the determination of prices and price changes under oligopolistic conditions and of wages and wage changes under collective bargaining, and discussing the alternative approaches to savings, investment and money. In Chapter 6, these 'building blocks' are brought together. The first task is to examine some of the relationships between endogenous and exogenous variables within the model, particularly the determinants of the average level of unemployment. However, there are elements within the model which indicate that the model is cyclical and we next explore that cyclical nature. Chapter 7 briefly surveys some relevant empirical material to indicate support for the approach taken. Finally, in Chapter 8 we present some brief concluding remarks.

Notes

1 The so-called reappraisal of Keynesian economics began with Clower (1965) with a major contribution by Leijonhufvud (1968); for a summary see Hines (1971). The title of the second indicates its approach —*Keynesian Economics and the Economics of Keynes*.

2 The original papers by Kalecki are printed in English in Kalecki (1971), Chapters 1, 2, and 3. Only in his introduction to that book does Kalecki make claim to prior discovery of the principle of effective demand. Klein (1975) has stated that 'Kalecki's greatest achievement, among many, was undoubtedly his complete anticipation of Keynes' *General Theory*', whilst Joan Robinson (1975) writes that 'Michal Kalecki's claim to priority of publication is indisputable', Robinson (1975) Part II, (1977) provides an outline of many of the essential ideas of Kalecki and makes comparisons with the ideas of Keynes. She also argues that 'Michal Kalecki produced a more coherent theory of the *General Theory*, which brought imperfect competition into the analysis and emphasized the influence of investment on the share of profits. Kalecki's

version was in some ways more truly a *general* theory than Keynes' '
(Robinson, 1972). Feiwell (1975) discussed the ideas of Kalecki at
length. A symposium in the *Oxford Bulletin of Economics and Statistics*, February 1977, discusses many aspects of the work and personality
of Kalecki.

3 The title of Skidelsky (1977) is, for example, *The End of the Keynesian
Era*.

4 Modigliani (1977) argued that 'the distinguishing feature of the monetarist school and the real issues of disagreement with the nonmonetarists is not monetarism, but rather the role that should probably be
assigned to stabilization policies.' He continues to say that nonmonetarists believe the economy 'needs to be stabilized, can be stabilized',
whilst monetarists 'take the view that there is no serious need to
stabilize the economy.'

5 Perhaps the best-known expression of this change is that of Prime
Minister James Callaghan when he said at the Labour Party Conference
1976 that '[w]e used to think that you could spend your way out of a
recession, and increase employment by cutting taxes and boosting
government spending. I tell you in all candour that that option no longer
exists, and that in so far as it ever did exist, it only worked . . . by
injecting a bigger dose of inflation into the system.' For discussion of a
shift away for concern over the level of unemployment to concern over
inflation see Deacon (1981).

6 Monetarist policies and monetary policies are not synonymous.

7 For definitions of monetarism see Laidler (1981), Purvis (1980), Mayer
(1978). For discussion of the shifting grounds of debate see Burrows
(1979), Morgan (1978), Vane and Thompson (1979).

8 Keynes did not make explicit his assumptions about the nature of labour
and product markets, a habit generally followed by macro-economists.
But, it is difficult not to believe that he was assuming perfect competition, particularly in Chapters 2 and 21 of the *General Theory*. Ohlin
wrote that 'in this respect [assumption of perfect competition] as in
other respects Keynes does not seem to me to have been sufficiently
radical enough in freeing himself from the conventional assumptions.
When reading his book [Keynes (1936)] one sometimes wonders
whether he never discussed imperfect competition with Mrs. Robinson.' This last remark relates to the publication by Mrs. Robinson of a
book on imperfect competition in 1933 (Robinson, 1933). Keynes
replied that 'the reference to imperfect competition is very perplexing'
(Moggeridge, 1973). The debate between Keynes and Ohlin involved in
part the question of whether employment could increase without a
reduction in the real wage. Shove complained to Keynes that he
'thought you [Keynes] were too kind to the classical analysis as applied
to the individual industry and firm.' Keynes' response was that Shove
was 'probably right' and that 'I have been concentrating on the other
problem, and have not . . . thought very much about the elements of
the system' (Moggeridge, 1973).

9 In most formal models no division of income into wages and profits is
made although there may be some informal discussion of the effects of

changes in the distribution of income on the consumption function. Kaldor (1955) postulated differential savings propensities out of wages and profits which in conjunction with exogenously determined investment determine the distribution of income between wages and profits. Kaldor labels this a Keynesian theory of income distribution mainly because of the key role played by investment. However he notes that 'Keynes, as far as I know, was never interested in the problem of distribution as such' (Kaldor, 1955). Pasinetti (1974) notes that 'more than Keynes, a notable precursor of Kaldor is perhaps Michal Kalecki, who was however interested in short-run situations and tended to emphasize the role of the degree of monopoly.'

10 In a different context (the re-switching debate which is referred to below p.26) and from an opposite point of view, Ferguson (1969) stated that 'until the econometricians have the answer for us, placing reliance upon neoclassical economic theory is a matter of faith. I personally have faith . . .'

11 In the literature on labour-managed firms (LMF) much has been made of the 'perverse' result that LMF respond to an increase in demand by reducing output, see for example Meade (1972). This illustrates the point that macro-economics must be built on a view of how firms operate, and the assumptions of macro-economics chosen accordingly.

12 However, some studies (e.g. Davidson *et al.*, 1978) have related consumption or consumer expenditure to personal disposable income. The latter includes dividends received by the personal sector but excludes the retained earnings of corporations. Thus the implicit assumption is made that for households wages and dividends have the same impact on consumption, but that retained earnings have a zero direct effect on consumption. There may be an indirect effect if retained earnings affect the share values of the corporations which in turn may affect the wealth and thereby the consumption of households.

13 Several prominent economists have argued that the economics profession has played too little attention to empirical matters and too much to theorising unhibited by 'reality'. On this point see Phelps Brown (1972); Worswick (1972); Leontief (1971).

14 There are numerous problems associated with empirical validation exercises, with substantial problems in measuring crucial variables. This is particularly acute in testing the expectations-augmented Phillips' curve (pp.67–82 below), where there are many alternative measures of wages available, and variables like excess demand and expected price changes are not directly measurable. The accuracy of the results of empirical work depends on the honesty of the investigators. In many of the natural sciences, attention is given to replication of experiments and results, which makes false results more easily detectable. In economics, replication (using same data set) is rarely tried, and the use of different data sets can easily generate different results. In the natural sciences there has been some recent disquiet over forged results (*New Scientist*, 10 April 1981). The advent of computers has created a problem which is probably much more widespread than deliberate dishonesty. Once data

have been collected, it is relatively easy to estimate a large number of regressions and then select those which support one's prior beliefs and prejudices or which generate positive conclusions which are more publishable than negative ones. At a minimum, the estimation of numerous regressions brings the use of standard statistical tests of significance into question. For further discussion and some proposals to reduce these problems see Mayer (1980).

15 Katouzian makes reference to Knowles and Winsten (1959) as expressing 'critical doubts' about the Phillips relationship; see also Routh (1959).

16 There are also aggregation problems. The relationship between consumption and income, for example, begins at the individual level. The question arises as to the conditions under which there is an analogous relationship between aggregate consumption and aggregate income. We will follow, without justification, the macro-economic convention and assume away these aggregation problems.

17 Machlup (1967) has discussed this type of problem in the context of the theory of the firm. He has argued that 'to confuse the firm as a theoretical construct with the firm as an empirical concept, that it, to confuse a heuristic fiction with a real organisation like General Motors or Atlantic and Pacific, is to commit the "fallacy of misplaced concreteness". This fallacy consists in using theoretic symbols as though they had a direct, observable, concrete meaning.'

18 Leijonhufvud argued that both Keynes and Keynesians begin with five types of goods and assets, namely consumer goods, bonds, physical assets, labour services and money. But only three relative prices are used which implies the use of only four types of goods. He argued that Keynesians aggregate the first and third items in the above list, whilst Keynes aggregated the second and third items. However, Keynes still had considerable influence on the items entered on the list. The characterisation used tends to neglect matters such as the use of internal funds and bank loans to finance investment, and the division of income between wages and profits.

19 Eltis (1976) argued that the characterisations used by Keynes were understandable in the context of the 'thirties but inappropriate for much of the post-war period. 'Keynes' simplification that money and bonds are the only portfolio assets has been even more damaging than has so far been suggested, because it has left Keynesians with an extremely unrealistic theory of the rate of interest.' 'Keynes' assumption that the British interest rate is independent of foreign interest rates and that government bonds are a typical portfolio asset are comprehensible in the context of the 1930s.' 'So the quasi-stationary state economics of 1936 was unable to provide what was needed for Britain's growth opportunities of the 1950's, 1960's and 1970's.'

20 Our starting point and background is the British economy, and our institutional assumptions are no doubt derived by experience of that economy. We would argue though that our analysis is relevant to many other advanced capitalist economies. However, some economies, notably Japan, may require different assumptions.

21 'The third and probably the most important single difference between Kalecki and Keynes concerned the relative weights attached by them to institutional and political factors as compared with pure knowledge, or ideas, in determining economic policy and development' (Eshag, 1977).
22 By neo-classical we mean here that economic agents are assumed to be maximising agents (of utility or profits) under conditions where they are price-takers.

2 The Building Blocks of Conventional Macro-Economics

Introduction
The central purpose of this chapter is a critical appraisal of the main building blocks of conventional macro-economics (whether Keynesian or monetarist) on which the orthodox macro-models rest, though they use simplified versions of the building blocks.[1] The four topics considered are consumption/savings, investment, and the demand for money and the supply of money. In Chapter 5 we will present alternative approaches to each of these four areas, often using the criticisms made of orthodoxy in this chapter as a starting base. In this chapter, we want to expose the neo-classical nature of much of the conventional analysis in that it is based on utility-maximising individuals or households and profit-maximising firms operating in perfectly competitive environments.

Consumption and savings[2]
It is significant that consumption and savings are treated together in most text-books since the decisions on both items are seen as taken by the same group of economic agents—that is households. Since consumption plus savings add up to disposable income for a household, the determination of one leaves the other determined as a residual (when, as is often the case, income is taken as fixed for the household). The separation of savings and investment, and the possibility that planned savings and planned investment could differ was one of the major innovations made by Keynes in the *General Theory* (Keynes, 1936). Keynes did not always make a sharp distinction between households and firms, but a frequent interpretation has been that households are the major (if not the only) source of savings and are typically 'surplus units' (i.e. income exceeds expenditure) whilst firms are the major users of savings, the major investors and are typically 'deficit units' (with expenditure exceeding income).

Savings is seen as mainly depending on household decisions. Two major problems arise with this type of approach. First, savings by firms (largely the retained earnings of corporations) are largely overlooked.[3] Second, little is said on the mechanism by which savings are passed from households to firms. In most macro-models there are only two financial assets—money and bonds. Implicitly, banks operate as links between households and firms by accepting deposits and making loans and there is a bond-market in which firms sell new bonds to households. The sources of finance for investment as modelled by Keynes and most macro-economists can be compared with those which underpin the macro-economics of Kalecki. In his work the major sources of finance are retained earnings (i.e. savings out of profits by firms) and bank borrowing (e.g. Kalecki, 1971, Chapter 3). The precise sources of savings and of finance for investment may appear to be minor matters, but the change from the Keynes' approach to the Kaleckian approach has two important consequences which are explored below. These are that the distribution of income between profits and wages is relevant to the level of savings with different propensities to save out of profits and out of wages and salaries and the role of banks and their ability to create money to finance investment (as well as other forms of expenditure) are introduced. The consumption function introduced by Keynes focused on the relationship between consumption and income (although many other factors which could influence that relationship were discussed in Keynes, 1936, Chapters 8 and 9). The rather obvious statement that a household's consumption depends on its income was seen by Keynes as central to his theory,[4] and has been placed at the centre of Keynes' contribution to economic theory by Clower in his re-interpretation (Clower, 1965); see pp.59–62 below). In a fully neo-classical approach, a household is assumed able to vary consumption and labour supply in pursuit of maximising utility, subject to the constraint that income and expenditure balance at the current wages and prices. Thus, the household decides on its consumption and labour supply and, indirectly as a result of that maximisation procedure, its income. The choices over consumption and labour supply (and hence income) are influenced by the relative prices of consumption goods and of labour, so that it is relative prices, rather than income, which determines consumption. The approach of Keynes marks some movement away from a view of the economy in which all economic agents are able to choose (against a background of relative prices)

is a measure of average expected future income. Aggregating over individuals within age-groups (who are assumed to have similar values of d_1), and then over age-groups, we arrive at $C = a_1.Y + a_2.Y^e + a_3.A$ where C is aggregate current consumption, Y current income, Y^e expected future income and A assets. The values of a_1, a_2, a_3 will depend upon the relative sizes of the different age-groups.[7] The influence of current income on current consumption is much reduced in this approach as compared with the traditional Keynes' approach. An increase of one pound in current income which does not influence expectations about future income leads to a small rise in current consumption of d_1, and further rises in future consumption of d_2 in period 2 through to d_N in period N.

A number of problems arises with this approach. First it is not clear whether the analysis is designed to apply to an individual or to a household. The analysis is often presented as an individual maximising utility over an individual's life cycle, but discussion of the analysis often makes reference to family or household (e.g. Modigliani, 1975). A household may be the effective decision-making unit at a moment of time[8] (or at least members of a household heavily influence each other's decisions), but the composition of a household changes over time and an individual may be a member of several households during a life-time. The age-profile of (non-property) income which is assumed tends to be either that income is constant with respect to age up to retirement (as in the illustrative calculations by Ando and Modigliani, 1963) or that income rises with age up to the age of 50 to 60 years and then declines (e.g. in the presentation of Branson, 1979). Whilst these age-profiles may provide a reasonable approximation for men, they omit any treatment of the sharp dip in the earnings of women when they leave the labour force (in earlier periods typically around the time of marriage, now more often around time of birth of first child). If a household is being considered, then the evolution of real income over time will have its ups and downs. This will partly reflect entry into and exit from the labour force by its members. As the size and age composition of the household changes so real income per head (or per adult equivalent) varies. Households with young children and those of retired people are likely to be experiencing relative austerity.[9]

Much of government activity can be viewed as transferring real income from households in the relatively affluent stages of the life-cycle to those in the relatively austere stages. Such government activities include provision of education, health care and social security. Thus the transfer of income between different stages of the life-cycle is effected through the public sector rather than through the capital market (as is assumed by the LCH). Indeed the wide-spread involvement of the public sector in activities such as education, retirement pension provision may serve to indicate the inadequacies of the capital and other markets to effect the transfers which people wish to make.

Second, the LCH incorporates precision for the individuals concerning future income and length of life (expressed as N periods in the above formulation). Essentially the individuals are assumed to spend their last penny as they breathe their last breath. The seriousness of such a criticism depends on two factors. The LCH could be regarded as providing an insight into one of the factors influencing savings (which is how we regard it below). However, the originators of the LCH appear to regard it as a complete explanation of savings (Modigliani, 1975).

The second factor involves a comparison of the nature of actual financial markets with that assumed implicitly by the LCH. We can note that a perfect capital market is assumed such that an individual is able to borrow and lend as much as s/he wants at the going rate of interest. The life-time budget constraint above does not distinguish between borrowing and lending, with the assumption that the interest rate on borrowing is equal to the rate on lending. It is often assumed in the development of the LCH that the period of positive saving (roughly working life) precedes the period of negative saving (roughly retirement), which overcomes the problem that the individual is assumed to be able to make unsecured borrowing at a constant rate of interest. But the observation of saving preceding dis-saving (if it is correct) may reflect imperfections in the capital market and could constitute a refutation of the life-cycle hypothesis if there were any way of knowing what the utility function given above actually looked like. An important element in the financial markets of advanced capitalist countries (particularly the UK and USA) is the existence of pension funds. Individuals are able, to an extent, to take out contracts with pension funds which, in exchange for contributions during working life, provide a stream of income generally from retirement to the time of death. It could be argued that the LCH provides some explanation for the development of pension funds. However, the recognition of pension funds raises some interesting points. It is often the case that membership of an occupational pension scheme is a condition of employment with a rate of contribution which cannot be varied by the individual and which is partly paid by the employee and partly by the employer. In those cases, the payments and their timing into the pension fund (and hence the final pension) may not be close to those which would have been freely chosen by the individual. The growth of pension schemes places considerable funds at the disposal of pension funds which may serve to concentrate power over the direction of investment funds into the hands of the controllers of a relatively few pension funds.[10] It is also the case that a considerable amount of pension provision (particularly via social security) is through unfunded schemes. Under such arrangements, current pensions are financed by current contributions from the working population (usually through social security taxes) rather than by interest returns on and running down of previous savings. Thus whether behaviour along the lines of the LCH generates savings would depend on the nature of the pension arrangements in operation. Further, when unfunded schemes operate then the net worth of individuals includes their rights to future pensions.[11] But that net worth is not backed by real assets but rather by the commitment of future generations to pay the necessary contributions.[12]

The general point is that the analysis of consumption and savings behaviour is derived from a model of household behaviour (of a utility maximising form), and that little attention is paid to savings by corporations nor to differential savings out of wages and out of profits. Further, work on the consumption function has tended to stress a life-cycle type of approach under which individuals are allocating their life-time expenditure over their life in a utility-maximising manner. In that approach, a perfect capital market is usually implicitly assumed, and little regard paid to the institutional arrangements.

Investment

Discussion of investment faces two related difficulties. First, there is an uneasy relationship between the various theories of investment which have been evolved and the simplified equation for investment which enters most macro-models. Typically that equation is of the form $I = I(r, y)$ where I is investment expenditure, r the real rate of interest and y output (which is often omitted). Equilibrium requires that $I(r, y) = S(r, y)$ where S is savings, and some important differences between the nature and determinants of investment and of savings are largely ignored. Investment is essentially forward-looking undertaken for profit by firms, whereas savings is more passive and undertaken by households. The theories of investment often stress other factors such as changes in output (the accelerator), profitability and liquidity and expectations about the future.

Second, there are many approaches to investment which reflect substantial differences in attitude to how the economy works.[13] These range from a neo-classical approach (with perfectly competitive firms and perfect capital markets) through to a fixed capital-output ratio accelerator model. Our immediate task is to present the main ingredients of these varying approaches.

We begin with the neo-classical model developed by Jorgenson (e.g. Jorgenson, 1967), in which the investment of an individual firm is examined. The basis of the model is a perfectly competitive firm which maximises its net worth, which is the present value of the expected future profits discounted at a constant discount rate over an infinite time horizon.[14] In order to produce output, the firm requires a flow of capital services. The implicit assumption is that a firm must purchase capital equipment if it is to have a flow of capital services, although it can re-sell that equipment easily in the future. The demand for capital services is thereby translated into a demand for capital equipment. In contrast, labour can be hired for a single period of time with no commitment to future employment.

From the maximisation procedure, the firm has a desired labour force at time t with the marginal product of labour equal to the real wage, and the desired stock of capital equipment with the marginal product of capital equipment equal to the ratio of the cost of capital to the price of output. These can be written formally as

$$\partial Q(L,K)/\partial L = w/p \text{ and } \partial Q(L,K)/\partial K = c/p$$

where Q is output, L is labour, K capital equipment, w wage, p price of output and c the cost of capital services (discussed below). From these two equations, the desired levels of labour and capital equipment can be determined as $L = f(w/p, c/p)$ and $K = g(w/p, c/p)$.

Several important consequences flow from this result. First, the demand for labour and for capital equipment depends only on relative prices and not on output. The firm is not constrained in terms of the amount of output which it can sell, but rather is able to choose the level of output which maximises profits in the light of the prevailing relative prices. The chosen level of output can be read off from the production function faced by the firm given the labour and capital equipment demanded. Second, it is the demand for capital equipment which is a function of relative prices (and the cost of capital, c, includes a rate of interest). Thus, in equilibrium, when relative prices are constant, the desired net capital stock would be unchanging, and the only demand for investment goods would arise from the desire to maintain the net capital stock, that is, gross investment would be equal to the depreciation on the existing capital stock. Out of equilibrium, the demand for investment goods would be generated by changes in relative prices which cause changes in the desired stock of capital equipment, which could be positive or negative. Third, the cost of capital services, which is equal to the cost of holding capital equipment, is $c=q(r+\delta)-dq/dt$, where q is the cost of investment goods, r the rate of interest and δ the rate of depreciation. In other words, the cost of capital services has an interest component $(q.r)$, a depreciation component $(q.\delta)$ and the gain or loss from owning the capital equipment (dq/dt). Thus the rate of interest is only one factor determining the cost of capital services. However, its importance is increased if certain conventional assumptions are followed. Often consumption goods and investment goods are aggregated, which is equivalent to assuming that the ratio q/p is constant. The rate of depreciation is often taken as constant and dq/dt ignored, which leaves variations in c arising from variations in r. Fourth, in this analysis, it is assumed that capital equipment, as well as labour and output, are continually divisible, and that there are no problems involved in measuring the number of units of capital equipment in use. Since there are no transactions costs involved in changing quantity of capital equipment used, the firm always adjusts the capital equipment level to that desired. In other words, there is never any excess capacity held by the firm.

Finally, this analysis relates to a single firm, and there are doubts on its applicability and relevance at the aggregate macro-level. This has three aspects. First, whilst the price of capital equipment may be fixed so far as a single firm is concerned, how is the price determined at the aggregate level? For new capital equipment, the price may be determined by the interaction of the demand and the production costs for that equipment. But the neo-classical model assumes a well-developed second-hand market in capital equipment, and the production costs argument does not apply there. The second-hand price of capital equipment needs to be determined. The problem arises that the rate of profit on second-hand equipment depends on the price of that equipment, and the price will depend on the rate of profit on the equipment. At the aggregate level, the price of equipment will be bid up if the rate of profit is relatively high, and bid down if the rate of profit is low. In equilibrium, the price of second-hand equipment would be such that the rate of profit on that equipment at the prevailing price equals the rate of interest.

Second, it has been implicitly assumed in the analysis above that the firm employs just one type of capital equipment. The first-order condition relating to capital equipment can be re-written

$$(p\partial Q/\partial K - q.\delta + dq/dt)/q = r,$$

which can be interpreted as rate of (net) profit equals rate of interest. From this a demand for capital equipment function can be derived, i.e. $K^d(r)$ with $\partial K^d/\partial r$ negative (for a lower value of r requires a lower value of $\partial Q/\partial K$, which with declining marginal product of capital equipment requires a higher value of K). When the firm employs m different types of capital equipment then K in the profit function is interpreted as a vector $(K_1, K_2, \ldots, K_m)$ and for each type of equipment $\partial K_i/\partial r$ $(i=1, 2, \ldots, m)$ is negative. The question arises whether it is possible to derive an aggregate demand for 'capital' equation in which the demand for 'capital' is a decreasing function of the rate of interest (which is equal here to the rate of profit). There are different types of capital equipment which would need to be reduced to a single aggregate called 'capital'. One approach would be to use a measure of 'capital'

$$K^* = \sum_{i=1}^{m} q_i K_i$$

(where q_i is the cost of K_i). However, the re-switching debate indicates that the relationship between aggregate 'capital' measured thus and the rate of interest cannot be unambiguously signed.[15] The basis of this conclusion is that for the production of a particular level of output, the firm could use either an amount K_1^* of the first type of capital equipment or an amount K_2^* of the second type. At relatively high rates of interest and also at relatively low rates of interest it would be more profitable for the firm to use K_1^* but in the middle range of interest rates more profitable to use K_2^*. Then as conceptually the rate of interest is gradually lowered, the firm would switch from K_1^* to K_2^* and then at a lower rate of interest it would switch back from K_2^* to K_1^*. Whilst one of those switches would involve moving to a higher value of K^* measured as indicated above, the other switch would involve moving to a lower level of K^* in response to lower interest rate.[16]

Third, the individual firm is assumed to be able to purchase as much labour and investment goods, to sell as much output and to borrow and lend as much finance as it wishes at constant prices. The use of a monopoly assumption in the product or labour markets would not make a fundamental difference to the analysis. But significant differences arise from alternative assumptions for the finance capital market. If, for example, past profits performance influences the availability of finance for a firm (whether directly through retained earnings or indirectly through a greater willingness of the finance capital market to lend to more profitable firms), then in contrast to the results derived above past profits can influence finance, its costs and thereby the investment demands of a firm.

The neo-classical model is essentially one of the demand for capital equipment, though it is often implicitly assumed that the demand for capital equipment (and the related demand for finance) is met. At the aggregate level, there are limits on the supply of capital equipment and on the supply of finance. These limits can be taken into account by, for example, the use of supply of capital equipment schedules alongside the demand schedule to determine the price of capital equipment (i.e. q), and similarly in the finance capital market. But in a disequilibrium situation where supply of capital equipment fell short of the demand, then there would have to be some rationing of firms for not all their demands would be met. The quantity constraints on economic agents in disequilibrium situations is further discussed in Chapter 3 (pp.000–000).[17]

The two points of particular importance which arise out of this section are that the demand for investment goods is analysed at the firm-level rather than the aggregate level and that perfectly competitive markets are assumed throughout.

The second basic approach leads directly to the view that $I=I(r)$ and is often taken as a reflection of the views of Keynes as expressed in the *General Theory*. This is usually derived from a decision rule for a firm in the form: expand capital stock if the internal rate of return on additions to the capital stock exceeds the rate of interest. The internal rate of return, ρ, is the solution of an equation of the form

$$\sum_{t=1}^{T} R_t/(1+\rho)^t = C$$

where C is the cost of the addition to the capital stock (incurred only in the present period), and R_t and the net additions to revenue expected in period t if the investment is made, which are assumed to begin in period 1 and continue until period N (which can include the scrap value of the addition to the capital stock).[18] Then in a specific context (including the volume of capital equipment inherited from the past as well as expectations about the future) at the aggregate level a lower rate of interest is predicted to be associated with a higher volume of additions to the capital stock.[19] However, this is a one-period relationship in that in the next period there will be a different capital stock (including current period's investment) and a different set of expectations, so that there will be a different relationship between investment and the rate of interest.

An alternative derivation (e.g. Branson, 1979) is to argue that the desired capital stock is a decreasing function of the rate of interest and with net investment zero in equilibrium, gross investment equals the depreciation on the existing capital stock. Then $I = \delta . K(r)$, and investment is a function of the rate of interest.

It can be argued that the representation of the investment theory of Keynes by a relationship of the form $I = I(r)$, which looks like an out-moded first stab at the neo-classical analysis given above, is to overlook the central importance of investment, its relative instability arising from changing beliefs about the future and its links with the demand for liquidity. Keynes indicated factors other than the rate of interest, which affected the rate of new investment, as 'the physical conditions of supply in the capital goods industries, the state of confidence concerning the prospective yield, the psychological attitude to liquidity and the quantity of money (preferably calculated in terms of the wage-units).' Indeed, Keynes (1936) warned (p.145) of the trap into which much macro-models have fallen when he wrote that 'the rate of interest is, virtually, a *current* phenomenon; and if we reduce the marginal efficiency of capital to the same status, we cut ourselves off from taking any direct account of the influence of the future in our analysis of the existing equilibrium.' Further, 'in estimating the prospects of investment, we must have regard, therefore, to the nerves and hysteria and even the digestions and reactions to the weather of those upon whose spontaneous activity it largely depends' (p.162).

The combination of the notions that the investment schedule (as a function of the rate of interest) is liable to marked shifts with waves of optimism and pessimism[20] and that investment is the driving force in determining the level of income via the multiplier gives a rather different perspective on the operation of the economy from that given by the static *IS-LM* model. In a specific period, with a particular set of expectations (held with a given degree of confidence) and with particular level of the capital stock, an investment schedule can be formulated and fed into a macro-model to determine the levels of output/employment and rate of interest which could generate equilibrium *in that period*. But such an exercise tells us little about equilibrium in subsequent periods. Indeed, the capital stock is changing, through depreciation and new investment, leading to shifts in the investment schedule.

The third approach to investment leads away from an emphasis on relative prices and focuses on output and changes in output. The accelerator theory can be expressed as net investment for a firm

$$I_t = \lambda . (K_t^d - K_{t-1}) = \lambda . (v . Y_t^d - K_{t-1})$$
$$= \lambda . v(Y_t^d - Y_{t-1}) + \lambda . (v . Y_{t-1} - K_{t-1}),$$

where K_t^d is the desired capital stock in time t which is related to desired output, Y_t^d, via the target capital-output ratio v, and λ is the proportion of the difference between desired and actual capital stock made up within the period. The final part of the equation indicates that net investment is linked to desired changes in output and the relationship between the capital stock needed to produce Y_{t-1} (i.e. $v . Y_{t-1}$) and the actual capital stock (K_{t-1}). Thus investment is linked to changes in output and capacity utilisation. The naïve version of the accelerator corresponds to the case where $\lambda = 1$ and full capacity working (i.e. $v . Y_{t-1}^d = K_{t-1}$), so that $I_t = v(Y_{t-1} - Y_{t-1})$.

An important element in the accelerator approach, which is vividly illustrated in the naïve version, is that net investment rests heavily on increases in output. However, net investment adds to the capital stock, and insofar as it is labour-saving, reduces the level of employment of labour required for any particular level of output. Thus investment today adds to aggregate demand, raising output and employment, but stores up problems for employment tomorrow.

The accelerator approach can be modified by making the value of λ depend on the costs of adjustment (of the capital stock), and the value of v depend on the relative prices. But in order to leave the basic thrust of the accelerator approach intact, changes in transactions costs and in relative prices (and thereby the changes in λ and v) must be relatively minor compared with the changes in output. Further, the level of output must remain essentially determined exogenous to the firms (usually from the level of aggregate demand), and not, as in the neo-classical case, by the firms themselves in light of relative prices.

The accelerator approach, like the preceding ones, is a theory of the demand for investment, and pays little regard to the availability of finance and to the supply of investment goods. In Chapter 5, we adopt the accelerator approach to bring in the role of profitability and the availability and cost of finance. Finally, it is noteworthy that the accelerator theory links investment to changes in output, and thus says little about investment in a static equilibrium situation where changes in output are zero. Thus in models which rely on equilibrium analysis, such as the *IS-LM* model examined in the next chapter, the accelerator model has to be excluded.

Demand for money

It is conventional to say that the functions of money are threefold —to be a unit of account, a medium of exchange and a store of value. The various analyses of the demand for money place varying emphasis on these functions.[21] The transactions demand for money is closely related to money treated as a medium of exchange.[22] In the simplest form of the transactions demand, money is held for convenience between its receipt and its disbursement. The average holding of money then depends on the quantities in which money is received and the average time between receipt and disbursement, and leads to a transactions demand of the form $M^d = k_1$. times the volume of transactions in nominal terms, and the latter is usually assumed proportional to money income *(py)* to yield $M^d = kpy$.

In the inventory approach to the transactions demand for money (Baumol, 1952; Tobin, 1956) economic agents determine their transactions demand for money in the light of the costs involved. In the simplest version of this approach, an economic agent (household or firm) receives £Y of money at the beginning of a period which is gradually disbursed during the period. Before the disbursement, the economic agent can hold (non-interest-bearing) money or an interest-bearing asset. If the latter is chosen, then interest is received but costs are incurred when funds are switched back into money preparatory to making the disbursements. The agent is seen as determining the size of each transfer *(T)*. The initial receipts are Y, so that the number of transfers is Y/T, with a (fixed) cost of transferring funds of b per transfer and the rate of interest on the alternative asset is r. With an average holding of money of $T/2$ (i.e.

money holding rises to T and is then gradually run down), the costs of this operation are $bY/T+rT/2$, where the first part is the transfer costs and the second part the foregone interest by holding money rather than the interest-bearing asset. Costs are minimised when $T = (2bY/r)^{1/2}$ and the average money holdings is $(bY/2r)^{1/2}$. A number of extensions to this approach has been made to incorporate, for example, receipts and disbursements which are subject to uncertainty (Orr, 1970). But the key features of the transactions demand approach remain. These are, first, that the transactions demand for money is a (negative) function of the rate of interest. Second, the transactions demand is a demand for money which can be used as a medium of exchange. Thus money is narrowly defined (and corresponds to something like the *M1* definition of money), and the alternative financial asset is one with a constant nominal price which yields interest, and would correspond to parts of money broadly defined (e.g. the interest-bearing components of *M2* or *M3*). Third, the economic agent is usually taken as being in a kind of equilibrium in the sense that receipts and disbursement are equal over the period. However, as Davidson (1965) and others have argued, it may be more fruitful to regard the transactions demand for money as relating to future planned expenditure. Plans for expenditure cannot be brought to fruition unless they are backed by purchasing power, represented by generally accepted money or by credit arrangements. Thus any planned expansion of expenditure requires the economic agent to find the extra money to finance the gap between receipts and the increased level of planned expenditure, and that requires some expansion of the available media of exchange (which could include trade credit as well as narrowly defined money). This consideration will be brought to the fore in further discussion of money within the alternative approach in Chapter 5.

Other approaches to the demand for money, including the speculative demand, a portfolio approach, demand theory approach, stress the role of money as a store of value, or perhaps more accurately a store of wealth. Friedman (1974) argues that 'more recent work has gone still further [than Keynes] in this direction, treating the demand for money as part of capital or wealth theory, concerned with the composition of the balance sheet or portfolio of assets.' The speculative motive for holding money elaborated by Keynes (1936) essentially rests on wealth-holders comparing the return on money over their planning period (zero assumed by

Keynes, but more generally a constant rate of interest r_m) with the expected return on bonds $r_b + b$ where r_b is the interest rate on bonds and b the expected capital gain (expressed as a percentage).[23] Wealth is held in the form of money or bonds as $r_m >$ or $< r + b$. The alternative presentation of Tobin (1958) introduces the risk attached to the price of bonds. The price of bonds at the end of the planning period is not known, and the expected gain from bonds (b above) may not be the outturn. The comparison made by wealth-holders is between a riskless return on money of r_m and a return on bonds with expected value $r + b$ but subject to risk.[24] This leads into a more general portfolio approach in which each asset is characterised in terms of expected return and the variability of that return. The major characteristic of money is that its price does not vary with the general level of interest rates in the way that bonds do vary.

A general approach proposed by Tobin (1969) considers money as one of many assets, with the essential characteristic of money being that the rate of interest of money is exogenously determined. For the other assets considered, the rate of return on them adjusts until the demand for each asset is equal to the available supply. Consistency requirements are imposed that the sum of the demands for the different assets adds up to the wealth available, and that a change in the rate of return on one asset whilst generating changes in the demand for specific assets does not increase overall demand for assets.

Friedman (1956) follows a different tack in his restatement of the Quantity Theory of Money. Money is treated like any other durable and money is held for the unspecified 'utility attached to the services rendered by money' (Friedman, 1974).[25] The demand for money is a demand in real terms and depends on total wealth, the division between human and non-human wealth, expected rates of return on assets in addition to the variables determining the utility attached to the services of money. Friedman (1956) envisages four categories of assets in addition to money—bonds, equities, physical non-human goods and human capital. Thus far no mention has been made of the influence of income on the demand for money. In Friedman's treatment income does not directly influence the demand for money but is only indirectly related to demand for money through two possible routes. First, some forms of wealth (particularly human capital) are difficult to measure. The basic argument is that income $Y = r.V$ where r is a weighted average of relevant interest rates and V wealth, and Y/r can be substituted for V in the list of factors influencing the demand for money. Second, the utility attached to the services rendered by money may vary with the level of income.

In these approaches to the demand for money, money is regarded as one asset amongst many assets in which wealth can be held. The main characteristic of money is that its nominal price is always unity, reflecting the unit of account and store of wealth functions of money. The nominal rate of interest on money may be zero (Keynes, 1936; Tobin, 1958), a constant positive nominal rate of interest (Tobin, 1969) or it 'may be zero, as it is generally on currency, or negative, as it sometimes is on demand deposits subject to net service charges, or positive, as it sometimes is on demand deposits on which interest is paid and generally is on time deposits' (Friedman, 1974, p.12).

Thus the transactions approach focuses on the medium of exchange role of money whilst the other approaches considered here neglect that role. Further, following the Baumol/Tobin analysis, the appropriate definition of money within the transactions approach would be financial assets generally accepted as a medium of exchange, with a constant nominal value and yielding a nominal rate of interest close to zero. In practice, the definition of the money supply usually labelled *M1* would be a close approximation. In the other approaches an appropriate definition of money would seem to be those financial assets whose nominal price is fixed. This definition would extend beyond the *M2* or *M3* definitions of the money supply and would include, for example, deposits with building societies (UK) and savings and loan associations (USA). But treated as a store of wealth, the interest-bearing component of money would dominate the non-interest-bearing component. Indeed, it would be difficult to explain why anyone would hold the non-interest bearing money as a store of wealth.

With a broad definition of money, the particular significance of the money supply for the level of economic activity rests on the argument that an increase in wealth in the form of broad money is more likely to lead to an increase in spending than an increase in the form of, say, bonds. The differences between broad money and bonds would appear to rest on constant versus variable nominal price and possibly the level of transactions costs involved in switching from those assets into the form of money which is a generally accepted medium of exchange.

What are the characteristics of money which have led economists, particularly monetarists, to conclude that changes in the money supply are much more important than, say, changes in government bonds? Friedman (1969) traces through the effects of a once-and-for-all increase in the money supply, which is somehow dropped into the economy without anyone trying to increase their holding of money. Basically, he argued that the increase in the nominal money supply leads to economic agents with larger real money holdings than they desire, since at the first stage the price level has not changed. The excess money holdings lead to increased spending which continues until the price level has risen sufficiently to restore the real value of money holdings to the original level. Thus the price level rises to the same extent that the money supply was increased initially, and this restores an equilibrium balance between the goods and services in the economy (the level of which are assumed to remain unchanged) and the real value of the money supply. However the model used by Friedman is a very simple one with money as the only financial asset. Now we introduce a second financial asset of perpetual bonds each yielding one unit of nominal income per period throughout the future, and so having value of $1/i$ (where i is the rate of discount) to their owners. Initially suppose that economic agents are in equilibrium with purchase of goods and services of Z per period, and real value of money holdings of M/p and of bonds B/pi. An increase in the nominal value of money upsets that equilibrium, but, in general, changes in the price level cannot restore the old equilibrium since changes in the price level cannot change the relative real amounts of money and bonds. The only case where the price level will rise in the same proportion as the increase in the money supply is when the demand for real money stock depends only on the level of Z. In other words, the demand for money is a simple transactions demand (related to Z), and is not a function of interest rates or wealth. One could undertake the mental experiment of dropping bonds into such an economy, and again in general it would be expected that the price level and the value of bonds would change. Thus, we conclude that the apparent uniqueness of money in the Friedman analysis arises from excluding other financial assets from the model.[26]

There are two ways in which the above argument could be defused. First, it could be assumed that all financial assets have returns fixed in real rather than nominal terms. Thus in the case of bonds the government would offer a particular level of real interest payments rather than particular nominal interest payments. Second, it has been argued that bonds do not represent net worth to the community for although the bond-holders receive interest payments these have to be financed by taxpayers (Barro, 1974). Each bond issued yields one unit of nominal income per period to the bond-holder but commits tax-payers to paying taxes equal to one unit of income as tax to finance the interest payments. If tax-payers discount their future tax liabilities at the same rate of discount as the bond-holders use, then the liability has a present value which exactly offsets the asset of the bond-holders. Under this line of argument, the issue of bonds involves no net creation of wealth.[27]

The money which enters the model of Friedman (and more generally) is money of a very particular sort. First, it is money which does not have any intrinsic value. With commodity money, such as gold, there may be some utility gained from holding gold which depends on the physical amount as well as its real value in terms of other goods. In the model of Friedman considered above, the utility of holding money is based only on the real value of money. Second, it is money which represents net worth to the community. In other words, when the money supply is increased whilst the price level remains unchanged the community feels better off. This type of money is often described as outside money. However when there is credit money (such as bank deposits) then the creation of money involves the creation of assets and liabilities to the same extent such that there is no change in the overall wealth of the community. It is also difficult to conceive of credit money being 'dropped into' an economy for the essence of credit money is that it is created by banks in response to the demand for loans.[28]

The conventional approach to the demand for money is closely linked to an equilibrium approach. In the transactions demand, the economic agent is in equilibrium in that inflows and outflows balance over a relevant period. In the portfolio approach the individual has adjusted holdings of money and other assets so as to achieve equilibrium. Thus attention is diverted away from dis-equilibrium behaviour, and the way in which plans to vary expenditure and changes in the money supply are intimately linked. This will be a theme to which we return in Chapter 5.

The supply of money

There are four approaches to the determinants of the supply of money, which appear to a greater or lesser extent in macro-economic textbooks. The first and simplest one, embedded in the conventional *IS-LM* models, regards the money supply as exogenously determined, in the sense that the level of and changes in the money supply are not influenced, directly or indirectly, by other economic variables (such as income, interest rates). It is difficult to think of an economy which would fit exactly into this mould. A closed economy which had inherited a stock of gold (which was used as the sole money) and which could not mine further gold would fit the requirements. If that economy were opened up to international trade, the stock of gold in the country would change with the surplus or deficit on the international balance of payments, which would lead to inflows or outflows of gold. In that case, the determinants of imports and exports and international capital flows, such as domestic income, interest rates, would influence changes in the money supply.

The second approach builds on the first by introducing banks into the system. In this context, it is useful to identify high-powered money, as those financial assets which are acceptable as reserve assets of the banking system. In the post-gold standard world, high-powered money can often be identified with non-interest bearing government debt (i.e. cash, balances at the Central Bank). Banks are seen as required (by law or convention) to maintain a minimum ratio between high-powered money under their control and the balances held by the public as bank deposits. The latter are taken to be part of the money supply. With a minimum ratio of s, high-powered money of H can support bank deposits of H/s (and hence a broadly defined money supply of the same amount) when the public decides to deposit all the high-powered money with the banks.[29] This 'credit multiplier' result can be easily modified for the public holding a proportion h of its money M as cash (i.e. high-powered money) and a proportion $(1-h)$ as bank deposits. The high-powered money in the banks' vaults is then $H-hM$ which can support bank deposits of $(H-hM)/s$, so that money supply $M = hM+(H-hM)/s$ which can be solved to give $M = H/(h+s(1-h))$.

The third approach has mainly appeared in discussion of the 'government budget constraint'. In the literature on that constraint (e.g. Blinder and Solow, 1973; Currie, 1978), it is recognised that the balance between government expenditure and tax revenue has implications for the issue of money and bonds. Specifically $DH+DB/r = G-T$ where DH is the change in non-interest bearing government debt, DB is change in number of bonds each of which raises $1/r$, G is government expenditure and T is tax revenue. When non-interest bearing government debt can be identified with money then this indicates how the evolution of the money supply depends upon the balance between government expenditure and revenue and the division of any deficit or surplus between money and bonds. When the banks can create money following an increase in high-powered money a slight modification is required to translate DH into a change in the broad money supply of DH/s.

The government budget constraint serves to link together the IS-curve (in the closed economy case based on $I+G = S+T$) and the LM-curve (with demand for money equal to supply of money). It also indicates that fiscal policy (changing G and T) has consequences for monetary policy since money supply and/or interest rates (through changes in bonds) are influenced. It also has implications for the analysis of a change in G or T on, say, the level of income, for not only does the direct effect of the change in G or T have to be analysed but also the consequent changes in H or B.[30]

The fourth approach draws upon, but substantially expands, the second and third approaches. The essential feature of this approach is that the behaviour of banks and the public interact to determine the money supply. The second approach is expanded in that the ratios s and h are not arbitrary constants but reflect decisions taken by banks and the public. Our discussion uses a simplified version of a model used by Tobin (1969) (which he labelled model III). The simplifications are that the rate of inflation is taken as zero (rather than the constant rate used by Tobin) and to exclude real assets. In this model, the equity of bank shareholders is ignored and the net worth of banks taken as zero.

Banks pursue some objectives such as profit maximisation but it is not necessary to specify particular objectives. Instead we work with general forms of demand and supply functions. The banks accept deposits from the public, on which they pay interest of r_D, and these deposits form assets for the public and liabilities for the banks. The demand by the banks for deposits will depend on r_D and the returns on the uses to which they put the deposits, which here are making loans and purchasing bonds. We write $\bar{r}=(r_D, r_L, r_B, r_C)$ where r_L is the rate of interest on loans, r_B on bonds and r_C is the Central Bank discount rate charged on borrowing by banks. Then the banks have a demand for deposits, $G_3(\bar{r})$ and actual deposits are D. The banks are legally required to hold a proportion s of their deposits as reserves of high-powered money. The banks wish to allocate the remaining $(1-s)D$ between voluntary reserves, bonds and loans.

The voluntary reserves are held to reduce the probability that a run of heavier-than-usual withdrawals from a bank would leave the actual reserve ratio below the legal minimum, and force the bank to borrow from the Central Bank at the discount rate r_C. The proportion of the $(1-s)D$ held as voluntary reserves will depend on r_C and on the returns from the other sources, and we write the desired proportion as $g_1(\bar{r})$. Similarly, the proportion held as bonds can be written as $g_2(\bar{r})$ and as loans as $g_4(\bar{r})$. Since the banks' net worth is zero, liabilities equal assets so that

$$D = s.D + (g_1(\bar{r}) + g_2(\bar{r}) + g_4(\bar{r})).(1-s).D.$$

The net worth of the private sector is $V = H + B$ where H is currency and B bonds (both issued by the government), and since the net worth of banks is zero the net worth of the (non-bank) public is also V. The public's demand for currency is taken as a proportion $f_1(\bar{r})$ of net worth, demand for bonds as $f_2(\bar{r})$, for deposits $f_3(\bar{r})$ and for loans equivalent to $-f_4(\bar{r})$ of net worth (so that f_4 is negative). The over-all wealth constraint requires that $f_1 + f_2 + f_3 + f_4 = 1$.

Equilibrium requires that the demand by banks and public for currency and for bonds sum to the currency and bonds available, and that the demand for and supply of deposits and of loans are equal. This yields:

(a)   (for high-powered money) $(s + g_1(r).(1-s)).D + f_1(r).V = H$
(b)   (for bonds) $g_2(\bar{r}).(1-s).D + f_2(\bar{r}).V = B$
(c)   (for deposits) $G_3(\bar{r}) + f_3(\bar{r}).V = 0$
(d)   (for loans) $g_4(\bar{r}).(1-s).D + f_4(\bar{r}).V = 0$

The fifth equation is the definition of deposits $D = f_3(\bar{r}).V$. In situations where the rate of interest on deposits (r_D) is externally determined, then equation (c) would be replaced by $G_3(\bar{r}) + f_3(\bar{r}).V < 0$.

This system of five equations only contains four independent equations. The first term of each equation sum to the net worth of the banks (zero) and the second term to the net worth of the public $(H+B)$. Thus one of the four equations (a)–(d) can be considered redundant in that it is implied by the other three and the overall wealth constraints. The four independent equations can then be solved for four unknowns r_D, r_L, r_B and D leaving the value of r_C exogenously determined by the Central Bank.

The net worth of the public is equal to their holdings of high-powered money, bonds and deposits minus loans. For banks deposits are equal to bank holdings of high-powered money (i.e.

reserves) of bonds and of loans. Adding those equalities together gives net worth of the public equal to high-powered money plus bonds, i.e. $V = B+H$. The money supply (broadly defined) would be regarded as deposits plus public's holdings of high-powered money, i.e. $M = D+f_1.V$. From equation (a) $D = (H-f_1.V)/s_1$ where $s_1 = s+g_1(\bar{r}).(1-s)$, and from equation (c) $D = f_3.V$, and putting these together yields $H = (f_1+s_1f_3).V$. Then

$$M = (H-f_1.V)/s_1+f_1.V = (H/s_1).(1-(1-s_1)f_1V/H)$$
$$= H(f_1+f_3)/(f_1+s_1f_3).$$

This is similar to the formula given at the end of the second approach where $h = f_1/(f_1+f_3)$ and with no voluntary reserves $s = s_1$.

The significance of this approach is three-fold. First, it indicates clearly that the creation of bank deposits and of loans and thereby the creation of (broadly defined) money does not involve any change in net worth of either the public or banks. Second, the key feature of the banks is that their deposits are regarded as part of the money supply. But the mechanism by which they accept deposits and make loans does not distinguish them from many other financial institutions. Third, the demand and supply of loans affects the money supply. For example, an increase in the demand for loans could be expected to be partly met by the banks raising r_L and in part by raising the value of g_4. A rise in g_4 would usually imply a fall in g_1 and thereby an increase in the money supply. In the more general case of disequilibrium, banks may have more voluntary reserves than they want, so that they can expand loans when the demand for loans rises. Further since loans entail a cost to the borrower, an increased demand for loans will usually be linked to some expenditure plans so that there can be close linkages between the expansion of planned expenditure and expansion of the money supply.

Conclusion

The preceding discussion may be attacked on the grounds that it presents a caricature of the approaches taken by economists to consumption, investment and money. In particular, the equations embedded in empirical models of the economy are much more sophisticated than would be suggested by the above discussion. Our discussion could not in the space available deal in detail at a technically sophisticated level with these topics. Instead we have sought to indicate the nature of the approaches taken to these topics. These approaches, often in a simplified form, are fed into theoretical models of the economy, and the conclusions from such models heavily condition the way in which economists think about macro-economics. In contrast, econometric models often incorporate an eclectic collection of equations, which have the main purpose of forecasting future developments. In doing so, approaches at variance with those discussed above often emerge. For example, investment equations are likely to include factors such as output and changes in output. The investment equations in most theoretical models link investment with the rate of interest and ignore the changes in output. A major strand of our argument is that the approaches in a lot of empirical work are inconsistent with (or at least orthogonal to) the conventional approaches to macro-economics.

Notes
1 Any orthodox text-book on macro-economics provides details of the approaches discussed in this chapter. See, for example, Branson (1979), Gordon (1981), Levačić (1976), Dornbusch and Fischer (1981).
2 The orthodox theories usually relate to consumption rather than consumer expenditure, although the empirical tests of the theories are often cast in terms of consumer expenditure. Consumption relates to the flow of goods and services consumed by households, and the services include those generated by consumer durables in the possession of households. Consumer expenditure relates to the spending by households in a particular period.
3 It can be argued that firms are owned by households, and firms make savings decisions on behalf of their shareholders according to the wishes of their shareholders.
4 'This psychological law [that consumption depends on income] was of the utmost importance in the development of my own thought, and it is, I think, absolutely fundamental to the theory of effective demand set forth in my book' (Keynes, 1937b).
5 Modigliani and Brumberg (1954) introduced the LCH; see also Ando and Modigliani (1963); Modigliani (1975). The permanent income hypothesis (Friedman, 1957) is in many respects a variant of the life-cycle hypothesis, although the motivation of households and the capital market assumptions are not as clearly indicated as in the LCH. The permanent income hypothesis also involves the assumption that the length of life is infinite (Modigliani, 1975, p.6). Because of the similarities with the LCH, we omit separate consideration of the permanent income hypothesis in this brief over-view.
6 The 'proportionality' result (i.e. that there is no constant term in the equation in the text link C_t and V) is often used in connection with the LCH but is not an intrinsic part of it. Permanent income can be defined as $y_p = r.V$ where r is the rate of return on V, and hence $C = (d_t/r)y_p$.
7 For the full analysis see Ando and Modigliani (1963).

8 For example, the definition of a multi-person household used by the Economic Commission for Europe was 'a group of two or more persons who combine to occupy the whole or part of a housing unit and to provide themselves with food and/or other essentials for living. The group may pool their incomes to a greater or lesser extent. The group may be composed of related persons only or of unrelated persons or of a combination of both . . .' (quoted in Sawyer, 1976).

9 For a summary of the incidence of poverty in different groups see Atkinson (1975) Chapter 10. Fiegehen et al. (1977) conclude for the UK that 'both the risk and the numerical importance of poverty are especially high for the retired and single parent households.'

10 See, for example, the report of the Wilson Committee (Committee to Review the Functioning of Financial Institutions, 1980) Chapter 6; Minns (1980).

11 This has led into the controversy over whether unfunded social security pension arrangements have led to a reduction in savings. For some recent work on this topic see Green (1981).

12 With unfunded schemes there are liabilities to pay contributions to finance pensions which correspond to the assets of those entitled to a pension. However, the pensions of many of those currently working will in that sense be paid for by the contributions of those yet unborn.

13 For a survey of investment theories see Austin (1979), Junankar (1972); for a book of readings on investment Helliwell (1976). For variations on an essentially neo-classical theme see Nickell (1978).

14 The firm is seeking to maximise $V = \int_o^\infty e^{-rt}R(t)dt$ where $R(t)=p.Q(K,L)-w.L-q.I$ subject to $dK/dt = I-\delta K$, where q is the price of investment goods, w the price of labour, K is capital equipment (or equivalently the flow of capital services), and dK/dt the net change in the capital stock (= net investment) and δ the rate of depreciation of capital equipment. The rate of discount could vary over time without making any basic difference to the problem. The rate of discount is assumed to be equal to the market rate of interest, at which rate the firm can borrow or lend as it wishes.

Now
$$V = \int_o^T e^{-rt}R(t)\, dt + e^{-rT}\int_T^\infty e^{-r(t-T)}R(t)\, dt.$$
The second term could be interpreted as the scrap value of the firm at time T discounted to the present, and is held to represent the price which can be obtained for the firm at time T. Thus the use of an infinite time horizon is not as restrictive as it might sound, provided that there is a competitive market for firms in which the 'scrap' value can be obtained.

15 Space precludes further discussion, for which see Garegnani (1970), (1978), Harcourt (1975).

16 The decision on whether to use K_1 or K_2 would be based on whether
$$D = \sum_{t=0}^{T} (R1(t)-R2(t))/(1+r)^t$$
is greater or less than zero where $R1\,(t)$ is the net revenue from using K_1 in period t, and $R2$ from using K_2. The equation $\Sigma(R1(t)-R2(t))/(1+r)^t$

$=0$ may have more than one solution in terms of r which is positive and real (i.e. economically meaningful). Suppose there are two solutions r_A and r_B $(r_A > r_B)$. Then the sign of the expression D will differ for r between r_A and r_B compared with r greater than r_A or less than r_B.

It is necessary to slightly amend the profit maximisation problem presented in the text to include the constraints $K_i \geq 0$ for each $i=1,2,\ldots, m$. The first-order conditions then become, from the Kuhn-Tucker theorem, that

$$K_i \cdot (\partial Q / \partial K_i - c_i / p) = 0, \; i=1,2,\ldots, m$$

17 Grossman (1972) provides a model of investment demand where firms are constrained in terms of the volume of output which they can sell.

18 This equation has, in general, N roots and more than one of them may be admissible (i.e. real and positive). An alternative decision-rule is: invest if present value of returns on investment (i.e.

$$\sum_{t=1}^{T} R_t / (1+r)^t$$

where r is the rate of discount) exceeds the cost C. The two decision-rules give equivalent answers if the net returns are re-invested at a rate of interest equal to the rate of discount and if the rates are constant over time (Hirshleifer, 1958).

9 For the individual firm, a lower rate of interest may not lead to any increase in the additions to the capital stock. It is assumed that at the aggregate level, this type of 'discontinuity' does not arise. Again the re-switching controversy suggests that the relationship between additions to the capital stock and the rate of interest (=rate of profit) may not be monotonically decreasing (p.26 in text).

20 'In the case of durable assets it is, therefore, natural and reasonable that expectations of the future should play a *dominant* part in determining the scale on which new investment is deemed advisable. But, as we have seen, the basis for such expectations is very precarious. Being based on shifting and unreliable evidence, they are subject to *sudden and violent changes*' (italics added) (Keynes, 1936, p.315). See also Keynes (1936), Chapter 12.

21 For surveys see Goodhart (1975), Feige and Pearce (1977), Laidler (1977).

22 It would, perhaps, be more accurate to follow Goodhart (1975) and say that the transactions demand for money treats money as the medium of final payment, rather than as a medium of exchange. The difference between the two concepts arises particularly with trade credit which can be used as a medium of exchange but is not a medium of final payment.

23 The rate of interest on money is often assumed to be constant. It would be more appropriate to use the expected rate of interest on money over the planning period. Banks, for example, vary the rate of interest paid on deposit account balances, which are often regarded as part of the money supply. Capital gains or losses on bonds arise from changes in the rate of discount applied to the interest payments on bonds. If that rate of discount is expected to change, it could be argued that the rate of interest paid on money would be expected to change as well.

24 The return on money in the analysis of Tobin is taken as riskless. This is only riskless in nominal terms. Whilst there is no uncertainty over the nominal value of money there may, following the previous footnote, be uncertainty over the rate of interest.

25 We should here note the comment of Hahn (1971) on this approach of Friedman when he argues that 'Friedman has a lazy man's theory of the demand for money in that he explains it by unanalysed utility and productive services.'

26 Hahn (1980) expresses this point more formally when he says that 'when there is government debt the homogeneity postulate must also be false unless one can legitimately leave out the real value of bonds from the aggregate excess demand functions.' The homogeneity postulate is that the absolute price level does not affect real demands in the economy.

27 Thus there would be no overall wealth effect on demand in the economy. There could, however, be distribution effects in that some individuals will be better off and others worse off than before, thereby affecting the composition of demand.

28 Banks are broadly defined to include any financial institutions whose liabilities are accepted as a generally accepted medium of exchange. Banks are not excluded from taking the initiative in finding customers for their loans, but we do assume that agents taking out loans do so for a purpose.

29 For a fuller story of how this comes about see any macro-economic texts.

30 See, for example, Turnovsky (1977), for an indication of the differences which arise from an analysis which includes the government budget constraint as compared with one which omits that constraint.

3 The Keynesian–Monetarist Orthodoxy

Introduction

The central purpose of this chapter is an exploration of the similarities of the Keynesian and monetarist approaches which are, we argue, sufficiently close to merit saying that they share a common 'vision' of the world. Within that common 'vision', we are able to indicate the nature of some of the differences between the Keynesian and the monetarist. The common 'vision' of the world does not preclude apparently sharp differences of emphasis and in policy recommendations. At times, such as when this is being written in 1981, the differences over policy have important consequences for the extent of unemployment and inflation. However, the policy differences are contained within a relatively narrow range, relating to matters such as the relative use of fiscal and monetary policy, the size of the government deficit, the suitability of incomes policy, demand management and control of the money supply as methods for reducing the rate of inflation. Questions such as the extent of national planning, the private, public or cooperative ownership of industry, etc. are generally not raised. Some policy differences between Keynesians and monetarists arise from differences of opinion over where the economy is at a particular time (e.g. how much slack there is in the economy), but many differences derive from different interpretations within a basically common model. At one time differences over the size of certain key parameters (such as the interest elasticity of the demand for money and of investment demand) were much discussed. During the 'seventies, emphasis swung away from those differences and towards questions such as:

(a) the speed with which prices adjust to eliminate disequilibrium and to restore full employment;

(b) the way in which expectations about the future are formed.

These are related with (b) having an influence on (a), and (a) in some respects being concerned with the size of certain key parameters (with the speed of adjustment treated as a parameter).[1] Arising to some extent out of (a) there have been differences in the relative emphasis placed on the demand and on the supply side of the economy.

There are two basic models which macro-economists use. The first is the *IS-LM* approach and extensions thereto, and the second a general equilibrium approach. We use each of these in turn to illustrate the similarities and differences between the Keynesians and monetarists.[2]

The *IS-LM* approach

The simplest version of the *IS-LM* approach is for a closed economy with a zero rate of inflation (so that we do not have to distinguish between real and nominal rates of interest). The two equations involved relate to equilibrium in the goods market and in the money markets. The first leads to equality between *ex ante* leakages (savings S and taxation T) and *ex ante* injections (investment I and government expenditure G). This provides the equation $S(y) + T(y) = I(r) + G$, where r is the rate of interest and y real income. All the terms in this equation are expressed in real terms, and it can be seen that simple representations of the savings and investment functions are used. The resulting negative relationship between y and r is usually labelled the *IS*-curve. The second equation relates to equilibrium in the money market with the real demand for money $(L(y,r))$ in equality with the real stock of money (M/p), where p is the price level and M the nominal stock of money, i.e. $L(y,r) = M/p$. The resulting positive relationship between y and r is usually labelled the *LM*-curve.

The savings and investment functions could be made functions of both y and r, and the supply of money a function of the rate of interest without substantially altering the analysis.[3]

The conventional diagrammatic representation of the two equations is given in Figure 3.1. A lot of the debate between Keynesians and monetarists, particularly during the 'sixties, concentrated on empirical questions. Two major questions were what was the slope of the *IS* curve? and which zone of the *LM* curve (*A, B* or *C*) was applicable? Keynesians were seen as leaning towards the view that the *IS* curve was nearly vertical (representing low interest elasticities of investment and savings), and zone *A* as the applicable one (with very high interest elasticity of the demand for money). The combination of those views led to a stress on fiscal policy (repre-

sented by a shift in the *IS* curve) and the neglect of monetary policy
(which although leading to a shift in the *LM* curve would not change
the position of zone *A*). Monetarists, in contrast, were seen as
viewing the *IS*-curve as incorporating significant interest-elasticity
of investment, and the *LM*-curve a low interest elasticity of the
demand for money. Hence zone *C* was seen as applicable, where a
shift in the *IS* curve has no effect on income, leading to emphasis on
monetary policy rather than fiscal policy.

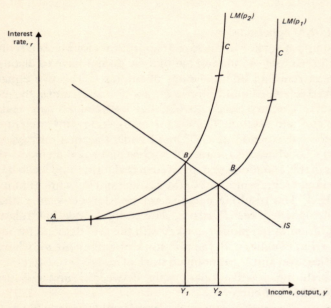

Fig. 3.1: Diagrammatic representation of the *IS-LM* approach.

A related debate was initiated by Friedman and Meiselman
(1963) who sought to contrast a naïve Keynesian position (corresponding to an economy operating in zone *A*) with a naïve monetarist position (corresponding to zone *C* and a horizontal *IS*-curve).
Friedman and Meiselman compared the correlation between
changes in money income and changes in autonomous expenditure
with the correlation between changes in money income and changes
in the money stock, and concluded that the latter were superior to
the former and evidence in favour of the monetarist position.[4]
An important aspect of these debates is that they were under-

taken within the context of a common approach. Indeed, it could be argued that their outcome was that the general position (corresponding to zone *B* and a downward sloping *IS* curve) was supported rather than either of the extreme versions.[5]

The two equations for the simplest *IS-LM* model contain three unknowns—*y*, *r* and *p*. The simple model above was completed by assuming that the price level was fixed. Friedman (1974) argued that one basic difference between Keynesians and monetarists could be seen in terms of (in his terminology) how the 'missing equation' is supplied,[6] with, he suggested, Keynesians viewing *p* as fixed whilst monetarists viewed *y* as fixed. The idea that the price level is fixed does not necessarily imply that the price level is constant but rather that it is unaffected within the period of analysis by economic factors such as the level of demand. One possibility would be that money wages were set by socio-political factors (for example, by trade unions), and prices determined as a fixed mark-up over unit labour costs.

The idea that the level of income is predetermined embodies the notion that prices are sufficiently flexible for the economy to move quickly to that level of income. The flexibility of the price level leads to changes in the real value of the money supply and consequent shifts in the *LM* curve in Figure 3.1, sufficient to generate equilibrium at the predetermined level of income. In turn, that level of income is often regarded as corresponding to full employment, determined by supply side considerations as will be seen below.

The counterpart to the idea that prices are fixed is that income adjusts to restore equilibrium following a shock to the system, whereas the counterpart to the idea that income is fixed is that prices adjust to restore equilibrium.

The view that Keynesians stress the role of quantity adjustment (in this simple case, income) rather than price adjustment, and that monetarists stress the reverse can be illustrated in numerous ways. The first relies on the use of an aggregate supply curve, which relates the amount of output which would be offered by firms to the price level (implicitly relative to costs of production). The aggregate supply curve is generally portrayed as upward-sloping, from the aggregation across firms of conventional upward-sloping neo-classical supply curves, based on rising marginal cost curves. From the two *IS-LM* equations, the rate of interest can be eliminated to provide an aggregate demand equation which links the price level and income in equilibrium on the demand side. The aggregate demand curve is a negative relationship between the price level and income, reflecting that higher prices imply a lower real money stock, necessitating lower demand for money and hence lower income if equilibrium is to be maintained. Equilibrium on the supply side will mean that firms are able to produce and sell the output indicated by the aggregate supply curve, and then planned output and income will be equal. Then we are able to draw the aggregate demand curve and supply curve on one diagram as in Figure 3.2. There zone *D* of the aggregate supply curve could be labelled the Keynesian zone, and corresponds to firms operating with spare capacity and with constant unit costs. Zone *F* could be labelled the monetarist zone, with firms operating at full capacity so that shifts in the aggregate demand schedule do not lead to changes in the level of income/output, but to changes in the price level.

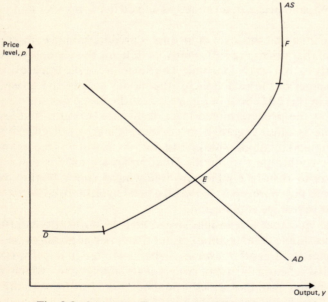

Fig. 3.2: Aggregate Demand and Supply Curves.

However this presentation obscures the role of relative prices in that the price changes are changes in price *relative* to costs. In order to draw out the role of relative price changes it is convenient to focus on the labour market. This is illustrated by Figure 3.3, where in quadrant I are the familiar *IS-LM* curves, and in quadrant II a

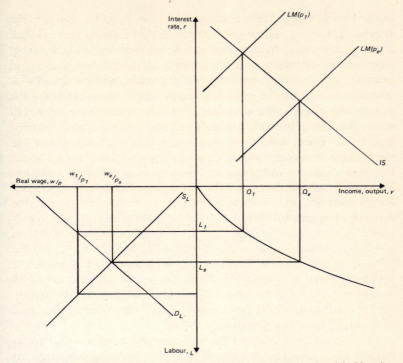

Fig. 3.3: Equilibrium in the Goods and Money Markets, with Varying Labour Market Situations.

short-run production function linking output and employment. In quadrant III, there are demand for and supply of labour curves, both of which are functions of the real wage.[7]

Let us begin with a particular real wage w_1/p_1 (where w is money wage) and real money stock M/p_1, where those values have been inherited from the past. These values may have been appropriate for a previous equilibrium, but not consistent for equilibrium now. At that real wage, the demand for labour determines employment at L_1 (with a demand below supply). Aggregate demand equilibrium (quadrant I) with a real money stock M/p_1 would generate income y_1 which is consistent with employment L_1.

At the prevailing wage, supply exceeds demand and there is unemployment. In this case, it could be said that both the real wage and the money supply are set incorrectly for the achievement of full employment, where the demand for and supply of labour are in balance, which requires a change in the real wage to w_e/p_e and a change in the real money supply. The speed with which the economy moves to full employment at L_e clearly depends, apart from the distance from equilibrium, on the speed with which the real wage changes in response to excess supply in the labour market, and the speed with which the price level or nominal money supply changes to take the real money stock to the required level. Keynesians have tended to stress the difficulties involved in wage and price changes, particularly when reductions in money wages and nominal prices are involved, whereas monetarists tend to argue that there is sufficient flexibility in wages and prices for equilibrium at full employment to be quickly restored.[8] Another, but related, difference between Keynesians and monetarists arises when the demand side of the economy (quadrant I) is out of balance with the supply side (quadrant III). For example, the real wage could be at its equilibrium level, which would generate employment L_e and output y_e, but the price level and nominal money stock such that the $LM(p_1)$ curve results generating equilibrium output of y_1. Keynesians could be seen as arguing for demand side dominance, so that in this situation output tends to y_1 whilst monetarists look to supply side dominance with output tending towards y_e.

This discussion illustrates the well-known conclusion that situations of unemployment in Keynesian models have, at some stage, to draw on price inflexibilities of some kind. These inflexibilities may be relative (e.g. wages relative to prices) or absolute (e.g. nominal prices). The practical relevance of the Keynesian position then clearly depends on the answer to the empirical question of whether in practice prices are or are not sufficiently flexible.

It could be argued that many of the problems of price inflexibility arise when absolute (rather than just relative) changes in prices are involved. In an inflationary era, reductions in absolute prices are generally not required. With the final variant of the *IS-LM* curve approach considered we move to an inflationary era. It is now necessary to distinguish between real and nominal rates of interest. The demand for investment is taken as a function of the real rate of interest, since the returns from investment are assumed to rise in nominal terms at the expected rate of inflation. However, the demand for money is a function of the interest rate differential between money and other financial assets. When money receives a zero rate of interest (whatever the rate of inflation) then the relevant differential corresponds to the nominal rate of interest.

The *IS-LM* equations now become:

$$S(y) + T(y) = I(r) + G \text{ and } L(y, r + \dot{p}^e) = M/p$$

where r is the real rate of interest, $\dot{p}^e$ is the expected rate of inflation and $r + \dot{p}^e$ is the nominal rate of interest.[9] Throughout the book the dot over the variable indicates proportionate rate of change of that variable, i.e. $\dot{x} = (1/x)dx/dt$. The revised *IS-LM* curves are drawn in quadrant I of Figure 3.4 where the *LM* curve has to be identified in terms of the prevailing price level and the expected rate of inflation. In quadrant II, there is the mapping between output y and unemployment U based on a production function linking output and employment. In quadrant III, we present a short-run expectations-augmented Phillips' curve (*PC*), that is, $\dot{w} = f(U) + b\dot{p}^e$, where $\dot{w}$ is the proportionate rate of change of wages. This Phillips' curve is

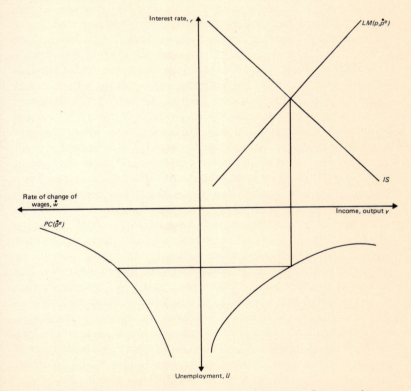

Fig. 3.4: IS-LM Curves and Phillips' curve for given set of expectations on inflation.

discussed in some detail in the next chapter. In the short run for a given value of $\dot{p}^e$, the level of output is essentially determined in quadrant I. Output determines unemployment (as in quadrant II), and unemployment (for given $\dot{p}^e$) determines the rate of wage inflation. However, in the next stage, these curves will begin to shift. The *LM* curve will shift for two reasons. First, following the rise in wages, prices will rise causing a change in the real money supply (unless there is an exactly offsetting change in the nominal money supply). Second, the expected rate of inflation may respond to the actual experience of inflation. This second factor will also cause the expectations-augmented Phillips' curve in quadrant III to shift. In the next period the *LM* and the Phillips' curves would have shifted and we could again work out the temporary equilibrium position. Instead of trying to follow the adjustment mechanism through we move straight to a consideration of medium-term equilibrium, in which, with no productivity growth assumed, $\dot{w} = \dot{p} = \dot{p}^e$ so that real wages are constant and expectations on inflation are fulfilled.[10] A stationary *LM* curve requires that the real money stock is constant so that $\dot{p} = \dot{M}$ so that the nominal money stock grows at the same rate as prices. For convenience, working with $\dot{p}$, rather than with $\dot{w}$ or $\dot{p}^e$, for quadrant III $\dot{p}\,(1-b) = f(U)$. The outcome now crucially depends on the value of b. If $b = 1$, then $f(U) = 0$ and the solution of this equation, say, U_N is the level of unemployment in equilibrium; and via quadrant II output is determined as well. The rate of increase of the money supply determines the rate of inflation, and the price level adapts until the *LM* curve reaches a position such that equilibrium in quadrant I is consistent with unemployment of U_N.

However, if $b < 1$, from $\dot{p} = \dot{M}$ we have $f(U) = (1-b)\dot{M}$. There is a long-run trade-off between unemployment and inflation, and the level of unemployment can be varied by changing the rate of increase of the money stock (and thereby the rate of inflation). The monetarist position has generally been that $b = 1$ and hence that there is no long-run trade-off between inflation and unemployment. Any short-run trade-off arises from the expectations about inflation not adjusting instantaneously to actual inflationary experience (see pp.68–70 below). With $b = 1$, unemployment in equilibrium is determined by the solution to the equation $f(U) = 0$. This solution, U_N, is often called the 'natural' rate of unemployment, and corresponds in most formulations of the expectations-augmented Phillips' curve to equilibrium in the labour market where demand for and supply of labour are equal so U_N corresponds to full employment (see p.68 below).

The Keynesian position has been a mixture of beliefs that b was substantially below unity and that expectations on inflation adjust slowly to actual experience, so that over a relevant time horizon there was a trade-off between inflation and unemployment. Again the central questions are empirical—here whether b is equal to unity or not and how quickly expectations about inflation adjust to actual experience.

When $b = 1$ this approach suggests that the level of unemployment (and hence of output) is sooner or later determined by conditions in the labour market, i.e. on the supply-side of the economy. This had led to a stress on the supply side and to de-emphasising the demand-side of the economy. However what happens on the demand-side may influence the supply-side, a theme to which we return in Chapter 6. Investment, for example, adds to productive capacity and may affect the position of the demand for labour curve.

Both Keynesians and monetarists present essentially equilibrium approaches, with the presumption of stable functions for consumption, demand for money, etc. derived in the ways summarised in Chapter 2. They differ over the degree of price flexibility and over how long the time-span is over which disequilibrium lasts, and these differences lead to considerable policy differences.

An equilibrium analysis can be used, of course, to predict what effects specified exogenous changes have on the functions involved and thereby on the equilibrium outcome. However, equilibrium analysis is likely to provide only limited insights if the functions involved are subject to continual change. For example, it could be argued that the investment function changes from period to period. In each period, the appropriate investment function could be entered into the *IS-LM* analysis and the equilibrium values of income and interest rate solved out. In doing so, it is implicitly assumed that the economy can adjust rapidly enough for that equilibrium to be achieved within the single period before the investment function moves to another position. The equilibrium analysis creates the impression that the equilibrium position is maintainable over time. But, if the functions involved are inherently cyclical (as we will argue for investment) then this feature is necessarily omitted from an equilibrium analysis.

There are two particular ways in which the *IS-LM* analysis may mislead.[11] First, it may not provide sufficient warning that the underlying functions for investment and the demand for money are liable to shift. The demand for investment and the speculative demand for money both rest on expectations about the future. But with the future inherently unknowable, expectations about the future are likely to be flimsily based and subject to change.[12] Further, there can be periods of time when the extent of uncertainty about the future changes, leading to changes in the demand for investment and for money. In Keynes' words, 'our desire to hold money as a store of wealth is a barometer of the degree of our distrust of our calculations and conventions concerning the future', and 'it is not surprising that the volume of investment, . . . should fluctuate widely from time to time. For it depends on two sets of judgements about the future, neither of which rests on an adequate or secure foundation—on the propensity to hoard and on opinions of the future yield on capital assets' (Keynes, 1937b).

Second, the impression has been created in the past that the *IS* and the *LM* curves are independent of each other. One consequence of that impression was discussion of economic policy in which fiscal policy was seen as shifting the *IS* curve whilst monetary policy involved a shift in the *LM* curve. The literature on the government budget constraint forcibly indicated that the *IS* and the *LM* curves were not independent (see pp.36–37 above). However an increase in planned investment can only take place in the short run before a corresponding increase in planned savings occurs if the supply of money and/or trade credit expands or the demand for money declines to allow the investment to be financed (see pp.116–117 below). Further the demand for investment and the demand for money may move together. Following the observations of Keynes quoted above, an increase in the degree of uncertainty may raise desires to avoid firm commitments for the future which is exhibited by a fall in the demand for investment and an increase in the demand for money.[13]

General equilibrium and disequilibrium

In this section, we utilise a different approach to illustrate the basic similarity of the Keynesian and monetarist approaches. In one sense, this section represents a generalisation of the preceding section in that, for example, consumption goods are treated separately rather than aggregated as a single good. But it represents a simplification in that the monetary sector is dealt with rather summarily and investment/savings are overlooked. A general equilibrium approach is used so that the contribution of the reappraisal of the economics of Keynes (Clower, 1965; Leijonhufvud, 1968), can be indicated.

We begin with a household which maximises a utility function of the form

$$V(d_1, d_2, \ldots, d_m, s_{m+1}, s_{m+2}, \ldots, s_n)$$

where there are n goods, of which the first m are typically demanded by households ('consumption goods') and those numbered $m+1$, $m+2$, . . ., n are typically supplied by household ('factors of production'). The household is subject to a budget constraint such that expenditure

$$\sum_{i=1}^{m} p_i d_i$$

equals income of

$$\sum_{j=m+1}^{n} f_j s_j + \propto \pi,$$

where p_i, f_j are prices of consumption goods and factors of production respectively and $\propto$ is this household's share of the profits earned by firms in the current period which are paid out to the households within the period. From this utility maximisation problem, the household derives demand functions $d_i(\bar{p}, \bar{f}, \propto\pi)$ and supply functions $s_j(\bar{p}, \bar{f}, \propto\pi)$, where $\bar{p}$ is a vector of consumption goods prices and $\bar{f}$ the vector of factor prices. From the household budget constraint, these demand and supply functions satisfy the equation

$$\sum_{i=1}^{m} p_i d_i(\bar{p}, \bar{f}, \propto\pi) = \sum_{j=m+1}^{n} f_j s_j(\bar{p}, \bar{f}, \propto\pi) + \propto\pi.$$

These demand and supply functions are homogeneous of degree zero, hence a proportionate increase in all prices and profits would leave the demand and supply unchanged, and there is no money illusion present.

Aggregation over households yields overall demand and supply functions of the form

$$D_i(\bar{p}, \bar{f}, \pi) \ (i=1, 2, \ldots, m)$$

and

$$S_j(\bar{p}, \bar{f}, \pi) \ (j=m+1, m+2, \ldots, n).^{[14]}$$

These aggregate functions will, from the summation of individual household budget constraints, satisfy equation (A):

$$\sum_{i=1}^{m} p_i D_i(\bar{p},\bar{f},\pi) = \sum_{j=m+1}^{n} f_j S_j(\bar{p},\bar{f},\pi) + \pi \qquad (A)$$

Firms are assumed to be profit maximisers with a profit function of the form

$$\pi_k = \sum_{i=1}^{m} p_i s_i - \sum_{j=m+1}^{n} f_j d_j$$

where goods *1* to *m* are supplied by firms to households, and goods *m+1* to *n* are factors demanded by firms from households. The maximisation procedure for a particular firm yields supply functions of the form $s_i(\bar{p},\bar{f})$ and demand functions of the form $d_j(\bar{p},\bar{f})$, which are related via the equation

$$\pi_k = \sum_{i} p_i s_i(\bar{p},\bar{f}) - \sum_{j} f_j d_j(\bar{p},\bar{f})$$

which serves to define profits for the firm. Aggregation across firms yields the equation (B):

$$\pi = \sum_{i=1}^{m} p_i S_i(\bar{p},\bar{f}) - \sum_{j=m+1}^{n} f_j D_j(\bar{p},\bar{f}) \qquad (B)$$

Adding equations *A* and *B* together yields

$$\sum_{i=1}^{m} p_i D_i(\bar{p},\bar{f},\pi) + \pi = \sum_{i=1}^{m} p_i S_i(\bar{p},\bar{f}) + \sum_{m+1}^{n} f_j S_j(\bar{p},\bar{f},\pi) - \sum_{j=m+1}^{n} f_i D_j(\bar{p},\bar{f}) + \pi$$

and hence

$$\sum_{i=1}^{m} p_i (D_i(\bar{p},\bar{f},\pi) - S_i(\bar{p},\bar{f})) + \sum_{j=m+1}^{n} f_j (D_j(\bar{p},\bar{f}) - S_j(\bar{p},\bar{f},\pi)) = 0.$$

This equation, generally referred to as Walras' Law, is of considerable significance in that it denies the possibility of overall excess demand or supply, by indicating that the sum of excess demands (over all products and factors) is zero. Positive excess demand in some markets would be compensated by negative excess demand in other markets. Perhaps the most surprising consequence of this equation is the view that general excess demand in the product markets (so that the first summation in the above equation is positive) would be accompanied by general excess supply in the factor markets (with the second summation negative).

Equilibrium in each market requires $D_k = S_k$ for $k = 1, 2, \ldots, m,$ $m+1, \ldots, n$. These n equations contain only $n-1$ independent equations, for from Walras' Law, equilibrium in $n-1$ markets ensures equilibrium in the remaining market. The $n-1$ independent equations may be solved for $n-1$ unknowns. These $n-1$ unknowns are the $n-1$ relative prices involved. As indicated above, the functions D and S are homogeneous of degree zero, so are functions of relative, rather than absolute prices. For example, take the nth good as numeraire, and measure other prices relative to the price of the nth good. We can write out

$$D_i(p,f) = D_i(p_1,p_2, \ldots, p_m, f_{m+1}, \ldots, f_n)$$
$$= D_i(p_1/f_n, p_2/f_n, \ldots, p_m/f_n, f_{m+1}/f_n, \ldots, f_{n-1}/f_n).^{15}$$

The number of unknown relative prices is $n-1$, in line with the number of independent equations, and in principle these equations can be solved for the $n-1$ equilibrium relative prices. The demand and supply of consumption goods and factors of production can be calculated for these equilibrium prices. In particular, the level of unemployment which would result is held to correspond to the 'natural rate of unemployment' (U_N above). Friedman (1968) says that

the 'natural rate of unemployment' . . . is the level that would be ground out by the Walrasian system of general equilibrium equations, provided there is embedded in them the actual structural characteristics of the labor and commodity markets, stochastic variability in demands and supplies, the cost of gathering information about job vacancies and labour availabilities, the costs of mobility, and so on.[16]

The use of the term the 'natural rate of unemployment' conveys a number of false impressions. The obvious one is that the use of the word natural implies that there is something inevitable about unemployment. Another is that there is a unique equilibrium outcome. There has been a long search for the conditions under which a general equilibrium system has a unique equilibrium with prices and quantities which are meaningful (that is non-negative). But Hahn (1971) notes 'the conditions for such an equilibrium to be unique are rather stringent. If there are many equilibria they will not all be stable for any adjustment theory we choose to use. It then follows that there is nothing in these models as such to allow one to conclude that the final equilibrium is independent of initial conditions and of monetary policy in particular.'

We can note that although production is included in this model many of the crucial features of production are overlooked. Production in this model takes place instantaneously so that the problems which arise from firms trying to forecast demand when making production plans do not arise (Chick, 1978). It has long been recognised that there are difficulties in finding a role for money in the general equilibrium framework.[17] Money is a barren asset, and within each period each household and firm balances income and expenditure. The easiest way of introducing money is to argue that economic agents require money for transactions demand purposes to cover the period between receipt of income and expenditure. Thus the demand for money M^d is linked to the nominal value of transactions in a simple way, i.e. $M^d = k.p.T$, where k is a constant, p is a measure of the absolute price level and T a measure of the volume of transaction. The volume of transactions is determined by the considerations discussed above, so that the absolute price level is determined by the nominal money supply from $M^s = M^d = kpT$. This leads to the 'classical dichotomy' under which relative prices and resource allocations are determined on the real side of the economy by the interaction of demand and supply, whilst the absolute price level is determined on the monetary side.

In many respects this general equilibrium approach underlies the (neo-classical) monetarist view of the world. Output and employment are determined by 'real' forces of demand and supply. Equilibrium is one of full employment in the sense that at the prevailing real wage the supply of labour is taken up by the demand for labour. There is a presumed tendency towards full employment arising from changes in relative prices. The prices of goods and factors in excess demand rise, whilst those in excess supply fall (see pp.67–77 below). The price level is determined by the money supply, and hence the rate of change of the price level (rate of inflation) is determined by the rate of change of the money supply. Yet, in this model money only matters for the price level, and it does not appear to matter for levels of output and employment.

There is a sense in which this general equilibrium approach relates essentially to a barter economy, and it has been argued that the contribution of Keynes was to shift the analysis of exchange from a barter economy into a monetary economy.[18] The analysis of household behaviour indicates, for example, that essentially the household exchanges consumption goods for factors of production. These exchanges are treated as taking place instantaneously so that there are no problems of temporary finance for the purchase of some goods and services prior to the sale of factor supplies. An economy which was in and remained in equilibrium might develop a credit arrangement system under which expenditure could precede income, provided that at the end of the period income and expenditure balances. But, the model is intended to work out of, as well as in, equilibrium. The problems of disequilibrium lead us to the view of Clower (1965) and others of the economics of Keynes.

Clower laid stress on the fact that in a monetary economy, goods exchange for money, but in general goods do not exchange for goods.[19] In particular, households do not directly exchange their labour supply (and other factor supplies) for consumption goods and services. Instead, they must first find a buyer for their factor supplies which they exchange for money, and then use that money to finance their purchases. In one sense this merely tells the same basic story at greater length. But it does serve to indicate that the first exchange (of factors for money) has to precede the second exchange (of money for goods). When the household is unable to find a purchaser for its labour, then it does not receive the income out of which it was planned to finance expenditure. In equilibrium, demands and supplies are matched so the problems of finding a purchaser have been solved. But out of equilibrium, there is a discrepancy between demand and supply so that at least one side of the market cannot carry through their plans. In Figure 3.5 at price P_1 planned demand is Q_D and planned supply is Q_S and these plans are incompatible. The market price may adjust very quickly to equilibrium price P_e so that the incompatibility is removed. But failing that quick adjustment, some market trading takes place at price P_1, and the amount bought and sold could lie between Q_D and Q_S. For simplicity, we follow the conventional assumption that in such circumstances the short side of the market dominates, so that the amount traded is the minimum of the quantity demanded and the quantity supplied (in this case Q_D). Now when the market is for a factor of production (particularly labour) and has a price (wage) above equilibrium, the quantity actually employed will be less than the quantity which the households wish to supply (at that price/wage), and the income of the household is less than planned.[20] The intended expenditure on goods and services cannot proceed since the income which was to finance the expenditure has not completely

The actual demands by the households, $d'_i (i = 1, 2, \ldots, m)$ are constrained by

$$\sum_i p_i D'_i = Y \leqslant \sum_j f_j S_j + \pi$$

where Y is income. The profit equation for the firms remains unchanged, and when combined with the above inequality yields

$$\sum_i p_i (D'_i - S_i) + \sum_j f_j (D_j - S_j) \leqslant 0.$$

The strict inequality holds except for situations of full equilibrium, when all plans can be realised.[21]

There has been a considerable literature based on the notion that prices are slow to adjust and that economic agents are quantity-constrained.[22] In the example given above, households were not able to supply the labour they wished (at the prevailing wage) but were constrained by the employment demanded. Following that quantity constraint on their actual supply of labour, their income fell and new consumption plans would be required. When there are quantity constraints, it is necessary to derive demand and supply functions which take into account those quantity constraints. The work of Barro and Grossman (1971, 1976), for example, seeks to ensure that the consumption demand by households is consistent with their factor sales and income, and that the demand by firms for labour is consistent with the output which the firms can sell. They analyse the equilibrium properties of models with such properties, which embody the idea that prices are rigid. However, if we compare those models with the *IS-LM* curve considered above we can note the following differences. On the 'plus' side, the Barro and Grossman model provides a more consistent treatment of the labour market in that the demand for labour is linked to the demand for output. On the 'minus' side, investment, savings and the role of money are largely neglected.

The achievement of general equilibrium clearly requires some device by which prices move in the required direction. As Arrow (1959) pointed out, there is the question of how prices change when all agents operate as price-takers. In the original formulation by Walras and others, there was 'the auctioneer which is assumed to furnish, without charge, all the information needed to obtain perfect co-ordination of the activities of all traders in the present and through the future' (Leijonhufvud, 1968). The auctioneer adjusted prices such that they rose in markets where there was excess demand and fell in markets with excess supply. Trading was only allowed to occur when the full set of equilibrium prices had been established. Much of the literature which followed Clower (1965) focused on the consequences of false trading in situations where there was no mechanism at all for changing prices so that prices were taken as fixed.

Two features serve to increase the instability properties of the model. The first is that prices are slow to adjust which leads to disequilibrium trading and quantity constraints. The second is the absence of stocks of any kind. The reduction in consumption expenditure by households following a fall in income is particularly sharp because there are no financial assets which can be run down to finance consumption demand. An extreme counter-example would run as follows. If households expect to be unemployed for T years during their working life, then they could plan their expenditure in the years of employment to be able to finance expenditure in the years of unemployment. In the periods of unemployment, expenditure can continue, financed by previous and future savings.[23]

This excursion into general equilibrium theory and the reappraisal of Keynesian economics literature indicates again the underlying similarity of the Keynesian and monetarist approaches. Throughout the 'real' side of the economy is assumed to be one of atomistic competition. The major difference between the two approaches revolves around the speed of adjustment of the system and the extent to which the economy responds to an exogenous shock by price adjustment or by quantity adjustment.

We conclude this section with two broad points, which we do not have space to develop fully. First, in a competitive general equilibrium model, equilibrium may not exist in a meaningful sense with non-negative prices and output, or there may be multiple equilibria. In the latter case, which of the equilibria is established would depend on disequilibrium behaviour and the actions of government. Second, there may be situations of 'non-Walrasian equilibrium' (Hahn, 1978). Out of Walrasian equilibrium, for reasons indicated above, economic agents cannot act as price-takers. Instead, agents hold beliefs about what would happen to relevant demand and supply if they changed the price. Non-Walrasian equilibrium arises when economic agents act on those beliefs and find that they are fulfilled. Thus economic agents are in equilibrium in the sense that, given those beliefs on the reaction of demands and supplies to changes in price, they cannot improve their own position and those beliefs are confirmed by the outcomes. In general, the markets in such a situation do not clear so that there is a divergence between the demand which would be forthcoming and the supply which would be offered if agents could operate as price-takers.

Conclusion

The similarities of Keynesians and monetarists stem in part from acceptance of an atomistic competition view of the world. The use of the atomistic competitive model to represent the supply-side of the economy creates a strong presumption in many minds that provided there is some price flexibility full employment will sooner or later be reached. Routh (1975) argued that a continuing theme in economic theory over 300 years has been the benefits of *laissez-faire* of which the Pareto-optimality of perfect competition in equilibrium is the most recent variant.[24,25] The alternative approach developed in Chapters 5 and 6 rests on an oligopolistic view of the world, which leads to conclusions that neither the level nor the structure of employment and output is likely to be in any relevant sense optimal.

Notes

1 'There are in reality no serious analytical disagreements between leading monetarist and leading nonmonetarists. Milton Friedman was once quoted as saying, "We are all Keynesians, now," and I am quite prepared to reciprocate that "we are all monetarists"—if by monetarism is meant assigning to the stock of money a major role in determining output and prices' (Modigliani, 1977). 'One purpose of setting forth this framework is to document my belief that the basic differences among economists are empirical, not theoretical . . .' (Friedman, 1974). 'Both monetarists and nonmonetarists are willing to discuss aggregate demand interpretation using the *IS-LM* model. . . . Nonmonetarists have accepted the major contribution of monetarist thinking. In the long run, stabilization policy cannot permanently reduce actual unemployment below the natural unemployment rate' (Gordon, 1981).

2 For descriptions of the gradually evolving debate between Keynesians and monetarists see Burrows (1979), Morgan (1978) and Vane and Thompson (1979).

3 For the *IS* curve provided that $\partial(S-I)/dY$ remains positive and $\partial(S-I)/\partial r$ remains positive. Similarly, for the *LM* curve provided that $\partial(L(Y,r)-M^s(r)/p)/\partial r$ remains negative. Following the analysis of the last chapter we could argue that the supply of money is a function of the difference in the market rate of interest and the Central Bank lending rate, so that a constant Central Bank lending rate would usually be assumed.

4 The original Friedman and Meiselman paper was criticised by Ando and
   Modigliani (1965) and DePrano and Mayer (1965). For a summary of
   the debate see Wonnacott (1978), Chapter 12.
5 See, for example, Morgan (1978), Chapter 4.
6 Note, however, Tobin's response where he states that he thought 'the
   main issue was . . . the shape of the *LM* locus' (Tobin, 1974).
7 In Keynesian terms there is an inconsistency in this approach in that
   the demand for labour is a function only of the real wage, and not of
   output. This point recurs in our discussion below of the Phillips' curve
   (p.72). The model of Barro and Grossman (1971), which arose out of
   the literature on the reappraisal of Keynesian economics, provides a
   consistent treatment of the labour market with the demand for labour as
   a function of output (see p.61 below).
8 Price falls may generate expectations of further falls. Those expectations tend to encourage current savings (to finance future consumption expected to be available at lower prices) and to discourage
   investment which will have to compete with future and cheaper investment. These changes shift the *IS* curve to the left thereby deepen-
   ing the recession. A number of economists (e.g. Minsky, 1976) have
   argued that price falls threaten the 'credit pyramid' of modern economies. Debt is denominated in nominal terms, and increases in
   real terms when prices fall. Recession and falls in prices make
   debt repayment more difficult. There is an increase in default on
   debt, which undermines the position of banks etc., who call in loans
   etc.
9 The rate of interest which appears on the market is the nominal rate of
   interest. It is assumed that the real rate is the nominal rate minus the
   expected rate of inflation. The expected rate of inflation is not an
   unambiguous concept. Apart from differences between people over
   their expectations for the future, the time span to which the expectations apply will depend on the nature of the contract. If, for example,
   the contract is for a loan over ten years with the interest rate specified at
   the beginning, then the expected rate of inflation over the ten-year
   period is relevant.
10 This is medium-term equilibrium only in the limited sense defined in the
   text. It ignores that investment is occurring and adding to the capital
   stock and that savings are adding to personal wealth.
11 It is often the case in economics that what is actually shown by a theory
   and the popular impression created by that theory differ. In this
   instance, we are not arguing that the *IS-LM* model cannot deal with the
   points raised, but rather that the conventional use of the *IS-LM*
   framework and the impression created by it do not allow for these
   points.
12 'Now a practical theory of the future . . . has certain marked characteristics. In particular being based on so flimsy a foundation, it is subject to
   sudden and violent changes' (Keynes, 1937b).
13 'For the same circumstances which lead to pessimistic views about
   future yields are apt to increase the propensity to hoard' (Keynes,
   1937b).

14 This aggregation rests on unchanging distribution of factor ownership and entitlement to profits.

15 From the definition of homogeneity of degree zero, we have
$$D_i(\lambda p_1, \lambda p_2, \ldots, \lambda p_m, \lambda f_{m+1}, \ldots, \lambda f_n)$$
$$= D_i(p_1, p_2, \ldots, p_m, f_{m+1}, \ldots, f_n)$$
$\lambda = 1/f_n$ generates the rest in the text.

16 Note the comments of Hahn (1971) on this quotation. 'As far as I know, no one has ever succeeded in writing down such equations nor in "grinding out" the natural level of unemployment from them. I also doubt that such a task is well formulated.'

17 '. . . much of the analysis of the micro-foundations of the economic system, choice-theoretic analysis of the determination of equilibrium prices in markets consisting of transactors with differing tastes and endowments, continue to be done on the basis of systems of certainty or certainty-equivalence, with the resulting tendency for equilibria to be achieved. Yet in such systems there is no role for money. Money is an asset whose very existence depends on uncertainty, transactions costs and the possibility of disequilibria' (Goodhart, 1975).

18 For example, a 'monetary economy, he [Keynes] argued, is not just a more complicated barter system. Rather an economy with modern capitalist financial institutions behaves in a manner fundamentally different from what he called a "real exchange"—that is, a barter —economy' (Moore, 1979).

19 Drazen (1980) argues that it is not money *per se* which creates the problems analysed by Clower, but the 'uncoupling of transactions'. Thus if good X was used as an intermediary in the barter transactions rather than money, then the same kind of problems could arise. For example, households could be prepared to exchange labour supply for good X, and then exchange good X for the desired goods and services, and a failure of the first transaction would lead to failure of the second. It could be argued that good X has, in those circumstances, acquired some of the properties of money.

20 The income may be more or less than would arise in equilibrium, i.e. $P_1 Q_D$ may be greater or less than $P_e Q_e$. But that is not the relevant comparison, which is between planned income of $P_1 Q_S$ and the actual income of $P_1 Q_D$.

21 This result of Clower arises from a mixture of planned and actual demands and supplies. When the analysis is entirely in terms of plans then Walras' Law is reached (as on p.56). When the analysis is entirely in terms of actual demands and supplies, an analogous relationship applies since by definition actual demand equals actual supply.

22 For example, Barro and Grossman (1976), Muellbauer and Portes (1978). A recent survey is Drazen (1980). He argues that 'one must say that in spite of Clower's brilliant contribution, the early work failed to really explain the causes of unemployment, and much of it ends up sounding like early interpretations of Keynes.' He also suggests that 'the main question . . . is not what happens when prices don't move, but *why* prices don't move. . . . What is necessary is a model of en-dogeneous price showing that prices don't move to clear markets, not

because they are exogeneously constrained from doing so, but because no price setting agent (or agency) finds it in his interest to change prices.'

23 The usefulness of future savings for this purpose will depend on the nature of the capital market and whether borrowing against future savings whilst unemployed is feasible.

24 'Despite all the warnings in the small print [in modern textbooks] the overall effect is soporific: if only competition could be left to itself, all would be well' (Routh, 1975).

25 For discussion on Pareto optimality and perfect competition see any text on welfare economics, e.g. Ng (1979), Winch (1971). 'It is in determining the volume, not the direction of actual employment that the existing system has broken down' (Keynes, 1936).

4 Inflation, Expectations and Unemployment

Introduction

In this chapter we discuss some of the inter-relationships in the orthodox approaches among inflation, expectations and unemployment. Inflation has often been defined as a persistent rise in prices, but the theories explored in this chapter purport to explain movements in some aggregate price level (of goods or of labour) which may not be persistent nor necessarily upwards. The explanations of changes in a general price level draw heavily on theories of changes of prices in individual markets, and the aggregation problems which could arise in such an undertaking are generally overlooked.

The wage change equation

Phillips (1958) presented evidence of a statistically negative relationship between the rate of change of money wages $(\dot{w})$ and the level of unemployment (U), i.e. $\dot{w} = f(U)$ for the period 1861–1913 which appeared to fit the experience of the period 1913–1957.[1] After the 'facts' came the theory, with Lipsey (1960) arguing that the Walrasian price adjustment mechanism postulated that the rate of change of a price (in this case the wage) was a function of the level of excess demand (of labour in this case), and that unemployment provided a (negative) proxy for the level of excess demand for labour. The two elements combined gave the rate of change of wages as a negative function of the level of unemployment. The coexistence of historically high levels of both wage inflation and unemployment from the mid-'sixties onwards focused doubt on the Phillips' curve. On the theoretical level, the response was the introduction of the expected rate of inflation to give the expectations-augmented Phillips' curve, i.e. $\dot{w} = f(U) + b\dot{p}^e$.[2]

The theoretical basis of the expectations-augmented Phillips' curve is that the rate of change of *real* wage is a function of the excess demand for labour, i.e. $\dot{\overline{w/p}} = a(D_L - S_L)$, arguing that the real wage rather than the money wage is the relevant price in the labour market which influences demand (D_L) and supply of (S_L) labour. However it is the money wage which is agreed by employers and employees, and the consequent real wage depends on what happens in the product market. The above equation can be expanded and re-arranged to give:

$$\dot{w} = a(D_L - S_L) + \dot{p}. \tag{1}$$

Equilibrium arises when the price is constant, so that labour market equilibrium leads to a constant real wage so that $\dot{w} = \dot{p}$. Equilibrium also implies that $D_L = S_L$. The combination of these two equilibrium requirements indicates that $a(0) = 0$. The translation of the equation into the expectations-augmented Phillips' curve requires two further assumptions: (i) money wage contracts are made for a period of time ahead, so that it is the expected rate of price inflation during the anticipated period of the wage contract which is relevant rather than the current rate of inflation; (ii) there is a (negative) mapping from excess demand for labour into unemployment such that $D_L - S_L = G(U - U_N)$ where $G(0) = 0$. Thus when there is zero excess demand for labour, and the labour market is in equilibrium then the unemployment rate is U_N, which is often labelled the 'natural' rate of unemployment. The substitution of these assumptions into equation (1) leads to:

$$\dot{w} = H(U - U_N) + \dot{p}^e, \text{ with } H(0) = 0. [3] \tag{2}$$

This equation will be used below as the representation of the expectations-augmented Phillips' curve.

Our discussion of the expectations-augmented Phillips' curve starts with a few preliminary remarks. First, excess demand only has a meaning in the context of atomistic competition, for it is only then that demand and supply functions and hence excess demand functions are defined. For example, the demand function indicates the quantity demanded at each price where the price is constant. But under monopsony conditions quantity and price are jointly determined by the purchaser.

Second, there is always the question of how prices change in a market of price-taking economic agents, for who changes the price? (Arrow, 1959). In the context of the labour market, it has been argued that in the short run a firm does not face an infinitely elastic supply of labour. An increase in the demand for labour by the firm leads it to raise money wages faster than prices in order to raise real wages to attract more labour. But in the longer term, when the knowledge that a firm has more jobs on offer becomes more widely known, it is postulated that the firm is then faced with an infinitely elastic supply curve.[4]

Third, expectations only come into the equation because it is assumed that wage bargains are struck for some period ahead, presumably because the costs of bargaining and negotiation inhibit continuous adjustment of wages. The theory says little about the length of the period for which the wage bargain is struck (which would presumably depend upon the costs of bargaining), and thus does not indicate the period to which the expectations of inflation related. If, for example, wage contracts are made for two years, then the expected rate of inflation would relate to inflation over a two-year period. The theory does not allow for any attempts to rectify the effects of mistaken expectations over price inflation within the period of the contract. At the subsequent wage bargaining, the real wage (which will in general differ from that anticipated) determines the demand for and supply of labour, and hence the excess demand for labour and thereby the level of unemployment. The excess demand for labour then determines the rate of wage change (given the expected rate of inflation).

Fourth, the long-run position arises when $\dot{w} = \dot{p} = \dot{p}^e$, so that the real wage is constant (from $\dot{w} = \dot{p}$) and price inflation is fully anticipated (so that $\dot{p}^e = \dot{p}$). Substituting these equalities into equation (2) yields $H(U-U_N) = 0$, and thus $U = U_N$. The labour market is then in equilibrium in that the unemployment level U_N corresponds to zero excess demand for labour. What happens when there is productivity growth is not clear. The equilibrium condition that $\dot{w} = \dot{p}$ would lead to continuously rising profits, whilst a constant profit margin would lead to $\dot{w} = \dot{p}+g$ where g is the growth of productivity.[5] In the latter case, substitution into equation (2) would yield $H(U-U_N) = g$, and the long-run rate of unemployment would diverge from the level of U_N.

Fifth, there is no theoretical justification for a belief in the coefficient of less than unity on the $\dot{p}^e$ term in the expectations-augmented Phillips' curve. Thus the use in some Keynesian models of an expectations-augmented Phillips' curve of the form $\dot{w} = H(U-U_N)+b\dot{p}^e$ with $b<1$ lacks a theoretical basis.[6] It is not legitimate to accept one half of a theory but not the other half.[7] The underlying reason, though, is clear. With $b = 1$, the economy in equilibrium operates at the 'natural' rate of unemployment U_N, apparently leaving no role for aggregate demand and government activity to influence the level of unemployment and output. With

$b<1$, there is a long-run trade-off between unemployment and inflation, given by $\dot{p}(1-b) = H(U-U_N)$ so that aggregate demand appears able to influence the levels of unemployment and inflation (see pp.50–52 above). Our discussion below indicates that the 'natural' rate of unemployment is not as immutable as this type of presentation suggests.

There are two major problems with the expectations-augmented Phillips' curve. The first relates to the mapping from excess demand for labour to unemployment, and the second to the use of a common real wage as appropriate for both sides of the labour market.

The mapping from excess demand to unemployment poses two groups of problems.[8] The first group arises from a consideration of the actual level of employment (and hence unemployment) which corresponds to a given level of excess demand. It is conventional to assume that the amount traded in a market in disequilibrium is the minimum of *ex ante* demand and *ex ante* supply. Thus in terms of Figure 4.1, at the real wage $(w/p)_1$, the actual level of employment would be L_1 under that assumption. The relationship between excess demand for labour and unemployment depends on how full employment is measured. We first take the case when full employment is defined as a fixed amount such as L_f in Figure 4.1. When the real wage is above equilibrium a negative relationship between excess demand and unemployment will hold. Comparing $(w/p)_1$ and $(w/p)_e$, it can be seen that the former real wage generates a higher degree of excess supply (and hence lower degree of excess demand), a lower level of employment (at L_1) and a higher level of unemployment (of L_f-L_1) than the latter real wage. But when the real wage is below equilibrium the reverse case holds. Comparing $(w/p)_3$ and $(w/p)_e$ indicates that the former involves a higher degree of excess demand but also a higher amount of unemployment (L_f-L_3) than the latter (L_f-L_e). Thus for situations of positive excess demand with full employment measured as a fixed amount there is a positive rather than a negative relationship between excess demand and unemployment.

We next take the case where full employment is defined as the amount of labour supply offered at the going real wage. For the real wage above equilibrium, excess supply of labour and unemployment measured in this way are always equal, leading to a negative relationship between excess demand and unemployment. When the real wage is below equilibrium level, then unemployment is always zero. We would anticipate that the actual measurement of full

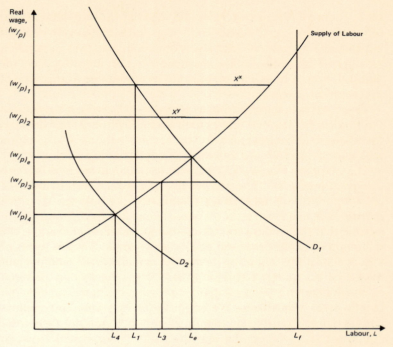

Fig. 4.1: Equilibrium and Disequilibrium in the Labour Market.

employment corresponds more to the first alternative (of a fixed level) than to the second. If that is so, then the negative mapping from excess demand for labour to unemployment only applies when the labour market is in situations of excess supply. It is ironic that the conventional approach appears to require that the labour market is generally in a state of excess supply of labour.

This problem is exacerbated if the assumption of employment as the minimum of demand and supply is dropped (Holmes and Smyth, 1970). For then actual employment may lie anywhere between the demand and supply curves. For example, if at real wage $(w/p)_1$ employment was at point X in Figure 4.1 and for real wage $(w/p)_2$ employment was at point Y, then however full employment was measured, unemployment would be higher at Y than at X even though excess demand was higher for real wage $(w/p)_2$ than for $(w/p)_1$. These circumstances could arise if the competitive labour market model was being used as a representation of a labour market in which there is collective bargaining with unions and firms bargaining over both wage and employment levels. Alternatively, when there are adjustment lags, then economic agents are likely to be off their demand and supply curves.

This now leads into the second problem that the scene above does not have any history, with no explanation of how or why the market came to be in disequilibrium. If a disequilibrium situation arose from a shift in one of the curves, then we have to consider that shifting curves led to shifting equilibria. In turn, shifting equilibria imply the breakdown of any clear relationship between excess demand for labour and unemployment unless unemployment is defined relative to *ex ante* supply. With a fixed level of full employment, then two different equilibrium positions would lead to different levels of unemployment despite each corresponding to zero excess demand.

The only partial escape (offered by Lipsey, 1974) is to argue that the short-run employment position has been determined by short-run demand and supply curves, but that long-run demand and supply curves exert their influence in determining the rate of change of real wages.

This point is particularly relevant to the Keynesian position. In Figure 4.1 (and in the derivation of the expectations-augmented Phillips' curve above), the demand for and supply of labour are taken as a function of the real wage only. However, a Keynesian approach would stress the role of aggregate demand in determining the demand for labour. Further it is the effective demand, not nominal or long-run demand, which is relevant in determining what happens in the market. In this context, it is the effective demand for labour which is held to determine the level of employment and the rate of wage changes. In terms of Figure 4.1, a leftward shift in the demand for labour curve from D_1 to D_2 arising from a fall in aggregate demand would be followed by a fall in the real wage (as there is excess supply at the previous equilibrium wage of $(w/p)_e$ with the demand for labour curve at D_2), and a fall in employment. A new equilibrium in the labour market could be established with employment at L_4, with lower real wage (of $(w/p)_4$) and higher unemployment of L_f-L_4. At the new equilibrium, real wages remain constant despite the higher level of unemployment. Thus a Keynesian analysis which stresses the role of aggregate demand in determining the demand for labour does not generate a Phillips' curve relationship, simply because a wide range of unemployment levels are compatible with zero excess demand for labour.

It could be argued that the expectations-augmented Phillips' curve (or some close approximation) could be derived from considerations of collective bargaining rather than the excess demand approach outlined above. Laidler and Parkin (1975) argue that

the rate of unemployment is a natural variable to use as an indicator of the relative bargaining strengths of the two parties and expected inflation variables have an identical role to play in both competitive and monopolistic markets. A theoretical basis for the relation between wage change and unemployment may thus be derived either from competitive or monopolistic analysis but in either case the prediction is that the relationship will be crucially influenced by some expected rate of inflation.

We take this argument to mean that a relationship of the form $\dot{w} = f(U) + \dot{p}^e$ can be derived from a collective bargaining approach as well as the excess demand approach. There may, however, be subsidiary predictions of the two approaches which may differ (Kahn, 1980). A collective bargaining approach does not necessarily generate an equation of the expectations-augmented Phillips' curve form, and indeed in the next chapter we derive a different one (although it does contain the Phillips' curve as a special case). Finally, even if the equations from the two approaches are apparently similar, the interpretation of the equations, and particularly of the role of unemployment, is rather different. In the excess demand approach, in equilibrium where $\dot{w} = \dot{p} = \dot{p}^e$ the demand for and supply of labour are in balance, and those not in work are regarded as voluntarily unemployed. In a collective bargaining approach unemployment serves to damp down wage increases. There may be an equilibrium level of unemployment, corresponding to $\dot{w} = \dot{p} = \dot{p}^e$, which we label U_X. But U_X is the level of unemployment which restrains wage inflation to the rate of price inflation, and it does not carry any connotations of full employment. In discussion below, we reserve the term 'expectations-augmented Phillips' curve' for the curve based on the excess demand approach, and use the term 'the bargaining Phillips' curve' for an equation of the form $\dot{w} = f(U) + b\dot{p}^e$ derived from collective bargaining considerations.

Thus the mapping from excess demand for labour into unemployment is suspect. It may be preferable to deal explicitly with the demand for and supply of labour rather than employ the mapping from excess demand for labour to unemployment. In doing so we can bring out the possible influence of government activity on the 'natural' rate of unemployment. The demand for labour by private sector employers is assumed to be based on the conventional neo-classical profit-maximising assumption, and hence is a function of the real wage plus employees' social security contributions, which we write as $D_L(w+t_s/p)$ where t_s is the nominal social security contribution. The public sector demand for labour, which is assumed to be exogenously determined at D_G is added to that demand to give a total demand for labour of $D_L(w+t_s/p)+D_G$. The supply of labour is assumed to be a function of the real post-tax wage and other income including the benefits of public expenditure, which is written as $S_L((1-t)w/p,G)$ where t is the appropriate tax rate and G the level of real government expenditure. The 'natural' rate of unemployment corresponds to excess demand for labour being zero, i.e. where

$$D_L(w+t_s/p)+D_G = S_L((1-t)w/p,G).$$

The effect of increased government expenditure is to raise the level of demand for labour through D_G, but to lower the supply of labour (since benefits of public expenditure raise the workers' income and hence their demand for leisure, provided that leisure is a normal good, and lower supply of labour). So whilst the economy may operate under equilibrium conditions at a 'natural' rate of unemployment, there is little that is 'natural' about such a rate of unemployment. In particular, government expenditure and taxation influence the level of employment which corresponds to the 'natural' rate of unemployment.

The second major problem with the expectations-augmented Phillips' curve is that the prices of labour and of output which are relevant to workers may differ from those relevant to producers. On the wages side, a major difference arises from taxation whereby labour is interested in post-tax wages and producers are interested in pre-tax wages plus social security contributions. Similarly, on the prices side, indirect taxation leads to differences in the output prices relevant to workers and to producers. But, additionally on the prices side, there may be a substantial aggregation problem. For workers, the relevant output price is the price of consumption goods. For a producer, the relevant price is the own-product price. It is implicitly assumed that there are no problems of summing these own-product prices to arrive at a composite price average, which corresponds to the price of consumption goods. A related problem is the requirement of agreement over the expected rate of price inflation.

It is inevitable that aggregation problems arise when dealing with macro-economic phenomena. This is particularly so when a macro-economic relationship is built upon micro-economic foundations. But in this case the aggregation problems appear particularly severe, and there does not appear to have been any attempt to investigate them.

The price change equation
In this section we ask whether there is an analysis for output price changes analogous to that for wage changes in that it is based on excess demand and expectations.

The application of the Walrasian adjustment mechanism to a product market yields $\dot{p} = F(X_G)$ where X_G is the excess demand for that product. In product markets, there is not the same justification for introducing expected price inflation as there was in the labour market, where essentially treating the real wage as the relevant price and with contracts made for a period ahead combined to introduce the expected rate of price inflation. A search of the relevant literature fails to yield any satisfactory explanations for the introduction of expectations into the price inflation equation. For example, Phelps (1967) puts forward an equation which in our notation reads $\dot{p} = f(Q-\bar{Q})/\bar{Q})+\dot{p}^e$ where Q is actual output and $\bar{Q}$ some measure of normal or capacity output. He says that 'the concept of the function $[f((Q-\bar{Q})/\bar{Q})]$ is more vulnerable to criticism. From the usual Phillips' curve standpoint, we have to regard the utilization rate as a proxy for the rate of employment to labour supply and to neglect rising marginal cost.' Laidler (1973) in advocating the same equation writes that 'The price formation hypothesised . . . is a version of the expectations-augmented Phillips' Curve, applied directly to the determination of the rate of price inflation however, rather than to the determination of a rate of wage inflation from which the rate of price inflation might be derived by way of some mark-up-adjusted-for productivity change mechanism.' This line of argument is explicit in Turnovsky (1977) when he gives, (p.95, converted to our notation)

$$\dot{w} = a_0+a_1U+a_2\dot{p}^e$$
$$\dot{p} = \dot{w}-g$$

where g is rate of change of productivity. Hence we arrive at

$$\dot{p} = a_0+a_1U+a_2\dot{p}^e-g.$$

The explanation of price inflation here is initially in terms of full-cost pricing, leading to a reduced form equation in which price inflation depends upon expected price inflation, the level of unemployment and rate of change of productivity. Thus the excess demand/expectations equation for price inflation has often been derived from an uneasy alliance between an atomistic competitive labour market and oligopolistic product market in which full-cost pricing is pursued.

It can be argued that there are costs of price change, as there are costs of wage change, so that each firm sets its price for a certain length of time ahead. In doing so the firm would take into account what it expects to happen to prices in its market and the state of excess demand in the industry. This would lead to a price change equation of the form $\dot{p} = F(X_G) + \dot{p}^e$. Another line of argument would be the inclusion of changes in production costs. But changes in production costs lead to shifts in the supply curve, and are thereby incorporated into the level of excess demand. Consequently, there is no reason for the independent entry of cost changes into the price inflation equation.

Parkin (1975) attempted to introduce expectations into a price change equation by the following route.[9] Take excess demand $X_i = G(c_i/p_i, p_i/p)$ where c_i is marginal costs of good i, p_i price of good i and p the general price level. The function G is derived from demand (which is a function of the relative price of good i, p_i/p) and supply (which is a function of costs relative to output price, c_i/p). It is postulated that firms change prices in order to eliminate excess demand within the decision period, so that $dX_i/dt = -X_i$. Assuming further that the function G is log-linear, then

$$X_i = a \log c_i + b \log p - (a+b) \log p_i$$

$$\frac{dX_i}{dt} = a\,\dot{c}_i + b\,\dot{p} - (a+b)\,\dot{p}_i$$

hence from $dX_i/dt = -X_i$;

$$\dot{p}_i = \frac{a}{a+b}\dot{c}_i + \frac{b}{a+b}\dot{p} + \frac{1}{a+b}X_i.$$

The price decision lasts for a period, so the firms use expected changes in costs and the general price level, with expectations entering because adjustment costs limit the firms to changing their price once a period.

No compelling reason is given why firms should want to eliminate excess demand within a period. In situations of excess supply, it is quite likely that firms as a whole would be better off with excess supply than they would be with zero excess demand. It has to be assumed that firms act as a collective in this way for otherwise we would be back with the situation where each firm would be pricing at the expected level.

There appear to be two forms of price change equation in general use. The first is of the form $\dot{p} = f(Q-\bar{Q})/\bar{Q})+b\dot{p}^e$, where $(Q-\bar{Q})/\bar{Q}$ is a proxy for excess demand for output.[10] The second is of the form $\dot{p} = \dot{w}-g$,[11] which is often combined with an expectations-augmented Phillips' curve to yield a price change equation involving unemployment and expected price changes (as shown above).

It is difficult to find any justification for the first form for, as indicated above, the Walrasian adjustment mechanism does not provide a rationale for the introduction of expectations. But even if b were set at zero, thereby excluding expectations from the equation, there remains the problem of using the term $(Q-\bar{Q})/\bar{Q}$ as a proxy for excess demand for output. Essentially the problems which surrounded the mapping of labour into unemployment occur here, and indeed may be intensified in the product market. In the case of the labour market, the severest problems arose when full employment was defined as a fixed level of employment. The process applied here is virtually identical, with deviations of output from a fixed level $(\bar{Q})$ being used.

The justification for the second form is usually in terms of full-cost pricing, with labour costs as the only costs of production. This latter assumption may appear to be fairly innocuous. However, the full-cost pricing argument only leads to this form of price change equation if unit costs are constant with respect to output.

An alternative justification, based on competitive market behaviour, would run as follows. If the product market clears instantaneously then $p = m.c.$ (marginal cost), and hence $\dot{p} = \dot{\overline{m.c.}}$. Treating labour as the only cost, and with the labour input per unit of output by $L(Q)e^{-gt}$ we have $p = w.L(Q).e^{-gt}$ at time t. Then we can derive that

$$\dot{p} = \dot{w}-g+(1/L(Q))dL(Q)/dt.$$

The second term can be expanded into

$$(Q/L)(dL/dQ)(1/Q)(dQ/dt)$$

which we write as $e_L.\dot{q}$. We arrive at $\dot{p} = \dot{w}-g+e_L\dot{Q}$, and the equation $\dot{p} = \dot{w}-g$ is the special case of constant unit costs, which corresponds to $e_L = 0$. Instantaneous market clearing in the product market, with constant unit costs, yields the equation $\dot{p} = \dot{w}-g$. But an equation more in the spirit of competitive market analysis would lead to $\dot{p} = \dot{w}-g+e_L\dot{Q}$.

Wage and price inflation

The expectations-augmented Phillips' curve is based on the equation $\dot{w} = a(X_L) + \dot{p}^e$, where X_L is excess demand for labour. The only way in which price changes can be consistent with that view in a neo-classical framework is for $\dot{p} = b(X_G) + \dot{w}^e$. This can be seen by proceeding as follows. With the labour and product market as the only two markets, applying Walras' Law (pp.56–57 above) $\dot{w}.X_L + \dot{p}.X_G = 0$, and then if X_L is positive, X_G has to be negative. Hence, with X_L positive $\dot{w}$ is greater than $\dot{p}^e$ so that the real wage is expected to rise, whilst with X_L negative $\dot{p}$ is less than $\dot{w}^e$ and the real wage is expected to rise from consideration of the product market. If other forms of the price change equation were used, then this element of consistency would be lost.

It should be noted that the price change equation of the form $\dot{p} = \dot{w}$, whether derived from full-cost pricing or instantaneous market clearing, is not consistent with the expectations-augmented Phillips' curve. For simply, such a price change equation implies that there is always zero excess demand in the product market $(X_G = 0)$, which would imply zero excess demand for labour (from Walras' Law) so that the Phillips' curve collapses to $\dot{w} = \dot{p}^e$. These remarks rely on the use of Walras' Law, and the re-appraisal of Keynesian economics literature raised doubts on Walras' Law as indicated in the previous chapter.

Expectations

The preceding discussion has indicated the importance which has been attached to expectations on future price changes within explanations of price and wage changes. In this section, we discuss two of the major alternative ways in which expectations have been modelled, namely adaptive and 'rational' expectations. With an adaptive expectations scheme, the expectations held prior to time t on the value which a variable will take in time t are based on the expectations held previously about future values of x and the previous values of x. The simplest form of this is

$$x_t^e = (1-a)x_{t-1}^e + ax_{t-1}$$

where x_t^e is the expected value of x for time t held at time $t-1$. These expectations are adaptive in the sense that expectations are gradually adaptive to what is happening to x, which can be clearly seen if we re-write the equation above as

$$x_t^e = x_{t-1}^e + a(x_{t-1} - x_{t-1}^e),$$

and the speed of adaption depends on the value of a.

Two particular problems arise with adaptive expectations. First, when there is a trend in x upwards or downwards, the adaptive expectations scheme indicated above would persistently under- or over-predict the actual value of x.[12] Second, the expectations about x depend only on the past behaviour of x and expectations about x. Thus other relevant information is excluded.

The 'rational' expectations approach, first developed by Muth (1961), postulates that economic agents form expectations based on all information available to them which are not subject to systematic error.[13] This can be summarised by
$$x_t^e = E(x_t|I_{t-1}) = x_t + e_t.$$
The first part says that expectations formed at time $t-1$ are based on the expected value of x_t given the information available at time $t-1(I_{t-1})$, where the expected value is the 'prediction that would be made by the relevant (and correct!) economic theory' (Buiter, 1980). The second part indicates that the expected and actual values of x_t differ only by a random term (e_t) which has a zero mean.

The power of the 'rational' expectations assumption can be seen by applying it to the set of two equations in the wage and price inflation section above. We put $\dot{p}^e = \dot{p} + u, \dot{w}^e = \dot{w} + v$, where u and v are random terms and this gives $\dot{w} = a(X_L) + \dot{p} + u$ and $\dot{p} = b(X_G) + \dot{w} + v$. Solving this yields
$$a(X_L) + b(X_G) + u + v = 0,$$
and with substitution from Walras' Law we have
$$a(X_L) + b(-wX_L/p) = -(u+v).$$
The right-hand side is a random variable with a mean value of zero. One solution to the equation $a(X_L) + b(-wX_L/p) = 0$ is $X_L = 0$ (although there may be other solutions). The value of X_L fluctuates around the solution to the previous equation in a manner which corresponds to the random fluctuations in $u+v$. In other words, for the 'equilibrium' solution $X_L = 0$, the actual value of X_L moves randomly above and below the zero excess demand position.[14]

The concept of 'rational' expectations can be illustrated within the context of a single market, which shows the rapid market-clearing properties of 'rational' expectations. In the market situation illustrated in Figure 4.2 if price p_1 prevailed then the amount demanded (Q_D) and the amount offered (Q_S) are incompatible, and at least one side of the market cannot undertake planned transactions. Armed with the knowledge that current price diverges from equilibrium price (or equivalently that Q_D and Q_S were unequal), economic agents would know that their belief that they can buy or

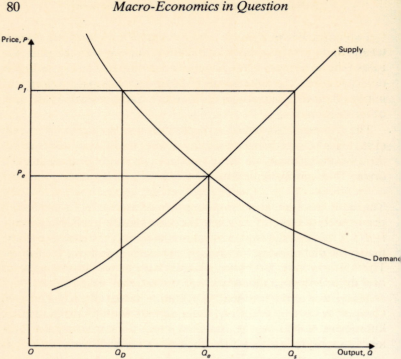

Fig. 4.2: Demand and Supply Curves.

sell as much as they wish at the going price was incorrect. They know that price will change, and will continue to change until the equilibrium price is reached. Suppliers realise that there is little point in trying to supply Q_S since there is insufficient demand. But they know that if they supply Q_e and charge a price p_e all will be well. In a world with flexible prices they know that p_e can easily be achieved. In other words, the belief, based on past experience of the operation of the market, that p_e will be reached causes the suppliers to operate in a way which speeds up the attainment of p_e. In this case, expectations are self-justifying, with a belief of quick adjustment leading to quick adjustment and the market moving into equilibrium.[15]

Leijonjufvud (1968) argued that 'the only thing which Keynes "removed" from the foundations of classical theory was the *deus ex machina*—the auctioneer which is assumed to furnish, without charge, all the information needed to obtain perfect co-ordination of the activities of all traders in the present and through the future' (see also pp.59–62 above). The assumption of 'rational' expectations and the associated price flexibility in many respects place the role of the auctioneer in the hands of economic agents. For as Buiter (1980) argues, 'the assumption of Muth-rational expectations . . . implies that all agents know each other's aims and anticipate each other's actions.'

The concept of 'rational' expectations serves to remind us that experience affects belief about the future, and those beliefs affect the outcome. But it is a large step from those general remarks to saying that economic agents have fairly full information and use economic theory to produce, on average, correct forecasts of the future. It is often jibed that a group of twelve economists will generate thirteen conflicting predictions on future economic events. It is not self-evident that economists have yet produced economic theory which provides, on average, correct forecasts for the future. There is a broader problem, which relates to the development of new models of the economy based on 'rational' expectations. It is assumed that economic agents within a model already know all about that model, and base their expectations of the future on knowledge of that model, and their other prior information. This leads to a model which is, in some sense, internally consistent, but that model cannot be an adequate explanation of the past. For until that new model was produced, how could economic agents know about its properties? It could be that economic agents know more than economists do, although that would require a schizophrenia whereby an individual knows about the model when acting as an economic agent but not when acting as an economist!

In a static economy where each period was basically a repeat of the previous period, it could be anticipated that economic agents would become conversant with the underlying model, perhaps in an informal way. Buiter (1980) concludes that 'the assumption that economic agents use the true model to make their (unbiased) forecasts suggests that Muth-rational expectations are likely to be most appropriate when the analysis is restricted to the tranquility of a long-run steady state. The positive economic question as to how economic agents form forecasts when they do not know the true underlying economic model still remains to be answered.' It could be further argued that a variety of adaptive expectations will also operate to provide unbiased forecasts in a tranquil state (although 'rational' expectations may lead the economy to that tranquil state more quickly than adaptive expectations). But an economy which is growing and evolving over time is likely to be rather different.

A modern capitalist economy usually experiences investment, technical change, movements in the degree of oligopoly, changes in the relative strengths of workers and capitalists, changes in the conditions of foreign trade, etc. Many of these changes occur 'beneath the surface' and yet have significant impacts on the way in which the economy operates. In an economy which is evolving over time and when the future is inherently unknowable, the notion that economic agents have accurate information on how the economy performs with which to make unbiased predictions about the future loses its appeal.

The 'surprise' supply function

The concept of a 'surprise' supply function is now often used in macro-economic models of an essentially monetarist flavour. Essentially, this concept postulates that deviations of supply (of labour or goods) from some normal or equilibrium level only arise from deviations of actual prices from anticipated prices.[16] Further, if 'rational' expectations are assumed, then deviations of actual from anticipated prices become a random variable with zero mean, leading to the deviation of supply from the equilibrium level being a random variable with zero mean.

Sargent (1973), for example, postulates an aggregate 'surprise' supply function, which in our notation is of the form:

$$Q_t = k_t + \propto (ln\ p_t - ln\ p_t^e) + u_t$$

where Q is output, k is capital stock (measured in units of output), p is prices and p_t^e prices expected at time $t-1$ to rule in time t and $\propto > 0$. The derivation of such supply schedules is not always clear in that it would usually be expected that supply was a function of prices relative to costs.[17] A similar approach is applied to the labour market. Santomero and Seater (1978) indicate three categories of theories in this vein:

(i) 'models in which the individual speculates on the distribution of nominal wages over current vacancies';

(ii) 'models in which the individual misperceives his real wage';

(iii) 'models in which the individual speculates over time on the normal level of nominal wages'.

Lucas and Rapping (1969) provided one of the first models of this genre, which illustrates a number of key features of this general approach. The supply of labour of a typical household is based on the maximisation of a utility function $U(C,C^*,L,L^*)$ where C relates to consumption and L to labour supply, where unasterisked variables relate to current period, asterisked variables to the future. The household faces a budget constraint

$$pC+p^*.C^*/(1+rn) = w.L+w^*.L^*/(1+rn)+A$$

where rn is the nominal rate of interest and A initial assets, p is the current price level and p^* the price level expected to prevail in the future, and w and w^* are the corresponding concepts for nominal wages. From this maximisation problem, the supply of labour in general terms is:

$$L = F(w/p,w^*/p^*(1+rn),p^*/p(1+rn),A/p),$$

and Lucas and Rapping take the log-linear form of this and put on time subscripts to yield:

$$lnL_t = b_0+b_1ln(w/p)_t-b_2ln(w_t^*/p_t(1+rn_t))$$
$$+ b_3(ln(1+rn_t)-ln(p_t^*/p_t))-blnA_t/p_t.$$

Full employment L_t^* is defined as the labour supply which would be offered in the current period if the household's previous expectations about future wages and prices had proved correct, i.e. $(w/p)_t = (w_{t-1}^*/p_{t-1}(1+rn_{t-1}))$ and $p_t = p_{t-1}^*$ with rate of interest rn_t^*. This gives:

$$lnL_t^* = b_0+b_1ln(w_{t-1}^*/p_{t-1}(1+rn_{t-1}))-b_2ln(w_t^*/p_t(1+rn_t))$$
$$+b_3(ln(1+rn_t^*)-lnp_t^*/p_{t-1}^*)-b_4lnA_t/p_t.$$

By subtraction with $rn_t^* = rn_t$, the following can be obtained:

$$lnL_t/L_t^* = b_1ln((w/p)_t/w_{t-1}^*/p_{t-1}(1+rn_{t-1}))+b_3lnp_t/p_{t-1}^*.$$

It can be seen that the actual labour supply L_t differs from full employment labour supply L_t^* insofar as real wages deviate from those expected (the first term on the right-hand side) and prices deviate from those expected (the second term). Thus, in this model, faulty perceptions generate unemployment. Lucas and Rapping then postulate an adaptive expectations regime for expectations about future wages and prices, and with an approximation for unemployment $U_t = g_0+g_1lnL_t^*/L_t$ arrive at an equation of the form

$$U_t = a_0-a_1ln((w/p)_t/(w/p)_{t-1})-a_2lnp_t/p_{t-1}+(1-a_3)U_{t-1}$$

where the coefficient a_3 depends on the speed of adaption of expectations (and corresponds to the parameter a in the formula for adaptive expectations on p.78). Since lnp_t/p_{t-1} is approximately equal to $\dot{p}_t$, there is a negative relationship between unemployment and price inflation.[18] This type of negative relationship is often used in the 'rational' expectations and related literature. It indicates that inflation reduces unemployment (through the generation of faulty beliefs about wages and prices) rather than unemployment reducing inflation. We note, however, that the effect of changes in real wages is overlooked. Further the nominal rate of interest is assumed to be the same in both the equation for lnL_t and that for lnL_t^*. If the real rate of interest were assumed constant then the term following b_3 would be the same in the two equations, leaving the final equation of the form

$$lnL_t/L_t^* = b_1 ln((w/p)_t/w_{t-1}^*/p_{t-1}(1+rn_{t-1})).[19]$$

This equation retains the basic property that unemployment is determined from the supply side and caused by misperceptions about wages.

There are several important features of this analysis. First, employment is seen as a voluntary decision of households, and unemployment arises essentially because of faulty perceptions (such that, for example, w_t/w_{t-1}^*). Second, the unemployment equation indicates that unemployment depends on changes in the real wage and changes in the price level (after using the adaptive expectations assumption). Many of the 'surprise' supply models draw upon the Lucas and Rapping model or similar, but drop without justification the changes in real wage element. Third, the analysis proceeds from the household decision on the supply of hours of work to the level of unemployment. Most unemployment is, however, not of the form of reduced hours of work but people without a job. This can be rationalised within the model by saying that households are deciding on supply of hours in, say, a year, and they actually achieve their desired supply of hours by working the appropriate number of weeks in a year and not working the remainder.

The combination of a 'surprise' supply function with the concept of 'rational' expectations soon leads to the conclusion that the only divergence between actual employment (or output) and equilibrium employment (or output) is a random term. The above discussion indicates that deviations from full employment rest in those models on misperceptions about the future, and under the 'rational expectations' approach misperceptions are not systematic. The 'rational' expectations and the 'surprise' supply function approaches have become influential variants of the general (neoclassical) monetarist approach, under which markets are close to perfect competition and quickly move to equilibrium. Under such circumstances, the economy hovers around full employment, and apart from slight hitches while prices adjust or misperceptions are corrected, any unemployment is the result of individual choices.

Whilst the last approach examined pushed matters to the extreme, nevertheless the neo-classical view underlies macro-economic orthodoxies. In the next chapters we begin to explore a macro-economics based on an oligopolistic 'vision' of the world, rather than a perfectly competitive one.

Notes

1 The equation used was $\dot{w} + 0.900 = 0.638U^{-1.3494}$. This was not estimated using standard regression techniques, but instead the average values of the rate of change of wages and of unemployment for each of six bands of unemployment levels were calculated, and an equation derived which best fitted these six points. For further discussion see Desai (1975).

2 The empirical response consisted in part of suggesting proxies for excess demand for labour other than unemployment (e.g. unemployment minus vacancies, registered unemployed plus hoarded labour as in Taylor, 1970), to postulating that the mapping from excess demand to unemployment had shifted and to adding extra 'intruder' variables.

3 From
$$\dot{w} = a(D_L - S_L) + \dot{p}^e = a(G(U - U_N)) + \dot{p}^e = H(U - U_N) + \dot{p}^e.$$
Since $a(0) = 0$, $G(0) = 0$, hence $H(0) = a(G(0)) = 0$.

4 Beginning with Stigler (1962), and pushed along by Phelps (1970); for a survey on search unemployment when the notion of price dispersion is applied to the labour market see Lippman and McCall (1976).

5 With labour as the only input, and with a constant mark-up m we can write $p = m.wL/Q$, and differentiating with respect to time yields
$$(1/p)dp/dt = (1/w)(dw/dt) + (Q/L).d(L/Q)/dt$$
(assuming $dm/dt = 0$). With productivity growth, $Q = Le^{gt}$, so that $(Q/L)d(L/Q) = -g$, and hence $\dot{w} = \dot{p} + g$.

6 See, for example, the essentially Keynesian models presented in Turnovsky (1977).

7 It could be argued that an expectations-augmented Phillips' curve with $b<1$ is a 'stylised fact', although the experience of the late 'sixties and 'seventies would not support that view. 'Until 1971, published empirical tests for the U.S. . . . yielded estimates of *[b]* which were significantly less than unity. . . . [But] the gradual acceleration of inflation during 1966–70 caused the computer to yield even higher values of *[b]* as the passage of time provided additional observations until finally . . . tests with a sample period including early 1971 were unable to reject statistically the hypothesis that *[b] = 1*' (Gordon, 1976). For the gradual rise of *b* in the UK Phillips' curves as the sample period was extended through the 'sixties and 'seventies see Henry, Sawyer and Smith (1976).

8 A third problem could be raised. Corry and Laidler (1967) pointed out that the rate of unemployment is affected by the extent to which workers quit jobs voluntarily. They argue that as job prospects improve, following an increase in the demand for labour, the voluntary

quit rate may rise. Thus an increase in excess demand for labour may be accompanied by a rise in unemployment generated by the increase in the voluntary quit rate.

9 For further discussion of the Parkin (1975) approach see Sawyer (1982c).

10 See, for example, Laidler (1973), Laidler and Parkin (1975), Metcalfe and Peel (1979) and Stein (1976).

11 Turnovsky (1977), for example.

12 In the simplest form for adaptive expectations given in the test, by successive substitution we can obtain

$$x_t = ax^e_{t-1} + (1-a)x_{t-1} = a^2x^e_{t-1} + a(1-a)x_{t-2}$$

$$+ (1-a)x_{t-1} = \ldots = (1-a) \sum_{j=1}^{\infty} a^{j-1}x_{t-j}.$$

In other words current expectations are a weighted sum of previous values. Clearly, when x is rising over time such a regime will under-predict future values of x.

13 For an easy introduction to 'rational' expectations see McCallum (1980) and a more technical survey see Kantor (1979). For recent discussion see the special issue (November 1980) of *Journal of Money, Credit and Banking* Volume 11 devoted to 'rational' expectations.

14 An easier, though in view of previous discussion misleading, illustration of this line of argument is given by Gordon (1976). In our symbols, he writes

$$\dot{p}_t = \dot{p}^e_t + \beta(U_t - U_N) + u_t$$

and inverting gives

$$U_t = U_N - (1/\beta)(\dot{p}_t - p^e_t) + u_t/\beta$$

With 'rational' expectations $\dot{p}_t^e = \dot{p}_t + u_t$ so that $U_t = U_N + e_t$ where $e_t = v_t + u_t/\beta$ is a random variable with mean zero.

15 Preston (1980) puts a similar point: 'If everybody reacts to events as if he believes that the quantity theory of money were true, does not a model of the economy have to include or at least be compatible with the quantity theory of money? If reflective individual decision-makers believe that certain kinds of external shocks lead to output contraction in the economy at large, does not a satisfactory model of the economy have to be based on a theory giving rise to such a prediction.'

16 For example, Sargent (1973), Lucas (1975), Sargent and Wallace (1976), McCallum (1978).

17 Sargent (1973) introduces the equation $y_t = k_t + \gamma(p_t - {}_tp^*_{t-1}) + u$ where $\gamma > 0$ where p_t is the log of the price level and ${}_tp^\cdot_{t-1}$ the log of the price level expected at time $t-1$ to apply at time t. The only justification which he gives for this equation is that it is

an aggregate supply schedule relating to the deviation of output from normal productive capacity directly to the gap between the current price level and the public's prior expectation of it. Unexpected rises in the price level thus boost aggregate supply, because suppliers mistakenly interpret surprise increases in the aggregate price level as increases in the relative prices of the labour or goods they are supplying. This mistake occurs because suppliers receive information about the prices of their own goods faster than they receive information about the aggregate price level.

A firm appears to be concerned only with price of its output relative to prices of other outputs, and not relative to costs. It could be argued that firms see costs rising faster than expected which leads to output reductions. Further, households see wages rising faster than expected but do not notice prices rising (faster than expected), whilst firms notice prices rising faster than expected but overlook wage rises above those expected. Tobin (1980) argues that the supply price equation 'says that output responds positively to price surprises. As I already observed, this specification is an implication not of rational expectations but of a particular asymmetrical gap in information. Its function is to make the model consistent with observed cyclical covariations of prices and output.'

18 For $ln(1+x) \approx x$ for small values of x. Then
$$lnp_t/p_{t-1} \approx ln((p_{t-1}+p_t-p_{t-1})/p_{t-1}) \approx ln(1+(p_t-p_{t-1})/p_{t-1}) \approx (p_t-p_{t-1})/p_{t-1} \approx \dot{p}_t.$$

19 For $ln(1+r_t) \approx r_t$, put $lnp_t^*/p_t \approx \dot{p}_t^*$, then
$$ln(1+r_t)-lnp_t^*/p_t \approx r_t - \dot{p}_t^*$$
which is the real rate of interest.

5   The Building Blocks of a Kaleckian Macro-Economics

Introduction

At the heart of our approach to macro-economics is the view that it must reflect the micro-economic and institutional realities of developed capitalist economies,[1] and that oligopolistic firms in the product markets and collective bargaining in the labour market are important elements of those realities.

The main feature of oligopoly is that a few firms dominate an industry in respect of price, output, investment and other decisions. The size of firms in an industry varies considerably and a summary measure of the dominance of a few large firms over small firms is required.[2] The most easily understood measure is the n-firm concentration ratio which is the share (as measured by, for example, sales) of the largest n-firms in an industry.[3] In the United Kingdom in 1975, the five-firm concentration ratio (in terms of net output) averaged 50.6 per cent in manufacturing industries (at the three-digit level), whereas at a lower level of aggregation the five-firm concentration ratio (in terms of sales) averaged 69.0 per cent in 1968.[4] For the manufacturing sector as a whole, the largest 100 firms accounted for 42 per cent of net output in 1977.[5] In the United States, the average four-firm concentration ratio in manufacturing (at the four-digit level) was 41.2 per cent in 1970 and the largest 100 firms accounted for 33 per cent of net output in manufacturing.[6]

These figures, and the vast collection of statistics of which they are only a sample, create the presumption that product markets are basically oligopolistic. They tend to understate the interdependence between firms since factors like collusion and interlocking directorships are not taken into account.

In Table 5.1 we present figures on the degree of trade unionisation in eight countries.[7] These figures clearly cover a considerable range from 25 per cent in the United States through to nearly 90 per cent in Sweden. However, they support the view that unions seek to influence wages and working conditions over a significant part of a modern economy. The proportion of wages which is determined through or influenced by collective bargaining is likely to be higher than the degree of unionisation.

Table 5.1. Union membership as percentage of workforce in eight countries, 1975

Australia	53.4	
Canada	34.6	
Denmark	66.6	
Germany	37.2	
Great Britain	49.2	(1974)
Norway	60.5	
Sweden	87.2	
United States of America	25.1	

Source: Bain and Price (1980), Table 10.1.

In developing the building blocks of the Kaleckian approach, our major concern is to derive relatively simple models of, for example, price behaviour, which will facilitate the exploration of macro-economic implications in the next chapter. At the same time, the models need to be broadly consistent with the empirical evidence and with non-neo-classical theorising in the areas of industrial and labour economics as appropriate.

We begin with a consideration of firms' price and investment decisions in an oligopolistic environment. The price decisions of firms lead quickly to the determination of the mark-up of price over costs, of profits and of price inflation. The determinants of investment emphasise the impact of output changes and capacity utilisation as well as profitability. Imperfect capital market conditions lead to a stress on internal financing of investment by firms, and the influence of profits (via retained earnings) on the over-all level of savings.

The starting point for wage determination is the modelling of changes in nominal wages, and the impact which unemployment and workers' demands for real wages have on wage changes. Finally, we pick up the discussion begun in Chapter 2 on the demand for and supply of money, with particular emphasis on the role of banks in the creation of money and the close linkages between changes in the level of aggregate demand and in the money supply.

Pricing

A basic distinction is made in elementary micro-economics between markets in which firms are price-makers and those in which firms are price-takers, which comes quite close to the distinction made by Kalecki between cost-determined and demand-determined prices (Kalecki, 1971, Chapter 5). The implication of earlier discussion is that conventional macro-economics relies on price-taking behaviour. We explore different approaches to price-making behaviour, with a view to arriving at a common equation for use in macro-economic models which incorporates varying approaches as particular cases.

There is a surfeit of theories of price-making behaviour. Theories of monopoly, and of oligopoly, managerial theories of the firm, satisficing theories (including full-cost pricing) and the administered price thesis are all in this vein. An essential feature of all these theories is that a firm sets price as a mark-up over cost. The determinants of that mark-up and the extent and manner of variation of the mark-up with changes in demand vary among the theories, as does the nature of costs considered (marginal or average). It follows then that changes in prices can be related to changes in the mark-up and changes in costs, and an exploration of price inflation is based on those two factors.

A full discussion of the theories of price would not be appropriate here, and we focus on the elements of three approaches.[8] The first approach is a generalised short-run profit maximising model of oligopoly.[9] In the simplest case there are n firms producing an homogeneous product, the price of which p depends on the total quantity produced for sale Q via the demand function, i.e. $p = p(Q)$. With q_i as the output of firm i $(i = 1,2, . . ., n)$,

$$Q = q_1 + q_2 + . . . + q_n.$$

With variable costs of $C(q_i)$, firm i seeks to maximise profits $\pi_i = p(Q).q_i - C(q_i)$. The first-order conditions for this are:

$$d\pi/dq_i = (dp/dQ)(\partial Q/\partial q_i).q_i + p(Q) - dC/dq_i = 0.$$

Put $\partial Q/\partial q_i = a_i$, and rearrange to give

$$(p - dC/dq_i)/p = -(Q/p)(dp/dQ)(q_i/Q).a_i = (1/e)s_i.a_i.$$

where e is elasticity of demand, s_i is share of firm i (i.e. q_i/Q). Write PC_i for left hand of last equation which is the mark-up of price over marginal cost relative to prices, then $PC_i = s_i a_i/e_i$. Forming a weighted average (with weights s_i) over all firms leads to price-marginal cost ratio

$$PC = \sum_i s_i PC_i = \sum_i s_i^2 a_i / e.$$

The term a_i can be regarded as a measure of the effective collusion between firms. At one limit when $a_i = 1$ then the only change in Q is the change in q_i. This corresponds to the Cournot theory of oligopoly where each firm ignores output responses of other firms to its own output decisions. Then

$$PC = \sum_{i=1}^{n} s_i^2 / e.$$

At the other limit

$$a_i = \partial Q / \partial q_i = Q / q_i$$

and then

$$PC = \sum_{i=1}^{n} s_i / e = 1/e$$

(since by definition

$$\sum_{i=1}^{n} s_i = 1),$$

which is the joint profit maximising outcome.

The profits-sales ratio can be written as

$$(p-atc).Q/p.Q = (p-mc)/p + (mc-avc)p + (avc-atc)/p,$$

and from the above formula for the price-marginal cost ratio this can be written:

$$\pi/R = \sum_{i=1}^{n} S_i^2 a_i / e + (mc-avc)/p + (avc-atc)/p \qquad 1$$

where π is profits, R is sales revenue, mc is marginal costs, avc average variable costs and atc average total costs. This formulation indicates five factors which influence the profit-sales ratio. The first is

$$\sum_{i=1}^{n} s_i^2,$$

which is the Herfindahl measure of industrial concentration, and the second is a_i which an indicator of the degree of effective collusion between firms in the industry (in this simple case, over output changes). The third factor is the elasticity of demand, which can be influenced by the activities of the firms through advertising, product differentiation, etc.[10] These three factors taken together have a close correspondence with the concept of the degree of monopoly stressed by Kalecki (Kalecki, 1971, Chapter 5) and indeed this approach to oligopoly can be seen as a formalisation of the Kalecki approach (Cowling, 1981). Below we will use the term 'degree of monopoly' to signify the term

$$\sum_{i=1}^{n} s_i^2 a_i / e$$

for which we will use the symbol d. Johnson (1973) and others have suggested that the degree of monopoly is merely the inverse of the elasticity of demand, which would be the case in a simple monopoly model (and in the joint profit maximising case above). Apart from the influence of industrial concentration and collusion, the elasticity of demand can be influenced by firms' activities such as sales promotion.

The fourth and fifth factors are connected. The term $(mc-avc)$ reflects the technical conditions of production (around the current level of output) in that constant costs yield $mc = avc$, whilst declining costs yield a negative value of $(mc-avc)$ and increasing costs a positive value. It is often argued that firms under oligopolistic conditions operate with excess capacity (which can form a barrier to entry (Spence, 1977)) which would suggest that variable costs are declining or constant. Kalecki (1971) generally assumed as a first approximation that variable unit costs were constant. The final factor arises from the term $(avc-atc)$ which is the negative of average fixed costs (i.e. overheads). This will be particularly affected by the level of demand and hence of capacity utilisation. A rise in the level of output will, from this factor, increase the ratio of profits to sales.

The allocation of total costs between the variable costs and fixed costs categories reflects two (possibly) conflicting considerations. The first is that variable costs are simply costs of inputs which are variable within the decision period of the firm. The balance between variable costs and fixed costs can depend on the degree of capital intensity, with higher capital intensity expected to be associated with higher fixed costs relative to variable costs. The nature of variable costs can also be influenced by the firm's expectations for the future. For example, a decline in demand which is not expected to last for long may lead the firm to maintain its labour force at the previous level, in which case labour costs would be a fixed rather than a variable cost.

The second consideration relates to the use of this approach as a theory of income distribution. The distinction is made between those costs which are marked up and those which are not. The type of costs entering variable costs (and thereby marginal costs) are marked-up such that

$$(p-mc)/p = \sum_i s_i^2 a_i / e.$$

Thus a general rise in variable (and hence marginal) costs does not disturb the ratio of profits to sales provided that the degree of monopoly remains unchanged. Fixed costs, on the other hand, are not marked-up so that an increase in fixed costs reduces profits paid out of a constant surplus of price over variable costs. This approach points to the factors determining the division of receipts of a firm into variable costs and a surplus. If, for example, variable costs could be identified with wages and the surplus with profits, then we would have part of a theory of the distribution of income between wages and profits. Thus this consideration points to identifying payments out of the surplus with the income of the owners and controllers of the firm (profits, managerial income, etc.) and the variable costs with the income of the workers and of foreigners (imported costs). Thus a distinction is made between incomes which arise out of the surplus and those which arise out of variable costs.

In our discussion below, we find that the first consideration is relevant to movements in the profits/sales ratio over the trade cycle, whilst the second consideration is relevant to the average profit/ sales ratio. We can illustrate this by a simple example. The costs which are marked-up are divided into those which vary directly with the level of output, and those which do not vary. The former we write as $C = aQ$ and the latter as $C' = bQ^*$ where Q is actual output and Q^* expected output to which the use of the second group of inputs is aligned. Then marked-up costs are $aQ+bQ^*$ and expansion of the expected level of output is subject to constant unit costs. When the degree of monopoly is constant with respect to output in the sense that the mark-up of price over costs at the expected level of output is maintained, we have $p = (a+b)/(1-d)$ (from $(p-mc)/p = d$ with $mc = (a+b)$ at the expected level of output). As output varies

$$(\pi+F)/pQ = (p-mc)/p = 1-(aQ+bQ^*)(1-d)/(a+b)Q$$

so that the ratio of profits plus fixed costs to sales fluctuates with output, and *a fortiori* the ratio of profits to sales fluctuates with output.

During the course of the trade cycle the degree of monopoly may also change. Kalecki (1971) argued that 'there is a tendency for the degree of monopoly to rise in the slump, a tendency which is reversed in the boom.' This arises as firms strive to protect their profits in the downturn as unit costs rise and bite into the surplus. We could expect that such moves would damp down the cyclical behaviour of profits share, without completely removing it. On the other hand, as Kalecki notes in a footnote there may be cut-throat competition during a depression, and hence a fall in the degree of effective collusion and in the degree of monopoly.

The average ratio of the surplus (i.e. profits plus fixed costs) to sales for an industry can be written $(\pi+F)/R = d$, where R is sales revenue and $R = \pi+F+W+MC$ by definition where W is total labour payments and MC material costs. Moving to the aggregate level creates two complications. First, if each industry were vertically integrated, then MC would correspond to imported inputs. The ratio of surplus to sales revenue at the aggregate level would be a weighted average of the individual degrees of monopoly, where the weights used are proportional to the sales revenue.[11] Second, when industries are not vertically integrated, then at the first stage of production prices are a mark-up over the costs of labour and of imported materials. At the second stage of production prices are a mark-up over costs of inputs purchased from the first stage as well as costs of labour and any further imported materials. Thus the labour and imported materials which enter at the first stage of production are subject to being marked up directly at that stage and then indirectly at the second stage.[12] The extent to which imported goods are marked-up depends on where they enter in the production chain. Raw materials may enter at an early stage and be subject to several layers of mark-up at the retail stage. An increase in imports of final consumer goods which replace domestically produced goods serves to reduce the level of profits since the latter will usually be subject to more mark-up than the former (within the domestic economy).

These remarks indicate that the aggregate degree of monopoly depends on the industrial composition of production. Industries differ in terms of the degree of monopoly and of the response of costs to changes in output, and the relative weights of different types of industries will affect the over-all picture. But from now onwards we will, unless otherwise stated, take the industrial composition as constant and use aggregate price equations, etc.

Above we wrote $\pi + F = d.R$ and $R = \pi + F + W + MC$, so that $\pi + F = (d/(1-d)).(W+MC)$. National income (= net output), $Y = \pi + F + W$ since MC is cost of imported inputs. Then the share of labour income in national income is

$$W/Y = W/((d/(1-d))(W+MC)+W) = (1-d)/(1+d.k)$$

where $k = MC/W$. Thus the share of labour income in national income depends (negatively) on the degree of monopoly and the ratio of imported costs to labour costs. The share of the surplus in national income, $(\pi+F)/Y$ is $d(k+1)/(1+dk)$, which is a positive function of d and k.

This approach has some clear implications for the evolution of the rate of profit. This can be seen if we write the rate of profit

$$\pi/K = (\pi/(\pi+F)). ((\pi+F)/pQ).(Q/Q^*).(pQ^*/K),$$

where K is the monetary measure of the stock of capital equipment, and Q^* capacity output. Since this equation is an identity, its usefulness depends on the four factors which are isolated being relevant. The third ratio measures degree of capacity utilisation, which will also strongly influence the first ratio. For a given degree of monopoly, the share of profits in the surplus will be greater the higher the utilisation of capacity and the mass of the surplus. The second ratio $((\pi+F)/Q)$ is determined by the degree of monopoly (and the ratio of imported input costs to wage costs). The fourth ratio, Q^*/K, is the inverse of the capital-output ratio and hence of capital intensity. Weisskopf (1979) examines the course of the rate of profits in the United States in the post-war period using a similar framework.

The only influence of the foreign sector on the analysis above comes through the price of imported inputs. In this analysis and particularly when a complete model is considered, the focus is on the implications of a specific relationship between foreign input price, n, and domestic prices, p. In general, we implicitly assume that the exchange rate (between foreign and domestic currency) is flexible and adjusts to maintain a constant ratio n/p. Any basic change in that ratio will lead to changes in the relationship between wages and profits. In considering imported inputs, the main feature is that they are not substitutes for domestically produced inputs. For an imported finished good still has to pass through the domestic distribution sector, and is thus still subject to some domestic profit mark-up. We explained above that the stage at which imported goods entered the domestic production and distribution system would influence the average degree of monopoly.

When imported goods compete with domestic goods then two consequences follow. First, in the short-term, the behaviour of the prices of foreign competing imports places some restriction on the short-term behaviour of domestic prices. The extent of such restrictions would depend in part on the nature of the exchange rate system, with fixed exchange rates placing more limitations than a flexible exchange rate. In the latter case, a faster increase in domestic prices than in import prices would be offset by a change in the exchange rate. Second, an increase in the attractiveness of imported goods reduces the demand for domestically produced goods, and in general would lead to a lower level of output. The consequences of this are explored in Chapter 6 (p.134). Foreign competition may also affect the degree of monopoly by lowering the effective degree of concentration and collusion, and through the introduction of close substitutes raise the elasticity of demand. The extent to which increased imports have this impact in practice will depend on, *inter alia*, the degree to which the imports come from multinational firms already established in the domestic market and the degree of international collusion (for further discussion on this point see Cowling, 1981, 1982).

This approach to oligopolistic pricing is clearly intended to apply to a capitalist economy, for payments to labour are regarded as a cost and the residual which is maximised accrues to the owners of capital. Thus, the macro-economic theory which involves the use of such an approach to pricing is specific to a capitalist economy. Wages and profits are clearly distinguished, and play quite different roles not only within the theory of pricing but also within the theory of savings and investment.

This approach (as well as the others to be discussed) indicates that the real wage is not determined solely in the labour market, but conditions in the product market are also relevant. For simplicity, take the case where variable costs are constant so that $avc = w.L/Q + n.N/Q$ (where w is wage, L labour input, n cost of material input and N quantity of material input). We have that $(p-avc)/p = d$ and by manipulation reach $p(1-d) = avc$ and then

$$(w/p)/(Q/L) = 1-d-(n/p)/(Q/N).$$

Thus the real wage (relative to output per employee) depends on the degree of monopoly (the *d* term) and the cost of material inputs. When Q/L and Q/N are constants, and the degree of monopoly invariant with respect to the level of output, the real wage is determined in the product market. In the more general case, the level of output influences the real wage, and that is examined of the general model considered in the next chapter.

The second approach which is examined is that of limit-pricing (Modigliani, 1958). For our purposes, it is sufficient to take a general form of the limit-pricing approach. Firms planning to enter an industry face various impediments such as those arising from economies of scale, advertising, product differentiation, excess capacity, absolute cost advantages of existing firms.[13] In view of these barriers, the existing firms perceive that they can charge a price above the competitive level without inducing firms to enter the industry. Thus barriers to entry permit profits to be gained in excess of the 'normal' or competitive level. The size of those profits will depend on the height of the barriers to entry, the enthusiasm or otherwise of potential entrants and the reactions of the existing firms to those barriers. The approach of Modigliani focused on economies of scale as the entry barriers, with existing firms acting cautiously and new entrants prepared to enter if post-entry profits are predicted to be at the competitive level or above. The barriers to entry may be added to in a variety of ways by existing firms, for example, by advertising or by operating with excess capacity.

The general notion of limit-pricing can be summarised by $p_L = ac.f(X)$, where p_L is the limit-price (the highest price which will prevent entry into the industry in the assessment of the existing firms), ac is average costs and $f(X)$ is a function of the vector X which indicates the heights of various barriers to entry. Rearrangement gives $(p-ac)/p = (f(X)-1)/f(X)$, assuming that the limit-price is actually charged. Thus, by an alternative route, we have again reached an equation in which the profit margin is determined by the degree of monopoly. In this case, the degree of monopoly is largely determined by the height of entry barriers, although the elasticity of demand and the level of concentration may influence the effectiveness of entry barriers in raising the profit margin.

The limit-pricing approach places an upper limit on the price (assuming existing firms wish to avoid entry). Firms may wish to pursue other objectives, or none at all, within the constraint formed by the limit-price. For example, firms may have a view on a 'satisfactory' profit margin and operate with that profit margin so long as it leads to a price which is below the limit-price.

The third approach which we briefly examine is the sales-revenue maximisation theory of Baumol (1959). This theory is intended to apply to a managerial-controlled firm, where the managers are interested in promoting sales in the belief that higher sales enhance their reputation and salaries. The managers are subject to a minimum profit constraint imposed by the shareholders of the corporation. When the profits constraint is binding (which is usually argued to be the case) then we have the profits constraint $A = p.Q - C(Q)$, which can be re-written as $p.Q = C(Q) + A$, and then $p = C(Q)/Q + A/Q$.

These three approaches (and others which we could have examined) yield a price equation of the general form $p = m(Q).C(Q)$. where m is the mark-up over costs, where both the mark-up and costs may vary with the level of output Q. The cost function $C(Q)$ will be taken as average costs (so that in the profit maximising case the relationship between marginal and average cost is incorporated in $m(Q)$). The mark-up may vary with the level of demand (proxied here by the level of output) for numerous reasons. In the generalised model of oligopoly discussed above, movements in the mark-up can be analysed in terms of movements in the elasticity of demand, the degree of effective collusion and the level of concentration.

From the general price equation it is straightforward to derive an equation for the surplus-sales ratio as

$$(p - C(Q))/p = (m(Q, Z) - 1)/m(Q, Z),$$

where Z is a vector of factors influencing the mark-up. For simplicity, we will refer to the surplus as profits, but it must be recognised that the surplus includes not only profits in the sense of income accruing to capital but may also include management expenses, rent, advertising, etc. This broader definition of profits is important when we come to consider expenditure and savings out of profits and the influence of profitability on investment.

The final subject of this section is price inflation. It is convenient to separate the causes of changes in costs into those which arise from changes in the level of output and those which arise from changes in the cost of inputs. Ideally we would wish to write $C(Q) = f.c(Q)$ where f is an index of input prices and $c(Q)$ is 'real' costs.[14] However the response by a firm to changes in the relative price of inputs may depend upon the level of output. In the case where the cost function has been derived from cost minimisation (subject to the input prices and the production function) the marginal rate of substitution between any two factors may depend on the ratio between the factors and the absolute level of the use of the factors. However, when the production function is homothetic,[15] and input price are constant as far as the firm is concerned, then we can write $C(Q) = g(f).c(Q)$, where f is a vector of input prices.[16] Using that result, we write the general price equation as $p = m(Q,Z).g(f).c(Q)$. When firms are able to adjust prices continuously (or if we are interested in, say, quarter-to-quarter changes in price then quarterly), we have by differentiation with respect to time:

$$\frac{1}{p}\frac{dp}{dt} = \frac{1}{m}\frac{\partial m.dQ}{\partial Q\ dt} + \frac{1}{m}\frac{\partial m.dZ}{\partial Z\ dt} + \frac{1}{g}\frac{dg.df}{df\ dt} + \frac{1}{C}\frac{dC.dQ}{dQ\ dt}$$

which we write as

$$\dot{p} = (e_m + e_c)\dot{Q} + + e_z\dot{Z} + e_g\dot{f}$$

where superscript $\cdot$ above a variable denotes a relative rate of change of that variable, that is,

$$\dot{x} = 1/x.dx/dt, \text{ and } e_m = (Q/m)\ (\partial m/\partial Q),$$
$$e_c = Q/c(dc/dQ), e_z = Z/m.(\partial m/\partial Z),$$

e_g is vector with elements $(f_i/g)(\partial g/\partial f_i)$. Thus the rate of change of prices depends on (i) the rate of change of output, (ii) the rate of change of the degree of monopoly and (iii) the rate of change of input prices. The effect of (i) depends on the elasticity of the degree of monopoly and of 'real' costs (with respect to changes in output).

There are many significant features of this price change equation, but space limitations reduce our discussion to two points.[17] First, price changes are related to quantity changes. Second, price changes and quantity changes are jointly determined by firms in pursuit of their objectives, and arise, *inter alia*, for changes in demand. Thus it is demand changes which influence price changes and not the level of demand (or of excess demand), and the division of demand changes into price changes and output changes depends on the firms and their objectives.

Investment

The discussion of investment in Chapter 2 indicated that much writing on the theory of investment dwells on investment by an individual firm operating in a perfectly competitive environment. Our concern here is with the aggregate demand for investment in an oligopolised economy. As far as we are aware there is not a well-worked-out theory of aggregate investment in such an economy, and here we indicate the main ingredients of the determinants of investment. Thus we are not able to spell out the precise mechanisms involved, but rather hope to isolate some of the key variables which influence investment. Our discussion focuses on private business investment and we do not attempt to say anything about public sector investment or personal consumer investment, except insofar as there are similar forces at work. Our final goal is the determinants of gross investment since the demand for gross investment (rather than for net investment) is an important component of aggregate demand which has to be financed by the firms. Net investment is important for any discussion of economic growth, but that is outside our remit here.

We begin with six factors which can be expected to influence the effective demand for investment goods. First, net investment is the change in the capital stock, and the desired level of the capital stock is linked to the expected level of output. From our discussion of the accelerator theory in Chapter 2, we write net investment

$$I_t = \lambda . v(Y_t^d - Y_{t-1}) + \lambda(v . Y_{t-1} - K_{t-1})$$

where λ is the proportion of difference between desired and actual capital stock made up within one period and v is the desired capital-output ratio. Thus net investment is linked to desired changes in output and to capacity utilisation (p.29 above).

Second, investment may be linked to a longer-term view of growth in output and changes in the technology for producing it. Some part of investment would then be linked to views on the underlying growth prospects for the economy. Technological developments may effect the rate of investment when a new technology has to be embodied in new capital equipment before it can effect the nature of the productive process (Kaldor, 1961, Kaldor and Mirrlees, 1962).

Third, investment has to be financed, with the return on it expected to accrue over several years so that the cost and availability of finance are relevant. The sources of finance for investment are (in typical order of importance) retained profits, bank borrowing and the issue of new shares and bonds (see p.167 below). The most readily available sources of finance for firms is savings out of profits (i.e. retained earnings for corporations) and other own resources. The term 'retained earnings' is used here to cover any savings out of profits, including that of unincorporated firms. Retained earnings have the advantage of being under the control of the firm itself and their use not subject to external scrutiny.[18] Whilst their use involves the opportunity cost arising from not putting them to other uses such as lending, it does not involve the transactions costs involved in raising external finance nor commitment to future interest payments.[19]

The cost of finance which is relevant to investment decisions is usually seen as the real rate of interest. If, for example, inflation proceeds at 10 per cent per annum and is expected to continue at that rate, then prices, costs and hence profits will all be expected to rise in nominal terms at 10 per cent per annum (faster than otherwise). Thus the nominal rates of profit and of interest are higher by 10 per cent per annum as compared with the corresponding real rates. This would indicate that the rate of inflation would be immaterial as far as investment decisions were concerned, and that the balance between the real rate of profit and real rate of interest was of importance. However, borrowing at a fixed rate of interest involves a long-term commitment, and a high nominal rate of interest would create problems for the borrower if the rate of inflation were to fall. Thus the rate of inflation may have some impact, and is likely to swing firms towards preferring retained earnings (which involve no financial outgoings) and borrowing at variable rates of interest (especially bank borrowing).

Three distinct ranges in the supply of finance function facing a firm can be identified, which are illustrated in Figure 5.1. In the first range, internal finance is available at an opportunity cost equal to foregone interest on lending. The second range relates to external borrowing available at a constant rate of interest. The difference in the cost of internal funds and external funds arises from differences in the lending and borrowing rates of (for example) banks and the transactions costs involved with external borrowing. The third range, where the supply of finance curve is upward-sloping, reflects the increasing risk arising from 'the greater the investment in relation to the entrepreneurial capital, the greater is the reduction of the entrepreneur's income in the event of an unsuccessful business venture' (Kalecki, 1971, Chapter 9). This also indicates that the position of supply of finance curve will vary between firms. The point *A* in Figure 5.1 may depend on the internal funds available in the relevant period and the extent to which previous investment had been debt-financed. Further, the extent of internal funds depends crucially on profits, and the more profitable firms have more finance for investment. Over the trade cycle, with profits rising in the boom and falling in the slump, investment may rise in the boom and fall in

subject to a great deal of uncertainty, and liable to substantial revisions. But a strong influence on expected profitability is likely to be actual profitability. A rise in profits and profitability (which in the short term with a constant capital stock are equivalent) can affect investment through two routes. Such a rise generates an increase in internal funds and shifts the supply of finance curve to the right, and may generate a rise in expected profitability. Both routes would lead to a rise in profits encouraging the effective demand for investment. Changes in profitability may also be relevant to investment decisions. The desired capital stock for a firm depends, *inter alia*, on profitability so that changes in profitability lead to changes in the desired capital stock and hence to investment.

The fifth influence is the cost of investment goods relative to other factors of production and the price of output. For the usual reasons, a rise in the price of investment goods would be expected to reduce the demand for investment goods. A demand schedule for investment goods could be constructed as a function of price (with changes in the other factors discussed above causing that demand schedule to shift) and place it alongside a supply schedule to determine price and quantity of investment goods produced. In our discussion below we do not intend to disaggregate goods into consumption goods and investment goods as that disaggregation does not appear to offer sufficient insights to offset the added complications. Thus we abstract from changes in the relative price of consumption goods and investment goods and treat the demand for investment as part of aggregate demand. Changes in the price of output relative to factors of production are subsumed into changes in profitability.

Finally, investment in capital equipment involves some commitment to its future operation, though the degree of commitment varies by type of equipment involved. At one end, the purchase of a car may involve a small commitment since well-organised markets exist for second-hand cars. At the other extreme, the second-hand market for some fixed capital equipment which forms part of an integrated production process is virtually non-existent. But the commitment of the economy as a whole is much greater than the commitment of a firm, for sale overseas or physical destruction are the only ways for an economy to dispose of capital equipment. These remarks have two implications. First, a firm's investment decisions are heavily conditioned by its assessment of the future. This is often taken to mean that since the assessment of the future is inevitably uncertain it is liable to sudden shifts, and the resulting instability in the investment function is a major cause of instability in the economy (p.28 above). But the assessment of the future by firms influences investment, which in turn affects the outcome in the future. Thus a belief that the economy will grow slowly yields low investment which 'justifies' the low growth prediction. Second, today's investment becomes part of tomorrow's capital stock, and unless further demands for investment arise tomorrow, aggregate demand will be lower tomorrow than it is today. Thus the capacity to produce is higher, the demand is lower. The naïve accelerator illustrates this point vividly. Net investment relies on growth, and unless the economy continues to expand net investment falls away.

The first influence discussed above relates specifically to net investment. As capital equipment wears out, firms are able to reassess their investment position. However, other things being equal, we would expect that gross investment was related to the capital equipment in existence and the depreciation on it. In turn, the capital equipment in existence is expected to be related to the level of output.

We can summarise the above discussion by the following general formulation of the function for gross investment as part of aggregate demand: $I = F(Q, \triangle Q, CU, \pi, \triangle \pi, \rho, g, r, E)$ where Q is level of output, $\triangle Q$ the expected change in output, CU capacity utilisation, π profits, $\triangle \pi$ change in profits, ρ the rate of profits, g the underlying rate of growth, r a summary measure of the cost of finance, and E the state of confidence. This investment function forms part of aggregate demand, and as with other components of aggregate demand, the extent to which the demand for investment is translated into effect depends on availability of finance and of supply. We could also anticipate in the case of investment lags between decisions on investment expenditure being made, that demand becoming effective and the investment coming into operation.

Saving

The central proposition of this section is that the propensity to save out of labour income is substantially lower than the propensity to save out of non-labour income. At one level, this proposition can be treated as an empirical 'fact' (some support for which we present in Chapter 7), and the macro-economic consequences explored. In some macro-econometric models there is some distinction between savings out of different types of income. This arises when personal consumption (and hence personal savings) is related to personal disposable income, which includes wages and salaries and distributed profits, but not retained profits. Thus savings out of wages are undertaken by the households, whereas savings out of profits are the sum of those undertaken by households out of distributed profits plus savings by corporations (i.e. retained earnings). Some recognition of differential propensities is made in some informal discussion of the effects of wage changes (e.g. Hansen, 1953, Chapter 10; Dillard, 1948, Chapter 9), with a reduction in wages shifting income towards profits and tending to depress consumption demand. But the idea of differential savings propensities does not usually enter formal macro-economic models, and the proponents of consumption functions based on the life-cycle hypothesis and the permanent income hypothesis explicitly reject the notion (Modigliani, 1975).

However, the differential savings propensities reflect a basic view about the nature of a capitalist economy. This has two aspects.[20] First, there is a belief that the propensity to save is larger for higher income households than for lower income households, and that the share of household income derived from non-labour income rises with income.[21] A shift from labour income to non-labour income is then seen as a shift towards households with relatively high savings propensities. Second, firms' decisions over retained earnings (which constitute savings) and investment are seen as the major determinants of savings in an economy. For the firms, competition forces them to seek lower costs, raise productivity and to invest in new machinery. 'Moreover, the development of capitalist production makes it necessary constantly to increase the amount of the capital laid out in a given industrial undertaking, and competition subordinates every individual capitalist to the immanent laws of capitalist production as external and coercive laws. It compels him to keep extending his capital, so as to preserve it, and he can only extend it by means of progressive accumulation' (Marx, 1976). In other words, high levels of savings are forced onto firms if they wish to survive the competitive pressures arising from the accumulation by other firms. Thus the nature of the competitive system dictates the propensity to save out of profits. The driving force towards savings is not a 'taste' for savings, but the survival and growth requirements of firms.[22]

This line of argument may need to be modified for a world of managerial-controlled oligopolies. Following Cowling (1981), the propensity to save out of the surplus generated by corporations may be lower under managerial capitalism than under competitive capitalism for two reasons. First, the pressure to accumulate may be less in that competitive pressures have been diminished. Second, some of the surplus is absorbed 'within the managerial hierarchy in the form of pecuniary and non-pecuniary income. Thus under managerial capitalism an increasing degree of monopoly will imply the replacement of worker consumption partly by corporate savings and partly by managerial consumption' (Cowling, 1981).

It is generally sufficient for our purpose that there are differential savings propensities. But we can observe that the life-cycle hypothesis (LCH) (pp.20–23) may be relevant for the savings decisions of workers out of labour income. Indeed that hypothesis is little more than the refinement of Kalecki's view 'that workers spend all their income and that they spend them immediately', by replacing 'immediately' with 'during their life-time'. Thus the LCH retains the assumption that workers are not in the business of saving long-term.

The view of differential savings propensities out of labour income and out of non-labour income arises from the nature of a capitalist income, and there is no particular reason to think that it applies elsewhere. In the next chapter it will be seen that some view the differential savings propensities as a central feature in the determination of the distribution of income (arising out of Kaldor, 1955). Further, when the profits share tends to rise in the upswing of the trade cycle, the differential savings propensities influence the movement of savings and consumption during the trade cycle.

Wages and wage changes

There has been relatively little effort made to introduce explicit consideration of the effects of collective bargaining into formal macro-economic models, although some wage inflation models have been built around collective bargaining (e.g. Hines, 1964). A major aim of this section is the development of a relatively simple model which encapsulates some crucial features of collective bargaining. The approach is developed for bargaining between trade unions on one side and employers in an industry on the other, and phrased in terms of unions and employers. Nevertheless many features of the approach would apply to non-union situations. For as Routh (1980) argued, it is a mistake to imagine that there is a sharp division between unionized and un-unionized workers, for trade unions cannot do much more than institutionalize and direct drives and aspirations that are already present in the individual workers. [However] unions protect individual workers against arbitrary acts; they give collections of workers more control over their own destiny than they would have as individuals and present the possibility of pursuing social ends that might not otherwise be attainable.

The approach of Wood (1978) stresses that there are two sets of forces operating on the level and structure of earnings. There are 'normative pressures' which arise from pay norms and notions about fair pay (or the 'just wage') and 'anomic pressures' which arise in other ways particularly from the forces of demand and supply (from which any influence of fair pay, etc. has been purged). Under the first heading there are '*real* norms (implying that beliefs about fair pay in money terms are revised in response to change in prices), and *relative* norms (implying that beliefs about fair pay in money terms for particular people or jobs are revised in response to changes in other rates of pay)' (Wood, 1978; italics in original). The major purpose of Wood (1978) is to explore how pay norms are set and change, and the interaction between normative and anomic pressures. Another author who stresses these normative pressures is Routh (1980), who argued that

there is something elemental in this attachment of a person to his level of income, measured in terms of its purchasing power (the maintenance of a standard of living) and in terms of the earnings of other occupations, that is not unlike the attachment of an animal to its young. It applies to the individual and leads individuals to act in concert with or without trade union organisation; a sense that their work has been devalued can turn a disciplined work force into a surly, disgruntled mob.

Arguments in a similar vein are given by, *inter alia*, Hicks (1975), Phelps Brown (1975), Kaldor (1976) and Paniç (1976). The argument of Hicks (1975) is perhaps the closest to the formalisation which we present below when he says that

the wage-earners' test for fair wages is not simply a matter of comparison with other people's earnings. It is a matter of comparison with his own experience, his own experience in the past. It is this which makes him resist a reduction in the purchasing power of his wage, and even a reduction in the growth of that purchasing power to which he has become accustomed. Thus there is a backlash of prices on wages—a Real Wage Resistance. . . .

The macro-econometric model of the Cambridge Economic Policy Group incorporates the concept of a target real wage which plays a major role in our model below (see Cripps and Godley, 1976).

The union, in setting its bargaining objectives for the coming round of negotiations, has to translate its basic objectives into a money wage objective, for bargaining takes place in money terms. The basic objectives are assumed to be threefold—maintenance of current real wage, progress towards obtaining a target real wage and some restoration of differentials (relative to other groups which are regarded as comparable). This we write, in a rather convoluted form for reasons which become apparent below, as:

$$w_t^* = w_{t-1} . (p_t^e/p_{t-1})^{a_2} . (T/(w_{t-1}/p_{t-1}))^{a_4} . (w_{ct-1}/w_{t-1})^{a_6}$$

where w_t^* is the money wage objective, w_{t-1} the current (at time of negotiation) money wage, p_t^e price level expected to prevail in time t, p_{t-1} (known) price level at time $t-1$, T is the target real wage, w_{t-1}/p_{t-1} is the current real wage, and w_{ct-1} is the average wage in industries which are regarded by unions in the industry under investigation as comparable with their own for wage-setting purposes.

The first two terms on the right-hand side indicate the starting point of the current money wage, which is uprated by the expected relationship between prices during time t and in time $t-1$. As Artis and Miller (1979) point out for a similar equation, there is not the same imperative for $a_2 = 1$ as there is for the coefficient on the expected inflation term to be unity in the expectation-augmented Phillips' curve. For if full compensation for price changes is not achieved this time, then next period the real wage is lower (than if full compensation were achieved) leading to a larger gap between target and actual real wage, and thereby a push for a larger wage increase next time round.

The third term expresses the desire to move current real wages towards a target real wage T. It could be argued that the larger the gap between the target and the current real wage, the greater will be the push by the union to close the gap, which could be represented by a more complicated function than the one used here. It can also be noted that this expression is symmetric for current real wages above and below the target real wage. Unions may be unlikely to plan for real wage declines when the current real wage is above the target real wage. The force of this argument depends on how the target wage is determined, as will be seen below. The equation could be complicated by making the third term subject to a minimum value of unity, so that real wage declines are not aimed for (although they may occur).

The fourth term represents attempts to restore differentials between the industry to whom this equation applies and other industries. In this equation we have conceptually separated the union's aims into a component which is linked to the absolute level of wages (T) and another component which is linked to this union's position within the wages hierarchy (w_{ct}). Thus the union is viewed as seeking to change the general level of wages and their position within that general level. In practice, separating out the two components would prove difficult, but here we make the theoretical distinction.

The achievement of the money wage objectives will depend on the extent to which the union is willing and able to push its claim, and the willingness or otherwise of the firms to concede the wage increases. The degree of militancy of the union will show up in terms of the values of coefficients such as a_4 and a_6. The extent to which the union presses its claim (including taking strike action) may be heavily conditioned by the state of the labour market, which we will proxy be the level of unemployment, though changes in the level of unemployment may also be important. The state of the labour market also influences the willingness or otherwise of firms to concede wage increases. We also postulate that the ability of firms is relevant to the wage increases achieved, and this is proxied by profitability.

Combining these ideas with the equation for the money wage objective gives achieved money wage

$$w_t = w_t^* . f(U_{t-1}).(P_{t-1}/P_{min})^{a_5},$$

where U is the rate of unemployment, P is profit rate on sales and P_{min} a minimum acceptable rate of profit for the firms. Writing this out in full we have:

$$w_t = w_{t-1}.(p_t^e/p_{t-1})^{a_2}.(T/(w_{t-1}/p_{t-1}))^{a_4}.f(U_{t-1})(P_{t-1}/P_{min})^{a_5}.$$

Taking logs of this equation, and using the approximation ln $(x_t/x_{t-1}) \doteqdot ln(1+\dot{x}_t) \doteqdot \dot{x}_t$ where $x_t = (x_t - x_{t-1})/x_{t-1}$ serves as an approximation for the rate of change of x, and a linerisation log $(f(U)) = a_1 + a_3 U$, we arrive at

$$\dot{w}_t = a_1 + a_2 \dot{p}_t^e + a_3 U_{t-1} + a_4(ln\ T - ln\ w_{t-1}/p_{t-1})$$
$$+ a_5(P_{t-1}/P_{min}) + a_6 ln(w_{ct-1}/w_{t-1})$$

(putting $\dot{p}_t^e = (p_t^e - p_{t-1})/p_{t-1})$) with a_2, a_4, a_5, a_6 positive and a_3 negative.

We have used a two-stage procedure of postulating the objective of the union and then looking at the factors influencing the achievement of that objective. These two stages could be compressed into one as the union learns about the constraints imposed by unemployment and profitability on the outcome of the bargaining process. We have paid little attention to the bargaining process itself, because we feel that the bargaining abilities of the two sides are of minor importance relative to the other factors involved, and tend to even out over the large number of separate bargaining situations which take place. Our major concern is with the overall wage outcome.

One further way in which this approach could be generalised is by postulating that the target real wage is a function of the level of unemployment, i.e. $T = T(U)$. But since unemployment already has an influence on wage increases and the achieved real wage, this generalisation would add complications without changing the basic nature of the analysis.

It appears from the above specification that the union can achieve any wage it desires by the suitable adjustment of the target real wage. But this is not the whole story. In the short run, there are likely to be further constraints than those given on the achievement of a particular money wage. Firms may feel that the extent to which they can raise prices is limited by demand conditions and the response of rivals, and this could place an upper limit on the wage increases which they are prepared to concede because of the implications for costs and prices.

In the short run, the union is concerned only with money wages (though based on a view about real wages), and not with unemployment. There are three reasons for this. First, the substitution possibilities between labour and other inputs are assumed to be small so that a rise in wages does not have any effect on employment through substitution. Second, at the industry level, labour costs form only a small proportion of costs.[23] Thus the rise in labour costs leads to a much smaller rise in costs and hence in prices, so that the impact on demand, and thereby output and employment is relatively small.[24] In addition, many other factors may be changing which serve to obscure the relationship between changes and employment. Third, when there are lags between cost changes and price changes, a wage change in a particular period will have an effect on future output and employment which varies over time. However, in the long run as indicated below (pp.126–129), there is a trade-off between the real wage and employment facing the unions, and it will be indicated there how a concern with employment may influence the target real wage.

The crucial element in this model of collective bargaining is the target real wage. How is that target set? There is a number of alternative mechanisms which can be suggested, and for our immediate purpose the major requirement is that for a particular set of wage negotiations the target real wage is predetermined.

A first view of the determination of the target real wage is essentially a satisficing notion. Workers are seen as holding ideas of what constitutes a satisfactory or acceptable wage. The value of T (and of w_{ct}) is generated by the expectations and aspirations of the union members. These, in turn, depend upon factors such as the militancy of the union and its members, the degree of social acceptance of profits and the profit motive, and beliefs about the dependence of employment and investment on profits. Essentially, then, T would be exogenously determined by social and political factors.

A second view, which could be seen as a special case of the first, is to take the target real wage as determined by (and perhaps equal to) the peak real wage achieved in the past. Thus unions operate real wage resistance in trying to maintain current wages and in seeking to regain previous real wage levels. This approach has advantages over the first view in that it serves to fix the target level and it could be modified to allow for the impact of achieved real wages to decline as time passes.

The target real wage is thus not a policy instrument of the unions, but emerges from the decision-making process within the union. However a maximising interpretation can be placed on the target real wage, and these form the third and fourth views on the determination of the target real wage.

A third view stresses the various costs associated with achieving a target real wage. These would include the costs of strikes in pursuit of a wage claim, and the maintenance of real wage achievements, and can be assumed to increase with the target real wage. For the union leadership, there are costs of the organisation of strikes and other evidence of militancy. But, further, since as will be shown below the higher the target real wage the larger the gap between target and actual, the more likely is membership discontent with the under-achievement of the target real wage.

A fourth view has to await its full expression until the interaction of the wage and price equations is considered. But its essence is that the target real wage determines where the economy operates in the long run on the real wage-unemployment trade-off presented to the workers by the firms. Thus the target real wage is seen as an instrument through which the union maximises a utility function with real wage and unemployment as arguments subject to the constraint presented by the oligopolists.

The aggregate wage change equation is taken as the weighted sum of industry wage change equations. On aggregation, the sum of the terms $a_6 ln(w_{ct-1}/w_{t-1})$ may cancel out, with some industries having wages above the 'comparison' wage, and some industries with wages below. An alternative would be that this component gives rise to a constant pressure on wage increases, with the industry-distribution of wages remaining unchanged relative to the distribution of 'comparison' wages. This is the assumption which we essentially make here. But particularly in the short run changes in the relationship of the two distributions mentioned may be an important cause of wage change.

Aggregating the wage change equation across industries, and incorporating the effect of final term (adjustment to differentials) into the constant term, we have the following

$$\dot{w}_t = a_1 + a_2 \dot{p}^e_t + a_3 U_{t-1} + a_4(ln\ T - ln\ w_{t-1}/p_{t-1}) + a_5(P_{t-1}/P_{min})$$

where the symbols have their previous meaning but now refer to aggregates or averages as appropriate. For ease of exposition in the next chapter we will take $a_5 = 0$, but that assumption does not affect the qualitative nature of the results.

The bargaining Phillips' curve is a special case of the general wage change equation with $a_4 = a_5 = a_6 = 0$. Thus if that bargaining Phillips' curve applied in some sectors of the economy, the incorporation of those sectors would not alter the basic aggregate relationship, although it could alter the size of the co-efficients.

We now look at the case of the economy in a kind of inflationary equilibrium in the sense that the money supply and nominal income level are rising at the same constant rate of $\dot{M}$. This merely describes the conditions of the equilibrium to be examined without implying anything about the direction of causation. When output is growing at a constant rate g we can write $\dot{p} + g = \dot{M}$. We assume a constant labour force and constant profit margin so that the real wage is also growing at rate g (i.e. $\dot{w} = \dot{p} + g$) and inflationary expectations are fulfilled so that $\dot{p}^e = \dot{p}$. Making those substitutions into the above equation yields:

$$ln \ w/p = a_4^{-1}(a_1 + a_3U + a_4 ln \ T + (a_2 - 1) \ \dot{M} - a_2 g).$$

We can note some interesting features of this equation. First, the relationship between the real wage and the level of unemployment is negative (since $a_3 < 0$, $a_4 > 0$), and the role of unemployment is to restrain the real wage achieved. Second, a rise in the target real wage leads to a rise in the actual real wage, other things, including the level of unemployment, being equal. But a rise in real wages would affect output and employment, and the rise in unemployment would damp down the actual real wage. In general a rise in the target real wage will lead to some rise in actual real wage and a rise in unemployment and an increasing gap between target and achieved real wage (p.130 below). Third, if $a_2 < 1$, a rise in the (permanent) rate of inflation lowers the real wage, with workers losing on each round by failing to achieve compensation for expected price rises. Fourth, with the real wage rising and $\dot{M}$ and g constant, some combination of falling unemployment and rising target real wage is required to maintain the above equality in effect over time. In the spirit of equilibrium analysis, this is taken to be the target real wage growing at rate g with unemployment constant. This may appear to be a stringent condition but arises from the imposition of an equilibrium analysis and constant unemployment requirement. A similar condition applies for the expectations-augmented Phillips' curve, where rising productivity leads to the demand for labour curve (in terms of real wages) shifting upwards, and unless the supply of labour curve shifts upwards at a consonant rate, the natural rate of employment and of unemployment will change.

The stress in this section has been on the aims of trade unions (or more generally workers), and their success or otherwise cannot be judged until the full macro-model is discussed in the next chapter. In one sense, our approach has tended to stress the normative (in the sense used by Wood, 1978, quoted above) approach above the anomic approach. The anomic pressures become more evident in the full macro-model. It can be objected that the target wage *(T)* is the *deus ex machina* of this approach. In one sense that is true, and indeed one of our objectives is to investigate the consequences of changes in the target wage. But we have sought to indicate the factors determining the target real wage. However, the strongest point to be made is that theories on the supply side of the labour market do not 'go very far back', and at a relatively early stage invoke a *deus ex machina*. In the case of conventional neo-classical analysis it is the utility function of the individual, whereas in our analysis it is the target real wage.

Money

The crucial feature of money is that it represents generalised purchasing power, and thus we focus on the medium of exchange aspect of money. In a monetary economy, intentions to purchase goods and services are inconsequential unless backed by possession of money or appropriate credit arrangements. Assets other than money and future potential income do not constitute immediate purchasing power though they may be usable in varying degrees to acquire money.

These remarks indicate a narrow definition of money as those financial assets which are currently generally accepted as a means of payment. In subsequent discussion money refers to this narrow definition, and we will assume that as a first approximation this corresponds to the *M1* definition of money, i.e. currency plus current account deposits (demand deposits in USA) which yield a zero nominal rate of interest. However concern over immediate purchasing power points to the inclusion of credit arrangements, though some credit arrangements relate to specific, rather than general, purchasing power in that they are tied to purchases from specified firms.[25] Although we exclude trade credit from our definition of money, for much of the discussion below the roles of trade credit and bank credit are very similar.

Items such as deposit accounts with clearing banks (time deposits in USA), which are often included in broad definitions of money, are excluded from this narrow definition of money on the grounds that they do not usually represent immediate purchasing power. Thus deposit account balances do not differ from, for example, government bonds in the sense that neither of them is a generally accepted medium of exchange. There are however two important respects in which those types of financial assets differ. First, the selling costs and the price uncertainty are greater for bonds than for deposit accounts.[26] The latter can be turned into narrow money at relatively low cost and at a constant price (i.e. one pound of deposit account yields one pound of current account). But the difference between deposit account balances and building society account balances (savings and loans associations in USA) may be rather slight on those grounds.

Second, deposit account balances can be created or destroyed by the unilateral action of the owner or potential owner of the balance. Thus the transfer of £100 from a deposit account to a current account reduces the former by £100 and increases the latter by £100. In this example stock of narrow money would increase by £100. The decision on such a transfer is in the hands of the individual and not the bank. The bank may respond by changing the interest rate paid on deposit accounts when there is a substantial net flow in one direction or the other. The importance of these remarks arises more at the aggregate level than the individual level. A general increase in, say, the desire for current account balances (which might arise as a prelude to a planned increase in expenditure) can take place and, as it does so, money is created. In contrast, bonds are not created or destroyed by the decision of the current or prospective owner alone. Whilst a bond may be sold by one economic agent, it has to be bought by some other economic agent on terms which are mutually acceptable, which can lead to variations in the price of bonds.[27] In the present context, however, the important feature is that the purchase and sale of bonds does not lead to net changes in the number of bonds or the amount of money in circulation (unless in this example the government is involved as buyer or seller).

Kaldor and Trevitick (1981) argue that 'in a credit money economy . . . the outstanding "money" stock can never be in excess of the amount which individuals wish to hold. . . .' It would perhaps be more accurate to replace 'can' in the quotation by 'need'. The mechanism involved is that if economic agents found themselves with more (narrow) money than they wished to hold, then the excess could be used to extinguish bank debt or be turned into near-moneys (such as deposit account balances). Monetarists argue that an excess holding of money spills over into an increased demand for goods and services, whilst Keynesians argue that such as excess mainly spills over into an increased demand for other assets. The Kaldor and Trevitick view is that the 'excess' money is mainly extinguished.

An economic agent can finance its expenditure in numerous ways—by sale of output or factors of production, by sale of assets, the running down of money balances, or by borrowing (including the use of trade credit). The first ways are the major sources of finance, and the consequences of failure to effect the sales was seen in the discussion of Clower (1965) in Chapter 3. The other ways involve the economic agent accepting the consequent changes in its portfolio of assets and liabilities. For example, if a firm held a stock of money which it felt on average to be barely adequate to cope with its day-to-day requirements arising from the non-synchronisation of inflows and outflows of money, then it would not feel able to run down its average holding of money to finance an increase in expenditure. But if a firm held 'idle balances' of money, then it could relatively easily finance an increase in expenditure.

We now look at a closed private sector economy in equilibrium, and trace the consequences of an increase in investment demand. Originally savings and investment were equal as well as the demand equal to supply of money. Now with a planned increase in investment expenditure, the previous level of savings is not sufficient to finance the higher level of investment. Whilst savings increase after the investment takes place, those increased savings are not available prior to the investment. Thus the gap between the higher level of investment demand and the existing level of savings has to be bridged by borrowing from the banks. Consider the financing position of firms on their capital account. Their sources of funds are their own savings (S_f), bank borrowing (BB_f) and issue of debt such as fixed interest bonds (D_f). For the investment expenditure to take place $I = S_f + BB_f + D_f$. Households save and use their savings (S_h) to purchase the debt of firms only in this simple case, i.e. $S_h = D_{fh}$. Substitution gives $I = S_h + S_f + BB_f$, where BB_f is the net creation of money by the banks. The willingness and ability of banks to create sufficient money to allow the expansion of investment to take place indicates how 'in general, the banks hold the key position in the transition from a lower to a higher scale of activity' (Keynes, 1937a).

The basic mechanism was described by Kalecki (1971) in the following way.

Let us assume that as a result of some important invention there is an increase in investment associated with its spreading. Now, is it possible for the capitalists to step up their investment, even though their profits have not increased (there was no reduction in wages) nor have they curtailed their own consumption *ad hoc* (this, indeed, is most unlikely). The financing of additional investment is effected by so called creation of purchasing power. The demand for bank credits increases and these are granted by the banks. The means used by the entrepreneurs for construction of new establishments reach the industries of investment goods. This additional demand makes for setting to work idle equipment and unemployed labour. The increased employment is a source of additional demand for consumer goods and thus results in turn in higher employment in the respective industries. Finally the additional investment outlay finds its way directly and through workers' spending into the pockets of capitalists (we assume that workers do not save). The additional profits flow back as deposits to the banks. Bank credits increase by the amount additionally invested and deposits by the amount of additional profits. The entrepreneurs who engage in additional investment are 'propelling' into the pockets of other capitalists profits which are equal to their investment, and they are becoming indebted to these capitalists to the same extent *via* banks.

With the creation of money by banks in response to demand for loans by firms, we have to consider the holding of that increased money stock. Between the two equilibrium positions, in the simple Keynesian case, income increases sufficiently to generate increased savings equal to the increased investment, i.e. $a \triangle Y = \triangle I$ where a is the marginal propensity to save. Taking the simple transactions demand for money with $M^d = k.Y$, then the changes between equilibrium are such that $\triangle M = k.\triangle Y$. Thus if the increase in investment demand dictates the required increase in income, that in turn dictates a required increase in the stock of money.[28] The latter can be brought about by a combination of two routes. First, the amount of money generated depends on the path back to equilibrium, for so long as *ex ante* savings and investment are unequal the money stock will continue to change. Second, economic agents can respond to an increase in their average holdings of money by seeking to convert the extra money into various near-moneys, and thereby help to generate a money supply more in line with the demand for money.

Two factors operate to reduce the apparent importance of banks in the above discussion. First, trade credit can serve as an alternative to bank credit in permitting the expansion of expenditure. Second, the existence of near-moneys which can be converted into money at the discretion of the holder reduces the power of the banks.

The creation of money is intimately linked in general with spending decision. In the case of high-powered money issued by the government, the linkage is with the deficit between government expenditure and revenue, and the proportion being financed by the issue of bonds. In the case of credit money, it is created in response to a demand for loans, which will usually be taken out for the purpose of financing expenditure. Surplus or deficit on the balance of payments, reflecting expenditure decisions on imports and exports, can also lead to changes in the money supply (depending on the extent of 'sterilisation' of the inflows or outflows by the Central

Bank). Conversely, expenditure decisions can only be put into effect if they are backed up by money (which here would include credit arrangements). In many respects, this view gives money a greater role than it receives within the monetarist approach. In that approach, an increase in the money supply leads to an excess holding of money which spills over into an increased demand for goods and services. In contrast, the approach taken here would see an increase in the money supply as arising from intentions to increase expenditure on goods and services, which can only take place if the money supply is increased.

Notes

1 'Although macro-economic models do not pay explicit attention to the internal composition of the aggregates, the relationships among aggregate variables that make up the models are intended to be consistent with theoretical and empirical knowledge of the behaviour of individual economic units and particular markets' (Tobin, 1970a). Our argument is that conventional macro-economics has started from the wrong theoretical viewpoint, that of atomistic competition, and has not been concerned with consistency with empirical knowledge.

2 For alternative measures of industrial concentration, see text-books on industrial economics, e.g. Sawyer (1981a). For a long list of alternative measures and some discussion of their properties see Aaronovitch and Sawyer (1975), Chapter 3. Hannah and Kay (1977) discuss the properties which they feel concentration measures should possess.

3 The immediate source of the figures quoted in this paragraph is Sawyer (1981a), Chapter 3, which cites the original sources.

4 This does not imply that concentration fell. The lower level of aggregation used in 1968 (as compared with 1975) would lead to more and smaller industries and, in general, higher measured levels of concentration.

5 For more details on the levels of and changes in concentration see Sawyer (1981a), Chapter 3; Aaronovitch and Sawyer (1975), Chapters 4 and 6; Hart and Clarke (1980); and Prais (1976). For concentration in non-manufacturing, see Aaronovitch and Sawyer (1975), Chapter 5.

6 Shepherd (1970) argued that figures such as those quoted in the text for the United States understate the degree of market power of large firms. In part this happens because the figures relate to national markets whereas markets are often regionalised in the USA, and concentration figures should then relate to regional markets. For further discussion of American concentration, see, for example Mueller and Hamm (1974), Stonebraker (1979) and White (1981).

7 Burkitt and Bowers (1979) provide figures on unionisation in thirteen countries (which overlap with those in our Table 5.1).

8 For full discussion see texts on theories of the firm, e.g. Sawyer (1979a).

9 This section draws heavily on Cowling and Waterson (1976), Cowling (1981), (1982).

10 For discussion on the effects of advertising on the elasticity of demand see Sawyer (1981a), Chapter 7.

11 For industry i $\pi_i + F_i = d_i R_i$, and so at the aggregate level

$$\pi + F = \sum_i (\pi_i + F_i) = \sum_i d_i R_i = \sum_i d_i (R_i/R) R = d.R$$

where d is the weighted average degree of monopoly and R aggregate sales revenue.

12 For each industry we can write

$$\pi_i + F_i = ((d_i/(1-d_i))(W_i + N_i) = a_i(W_i + N_i) \ (i = 1,2)$$

where N_i are material inputs and a_i defined as indicated. Sales of industry 1 are the material inputs of industry 2 so that $R_1 = N_2$. Then

$$\pi_1 + F_1 + \pi_2 + F_2 = \pi_1 + F_1 + a_2(W_2 + \pi_1 + F_1 + W_1 + N_1)$$
$$= a_2 W_2 \ (+ a_1 + a_1 a_2 + a_2).(W_1 + N_1).$$

13 Bain (1956) discusses at length the roles of economies of scale, product differentiation and absolute cost advantage as barriers to entry. Spence (1977) analyses the role of excess capacity, and suggests that under certain conditions, firms operate with sufficient excess capacity to deter both entrants as well as to maximise short-run profits. For a summary see Sawyer (1981a), Chapter 5.

14 This is essentially the line followed by Coutts, Godley and Nordhaus (1978), where they postulate that firms base their prices on 'normalised costs', which are those which would be in effect if the firm were operating at its normal or planned level of output. In terms of the equation $C(q) = f.c(q)$, this can be interpreted as saying that firms base their prices on the index f where the weights used in compiling that index relate to the normal level of output. Variations in costs arising from the $c(q)$ component are either negligible in importance and/or disregarded by firms.

15 A homothetic function is a monotonic transformation of a homogeneous function. A homothetic production function has the property that the ratio of marginal products depends only on the ratio of factors of production and not on the scale of their use. But, unlike homogeneous production functions, the returns to scale can vary (see Layard and Walters, 1978, Appendix 3).

16 For formal proof see Shephard (1970), Chapter 4.

17 For further discussion and empirical estimation of this type of price change equation see Sawyer (1981b).

18 However for a corporation with a large number of shareholders, distrust in corporate policy can be expressed through sale of shares, and thereby a depressed share price. This may open the way for a takeover bid, and this may provide a constraint on the activities of the corporation.

19 The use of external finance involves commitment to future interest payments. The larger are interest payments, the more likely it is that in a 'bad' year the surplus over operating costs will be insufficient to meet the interest payments.

20 A third aspect arises from the distinction made by tax laws between wages and profits. Labour income is subject to income tax and social

security contributions, whereas corporate profits are subject to corporation taxes and, as dividends, to personal income tax.

21 For some evidence see Sawyer (1976), Table 14.

22 For some further discussion along similar lines see Green (1979).

23 For example, at the three-digit level for British manufacturing industry, direct labour costs form about one-fifth of total costs. The prices of other inputs are, of course, influenced by labour costs, but those costs are not under the influence of the union in the industry under consideration.

24 Phelps Brown (1975) argues that

monetary restraint will not of itself stop the pressing of pay claims. Even if all employees understand that a general raising of pay against a limited increase in the stock of money is bound to result in unemployment, they will also see that it is only by the aggregate of pay rises that the sanction will be actuated, no one group will bring the sanction upon itself by pressing its own claim, nor escape it by not pressing its claim if other groups go ahead with theirs.

25 Thus trade credit is limited to use for the purchase of goods and services from the firm providing the credit. Credit cards are limited to use with shops which accept them. On the other hand, unused overdraft facilities can be used for purchases generally.

26 The price uncertainty may be an adverse feature of holding wealth in the form of bonds. But for an individual economic agent wishing to sell bonds on a specific day there is little price uncertainty, so that bonds can be exchanged for money at the going price.

27 However an increase in, say, the demand for bonds leading to a rise in the price of bonds may encourage firms and governments to borrow more through the issue of new bonds.

28 This can be compared with the analysis of Hillier (1977) for the government budget constraint.

6 The Kaleckian Approach to Macro-Economics

Introduction

In this chapter the elements of macro-economics discussed in the previous chapter are brought together. We begin with investigations of the short-run steady-state properties of some models which incorporate some or all of those elements. But since the Kaleckian approach leads to macro-economic models which are inherently cyclical it is necessary to discuss the cyclical properties of such models as well as their steady-state properties. Finally, we offer some brief remarks on the implications of the Kaleckian approach for the role of the State in macro-economics.

The almost automatic response of an economist faced with an economic model is to look for and at its equilibrium solution. In the case of a static model, this involves ensuring that values of all variables are constant, and for a dynamic model that variables grow at a constant rate. An outstanding feature of capitalist economies is that they do not exhibit either constancy and stagnation or constant growth. Instead they involve growth, change and fluctuations. Thus there must be a question mark against the use of equilibrium analysis as a guide to explaining and understanding economies which do not exhibit obvious conditions of equilibrium. At a minimum it means that the explanation of change in such circumstances must draw on factors which have been treated as exogenous in the analysis.

The short-run steady-state analysis undertaken below looks superficially like equilibrium analysis. This analysis explores the relationship between certain endogenous variables and exogenous variables under specified conditions. The steady-state situation is not one of equilibrium in the sense that there are not necessarily forces which lead the economy towards that situation nor which maintain the economy in such a situation if it were to be attained. An example may be useful. In a model which incorporates accelerator features, investment could be analysed in steady-state terms by placing the accelerator component equal to some average or 'base' value, thereby removing a major cause of cyclical fluctuation. With investment set at the 'base' level, the nature of the relationship between exogenous variables and the 'base' level of the endogenous variables could be explored.

The investment example leads into another problem with equilibrium analysis in macro-economics. As net investment occurs, the capital stock is growing. The static equilibrium analysis could be concerned with investment being constant, but with the capital stock changing in the background. Alternatively, the equilibrium analysis could focus on the capital stock being constant, and hence net investment zero. Whilst that has long been realised in the case of investment, it seems to be often overlooked in the case of other flows which add to stocks.[1] Differences between government tax revenue and expenditure lead to changes in money stock and/or bonds, which leads frequently to the imposition of equilibrium condition so that the government budget is balanced in order to have money stock and stock of bonds constant (Blinder and Solow, 1973). A positive level of savings will generally lead to accumulation of financial assets, and once again there is the choice between imposing savings as constant or zero as the equilibrium condition. The condition that the stocks (of capital stock, money, bonds or whatever) are constant leads to analysis of something close to a stationary state. In our analysis below, insofar as we are concerned with equilibrium, it will be of the short-run variety. Thus flows will be in equilibrium, but these will be adding to relevant stocks and we do not impose conditions that the stocks are unchanging.

In the steady-state analysis below, some important factors will be held constant or overlooked. First, whilst flows of investment and savings are taking place, their impact on the corresponding stocks will be ignored. Second, the evolution of the economic system arising from, for example, changes in the degree of monopoly (which we would expect to be generally on a rising trend as the process of concentration and centralisation proceeds), movements in the organisation of workers, and technical progress and innovation, are overlooked for the present. Third, the accelerator component of investment will be set at a constant level.

Steady-state analysis I

In the first part of the steady-state analysis explicit consideration of bargaining over wages is neglected, and the bargaining strength of the workers is reflected within the degree of monopoly of the firms. This follows Kalecki (1971, p.51) when he argues that 'a high ratio of profits to wages strengthens the bargaining position of trade unions, in their wage demands for wage increases since higher wages are then compatible with "reasonable profits" at existing price levels. . . . Thus, the degree of monopoly will be kept down to some extent by the activity of trade unions, and this the more the stronger the trade unions are.' Effectively, this envisages that on the workers' side they are mainly concerned with their share in income. On the firms' side there is an element of a 'kinked demand' curve argument (Sweezy, 1939) in the sense that firms face problems in raising prices in order to pass on cost increases (arising from wage rises).

In this analysis we bring together two basic strands of the work of Kalecki (1971), namely the differential savings propensities and the degree of monopoly. Asimakopulos (1975), (1977) presents similar analyses, and Cowling (1981) relies on these two basic strands. The first equation is:

$$s_w W + s_p \pi + TX + IM = I + G + X \tag{1}$$

where W is labour income, π profits (including in the terminology of Chapter 5, fixed costs F), TX taxes, IM imported inputs, I investment, G government expenditure and X exports. It is derived from the familiar injections equals leakages condition for an open economy. The second equation is derived from the pricing model developed in the previous chapter (cf. p.91), and is

$$\pi = (d/(1-d))(W + IM) \tag{2}$$

where d is the degree of monopoly, which for simplicity is assumed to be the same for wages and imported inputs, and to be constant with respect to output.

From equation (1), and the identity $Y = W + \pi$, we obtain

$$(s_p - s_w)\pi/Y = (I + (G - TX) + (X - IM))/Y - s_w. \tag{3}$$

Thus the share of profits in national income is indicated to rise with increases in investment, the government deficit and the balance of payment surplus (all relative to national income). This equation indicates that in terms of the determination of the share of profits in national income, investment, the government deficit and the balance of payments surplus play a similar role. In a more complicated analysis with, for example, tax rates on labour income and on profits differing, the roles of the terms on the right-hand side of equation (3) may not be as close as here. However, it can be seen that if investment falters relative to income through, for example, a decline in the rate of profit or the drying up of investment opportunities, then the gap left by investment can be filled so far as the profit share is concerned, by increases in the government deficit and in the balance of payments surplus. This can clearly lead to interpretations of the expansion of government expenditure (particularly defence expenditure) in the post-war world and of export drives as a means by which the share of profits in national income can be maintained in the face of declines in the ratio of investment to national income and/or rises in the savings propensities.[2]

Equation (3) represents a slight generalisation of the theory of income distribution of Kaldor (1955). By itself equation (3) determines the share of profits in national income (assuming that the ratios on the right-hand side are exogenously determined), but does not determine the level of income. Kaldor closed the model with the assumption that $Y = Y^f$ (the full employment level of national income). However, Kalecki (1971) used an equation similar to equation (3) but essentially closed his model with the equivalent of equation (2) as will be explored below.

The Kaldor theory of income distribution has been attacked along a number of avenues, of which two are relevant here. First, it is argued that any income group (e.g. recipients of property income) could achieve whatever share of national income it wished by an appropriate choice of its savings propensity (Tobin, 1959). This illustrates one of the pitfalls of the use of aggregates for, of course, in reality there are numerous receivers of property income who would have to be organised to achieve that result. The use of a single symbol (such as π) should not obscure the disaggregated reality which lies behind it. Further, as Kaldor (1959) argued, in most models of income distribution if the owners of one factor realised the determinants of the distribution of income, then they could collude to achieve an outcome more favourable to themselves.

Second, it is argued that a certain schizophrenia prevails in that an individual receiving wages and profits saves more out of a pound of profits than out of a pound of wages. However, an individual may save the same proportion out of wages as out of profits, but at the aggregate level there could be a differential savings propensity when the proportion of wages and profits varies with the level of income, so that the savings propensity varies with the level of income. Wages and profits are subject to different tax rates which would cause different propensities to save out of pre-tax wages and profits. However, the crucial consideration is that profits are subject to 'double savings' by corporations and by individuals, whereas wages are only subject to one level of savings. This creates at least an *a priori* expectation that there will be differential savings propensities.

Bringing together equations (2) and (3) yields:

$$(s_w + d(s_p - s_w))Y = Z - d(s_p - s_w)IM \tag{4}$$
$$(s_w + d(s_p - s_w))\pi = d(Z + s_w IM) \tag{5}$$
$$(s_w + d(s_p - s_w))W = Z(1-d) - ds_p IM \tag{6}$$

where $Z = I + (G - TX) + (X - IM)$.

A rise in investment by 1 unit raises income by $1/(s_w + d(s_p - s_w))$, profits by $d/(s_w + d(s_p - s_w))$ and wages by $(1-d)/(s_w + d(s_p - s_w))$. A rise in the degree of monopoly raises profits (provided that $s_w > 0$) but depresses wages (and thereby the level of aggregate demand) sufficiently that income overall falls.[3] A rise in imports (with a constant degree of monopoly) depresses income, profits and wages.

In the special case often used by Kalecki where $s_w = 0$, an increase in investment leads to the generation of higher profits such that sufficient extra savings are made which finance the extra investment. Wages also rise by $(1-d)/ds_p$ for each unit increase in investment, and income by $1/ds_p$. When $s_w = 0$, a rise in the degree of monopoly changes the distribution of income towards profits but leaves the *level* of profits unchanged. From equation (5) $s_p\pi = Z$ so that the level of profits is unaffected by changes in d. However, the level of wages and income falls. From equation (4) with $s_w = 0$, by differentiation or otherwise, it can be seen that a rise in d would depress Y, and hence depress W.[4] Essentially in this context, a rise in the degree of monopoly shifts income from wages and profits, which depresses the level of aggregate demand when investment and other injections are unchanged. Income and wages fall to restore equilibrium. Thus, in these circumstances, attempts by firms to raise the degree of monopoly will *not* lead to a rise in profits but to a fall in wages and income. The realisation of increased profits following a rise in the degree of monopoly requires an increase in injections (i.e. Z in the above analysis).

The above analysis has been conducted in money terms, and nothing has been said yet about movements in real incomes and in prices. However, the assumption made by Kalecki was that firms typically operate with excess capacity with the consequence that unit costs are constant with respect to output changes, so that in real income correspond to changes in money incomes, with prices unaffected. This does not imply that prices are constant but that prices are unaffected by the changes being discussed. Employment would be expected to broadly follow income and output changes.

Steady-state Analysis II[5]

The second stage of the short-run steady-state analysis focuses on the struggle between workers and firms over real wages and profits. The wage and price equations developed in Chapter 5 form the basis of this analysis. The situation which we examine is artificial in the sense that we do not expect that the economy would move to or remain in such a situation, but rather could be a situation around which the economy fluctuates, and we explore causes of fluctuations below. The short-run steady-state analysis allows us to focus on the relationship between some of the exogenous variables and the average values of endogenous variables around which the actual values of those variables would be expected to fluctuate.

The short-term steady-state is defined in terms of constant real wages, constant output, and expectations about inflation being fulfilled. For the wage change equation derived in Chapter Five (pp. 106–114), we make the substitution that $\dot{w} = \dot{p}$ (so that the real wage is constant) and $\dot{p}^e = \dot{p}$ (so that expectations are fulfilled). These short-term steady-state conditions yield:

$$\log(w/p) = a_4^{-1}(a_1 + (a_2 - 1)\dot{p} + a_3 U + a_4 \log T). \qquad (7)$$

For ease of exposition we take the case where the rate of change of productivity is zero. With the existing productive capacity, which is unchanged in the steady-state, there is a positive relationship between employment and output and thereby a negative relationship between unemployment and output, i.e. $U = U(Q)$. In using that relationship we are effectively assuming that it is only the level of output which influences the demand for labour and hence of employment, and that relative prices (e.g. of labour and output) have no influence.

Equation (7) provides a relationship between the real wage and output for the short-term steady-state, and this is sketched as the w-curve in Figure 6.1. This relationship is a positive one since a_3 is negative and a_4 is positive. The slope of the w-curve depends on the reaction of wage changes to unemployment (reflected in a_3), the effective pressure towards raising the real wage towards the target wage (a_4) and the relationship of output and unemployment. A rise in the target real wage would shift the w-curve upwards as would an increase in the rate of inflation. A once-and-for-all increase in productivity changes the relationship between output and unemployment, whereby for any particular level of output, unemployment is higher than before, and this is reflected in a downward shift in the w-curve. The basis of the relationship in equation 7 and the w-curve is that the higher the real wage (relative to the target real wage) the lower is the pressure for wage increases, and the lower the level of unemployment 'needs' to be to hold down wage increases to the rate of price increases, thereby maintaining a constant real wage.

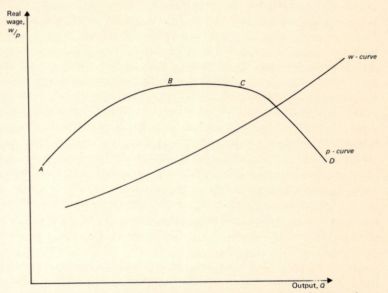

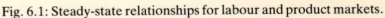

Fig. 6.1: Steady-state relationships for labour and product markets.

The aggregate price equation is $p = g(f).m(Q).c(Q)$ (from p. 99 above), where f is a vector of relevant input prices, $c(Q)$ the cost function and $m(Q)$ is the mark-up function. In the short-run steady-state, the level of capacity is held constant, the level of output is constant and fully anticipated by firms. We analyse the simple case where there is a one period lag of prices behind costs, and in which for simplicity of exposition we take $g(f) = (aw_{-1}+bn_{-1})$ where w is money wage, n foreign input prices and subscript -1 indicates a one period lag.[6] The rates of change of all prices are the same so that real wage and ratio of input price to output price remains constant. In this simple case the price equation becomes

$$p = (aw_{-1}+bn_{-1}).c(Q).m(q) \qquad (8)$$

Manipulation and rearrangement of this equation to provide an equation which clearly links the real wage with output yields:

$$w/p = a^{-1}(w/w_{-1})((c(Q)m(Q))^{-1} - b(n_{-1}/p_{-1})(p_{-1}/p)). \qquad (9)$$

In the steady-state the rate of change of w and of p are the same, and both reflect the general rate of inflation and the ratio (n_{-1}/p_{-1}) will remain constant.

The relationship between the real wage and output involved in equation (9) is illustrated in Figure 6.1 by the p-curve. We have drawn the p-curve for the case where the multiple $c(Q).m(Q)$ is initially a decreasing function of Q, then a constant function and finally an increasing function of Q. Since the inverse of $c(Q).m(Q)$ appears in equation (9) this leads to the relationship between w/p and Q being initially an increasing one, then a constant one and finally a decreasing one. This shape for the p-curve would arise from the following consideration. The cost function initially exhibits declining unit costs, followed by a range of output during which unit costs are roughly constant, and as full capacity is reached unit costs begin rising. The mark-up of price over costs gradually rises with output (relative to capacity), particularly as full capacity working is reached. This particular shape of the p-curve has been chosen as it appears to be a reasonable approximation of the p-curve in practice.[7] The point of intersection of the p-curve and the w-curve could be on the rising or horizontal sections of the p-curve rather than as illustrated, and there could easily be multiple intersections.

The effect of a rise in foreign input prices (relative to domestic prices) can be seen from equation (9) as leading to a downward-shift in the p-curve. A general rise in the degree of monopoly (i.e. an upward shift in the $m(Q)$ function) will have a similar effect. A higher rate of inflation would shift the p-curve upwards since the gap between last period's costs (on which output prices are based) and this period's wages is larger when inflation is faster. Inflation has an effect on the real wage so long as there is a lag between costs and output price. The cost function $c(Q)$ is a short-run one, with its position influenced by the level of capital equipment, so that an increase in capital equipment leading to a reduction in short-run costs (for any particular level of output) would be reflected in a fall in $c(Q)$ and an upward shift in the p-curve.[8]

In terms of the discussion in Chapter Five (pp.111–112) on the objectives of trade unions, the *p*-curve could be interpreted as the steady-state trade-off between real wages and output (and thereby employment) which faces a utility maximising union. When the *p*-curve is downward-sloping, such a union could be viewed as choosing a target real wage which would place the *w*-curve in such a position to achieve the steady-state combination of real wage and output (and employment) which is regarded as 'optimal' for the union in light of the *p*-curve.

The major and important conclusion derived from a consideration of the interaction of the wage and price equations, and illustrated by Figure 6.1 is that the level of real wages and of output (and thereby of unemployment) is strongly influenced by the wage demands of unions and workers and by the profit demands of firms. Although wage and price behaviour have been modelled here in a somewhat different way, the broad thrust of the analysis is similar to that of Rowthorn (1977). In both cases, the short-run steady-state level of unemployment 'is the level of unemployment at which the claims of the rival parties become mutually consistent'. For unemployment restrains the effectiveness of the wage claims of unions and workers, whilst level of output constrains the volume of profits and the profit margin of firms.

The level of unemployment which results from the interaction of the wage side and the prices side does not carry with it any connotations of full employment. This arises from a number of considerations. First, the role of unemployment is akin to the 'industrial reserve army' of the unemployed, which in the circumstances of the day keeps wage claims down sufficiently to hold the real wage in check. Thus whilst the conventional approach sees the army of unemployed as largely or entirely a volunteer army, this approach sees it as an army of conscripts. As with any conscript army, it may include some who would opt to join anyway, but the majority of the army and the conditions of service are dictated by, in this case, the 'needs' of the economy. Similarly the level of output serves to hold profits in check. Second, the position of the *p*-curve depends on the amount of capital equipment, and even if the level of output generated was equivalent to full capacity utilisation there is little reason to think that full capacity output would generate full employment. For example, after a period of prolonged depression and low investment the capital stock in place could, with existing technical knowledge be such that even if it were used at full capacity the demand for labour which would result could be insufficient to provide full employment.

The positions of the *p*-curve and the *w*-curve depend on numerous factors, including foreign input prices (relative to domestic prices), the degree of monopoly reflected in the mark-up function, the target real wage, government expenditure and taxation.[9] Changes in those and other factors would lead to shifts in the *p*-curve and/or the *w*curve, and the impact of such changes can be gauged from equations (7) and (9). When the steady-state values of output and the real wage are determined, then labour income and profits can be easily calculated.

The effects of a shift in the *w*-curve depend on the slope of the *p*-curve. When the *p*-curve slopes downwards (as in segment *CD* in Figure 6.1), then an upward shift in the *w*-curve leads to rises in the real wage and a fall in output. If the *w*-curve had shifted through a rise in the target real wage, then the rise in the actual real wage would be less than the rise in the target wage. When the *p*-curve slopes upwards (as in segments *AB* in Figure 6.1), then when the slope of the *w*-curve is greater than that of the *p*-curve an upward shift in the *w*-curve leads to falls in both real wages and output. However when the slope of the *w*-curve is less than that of the *p*-curve, an upward shift would lead to rises in both the real wage and output.

In the steady-state there will, in general, be a gap between the actual and the target real wage. When the *p*-curve is downward-sloping (as segment *CD* in Figure 6.1), a rise in the target real wage would open up the gap between the actual and the target real wage considerably. In situations where the gap is regarded as intolerably wide would be expected to lead to extra-market activities. At the other end of the spectrum, there are economies in which in some significant sense there is only a small gap between the actual and the target real wage. This could arise, for example when the target real wage was heavily influenced by the actual real wage. A relatively pliable and subservient work-force would be represented by a situation where effectively there was little difference between actual and target real wage.[10]

An interesting simple case, based on widely-used simplified versions of the wage change and price equations, is illustrated in Figure 6.2. On the wage side, the bargaining version of the Phillips' curve, $\dot{w} = b\dot{p}^e + f(U)$ yields the steady-state relationship $f(U) = (1-b)\dot{p}$ when the real wage is constant (so that $\dot{w} = \dot{p}$) and inflation expectations are fulfilled (so that $\dot{p}^e = \dot{p}$). With unemployment depending on output (i.e. $U = U(Q)$), this provides the w-curve in Figure 6.2 where for $b \neq 1$ the position of the curve depends on the rate of inflation $(\dot{p})$. A price equation with a constant mark-up (m^*) over constant unit costs (c^*) would be $p = m^*.c^*.(aw+bn)$, and hence a p-curve with the form $(w/p) = (c^*/am^*)-(bn/ap)$. Thus the p-curve is horizontal as it does not depend on output. It can be seen that, in this case, the real wage is essentially determined in the product market and depends on costs (c^*), mark-up (m^*), and foreign input prices (n/p). The steady-state level of unemployment (and hence that of output) is essentially set in the labour market at a level which restrains wage increases in line with price increases so that the real wage set in the product market is maintained.

There are three sets of circumstances of interest which could lead to shifts in the p-curve and the w-curve such that the steady-state

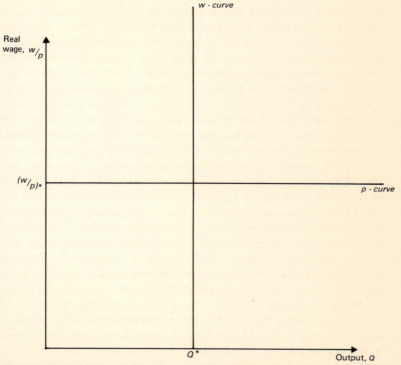

Fig. 6.2: Particular case of steady-state relationships for labour and product markets.

levels of output and real wage rise, whilst the gap between actual and target real wage is reduced. The first case arises when the price of imported inputs falls relative to the price of domestic goods, i.e. the ratio n/p falls. From equation (9) it can easily be seen that a fall in n/p leads to a rise in the real wage w/p for any given level of output, i.e. the p-curve shifts upwards. In terms of Figure 6.1 such a shift leads to a rise in steady-state output and real wage (and a consequent closing of the gap between actual and target real wage). With a constant degree of monopoly, a fall in imported input price leads to a fall in the profit share in national income since there are lower costs to which the mark-up is applied (pp.90–99 above). The change in the level of output may change the degree of monopoly, and the volume of profits increases with a constant degree of monopoly when the volume of output rises.

The second case arises when buoyant conditions of demand produce relatively high levels of investment and economic growth. The capital investment and associated technological change cause the real costs of labour and materials per unit of output to fall. Thus the $c(Q)$ function shifts downwards, and (from equation (9)) the p-curve shifts upwards. On the wage side, there is a change in the unemployment-output relationship, with a particular level of output now being associated with lower employment and higher unemployment. This is reflected by a downward shift in the w-curve. The combination of the shifts in the two curves would lead to a rise in steady-state output and an indeterminate (from available information) change in the real wage. As growth and investment proceed, the p-curve and the w-curve would continue to shift. However, two factors operate to slow down the upward march of output. First, the lowering of real costs is likely to shift the distribution of income away from wages towards profits. The level of savings rises because of the rise in output and the shift towards profits. Thus unless investment and other forms of exogenous demand increase sufficiently to mop up these extra savings, a deflationary situation arises. In other words there would be problems in sustaining the higher levels of output from the demand side. Second, the target real wage may begin to adjust to the evidence of higher productivity and profits. This is represented by an upward shift in the w-curve, which leads to rises in the real wage which would help to alleviate the demand problems which arise from the first factor.

The examination of the third case of an increase in public expenditure financed by an increase in taxation on wages requires the expansion of the wage change equation. With w as the wage bill per worker paid by the firm, $(1-t_1)w$ is the wage received by the worker, where t_1 refers to all taxation falling on wages including income tax and social security contributions (employers and employees). We treat p as the price received by the firms, so that $(1+t_2)p$ is the price paid by workers, where t_2 summarises the indirect taxes levied on prices. Workers receive benefits from public expenditure which we summarise as ΘG, where G is government expenditure, and Θ is a measure of the perceived benefits of public expenditure per pound of expenditure. Thus the real wage of workers becomes $(1-t_1)w/(1+t_2)p + \Theta G$. The modified version of equation (7) is:

$$\log(w/p) = a_4^{-1}(a_1 + (a_2-1)p + a_3U + a_4\log((1+t_2)/(1-t_1)).(T-\Theta G)) \tag{10}$$

An increase in public expenditure, provided it yields some perceived benefits to the workers, is equivalent to a reduction in the target real wage in terms of the effect on w/p. The effects of taxation are the reverse. The perception of the benefits from public expenditure has at least two dimensions. First, the perceived benefits arising from an increase in public expenditure will vary considerably between different types of expenditure. Second, an increase in expenditure may correspond to an increase in the 'need' for that expenditure. For example, an increase in expenditure on old age pensions which arises from an increase in the age group eligible for retirement falls into this category. But the perceived benefit of that increased expenditure may be very low in that neither the current retired population nor the working population (in respect of anticipated pension) is better off following the increase in public expenditure. Of course, in those circumstances a reduction in the level of pension to compensate for the increased retirement population could well lead to a reduction in perceived benefits. The point here is that the increase in the retirement population leading to an increase in public expenditure may, via the target real wage, influence the rate of wage change and then the actual real wage.

The influence of taxation and government expenditure on the target real wage, and thereby on the actual real wage and output, provides one of the major links between the demand-side and the supply-side of the economy. Other linkages arise from, *inter alia*, the effect of interest rates and inflation on the supply-side of the economy. First, firms may regard interest payments as a cost on which a mark-up is obtained.[11] Second, it may enter the cost of living directly through, for example, the effect on mortgage interest payments.

The rate of inflation can affect both the p-curve and the w-curve. An increase in the rate of inflation serves to shift the p-curve upwards when prices lag behind costs, as explained above, but serves to shift the w-curve downwards (if $a_2 < 1$).[12]

The foreign sector has so far been relatively neglected. The sole influence of the foreign sector has been on the price of imported inputs. On that front we are exploring the consequences of a particular relationship between domestic and foreign prices. We have not indicated how that relationship is determined, but implicit is the view that the ratio n/p (and the implied exchange rate) are set such that over the long haul the balance of payments is indeed in balance. Thus for the steady-state analysis, the n/p ratio can be taken as exogenously determined. During the course of the trade cycle, as incomes expand and contract the demand for inports will vary with some consequent effects on the exchange rate and hence on the n/p ratio. In Chapter 5 (pp.96–97) it was argued that the effect of an increase in the imports of finished goods was to shift the p-curve to the left, thereby reducing the level of output and the real wage.

The demand side of the economy can be relatively easily described as far as the steady-state is concerned, although the use of steady-state analysis removes much of interest on the demand side, notably the accelerator component of investment and the interdependence of expenditure changes and the money supply. The first equation on the demand side arises from the leakages equals injections requirement:

$$s_w(1-t_w)W + s_p(1-t_p)\pi + TX + IM = I\,(Q, r, \pi) + G + X$$

(11)

where t_w, t_p are tax rates on labour income and property income respectively. Real wage and output have been determined on the supply-side of the economy, and thereby total labour income and property income are determined. With G and X exogenously determined, and TX and IM depending on W and π, this equation serves to determine the value of r.

The nominal demand for money, related to transactions purposes, is represented by $M^d = M^d(pQ, r+\dot{p})$ where $r+\dot{p}$ is the nominal rate of interest. The supply of money will depend on the amount of high-powered money created on the path to the steady-state position, and the willingness of the public to hold bank deposits. The banks policy on loans is also important, and as argued in Chapter 2, this depends on the return on loans (proxied by the nominal rate of interest) and the discount rate of the Central Bank, r_d. The supply of money is summarised by $M^s = M^s(H, r+\dot{p}, r_d)$. Since money is narrowly defined here and a zero rate of interest on money is assumed, the appropriate rate of interest influencing demand and supply is the nominal rate of interest. The steady-state condition is then:

$$M^d(pQ, r+\dot{p}) = M^s(H, r+\dot{p}, r_d). \qquad (12)$$

This equation can be solved for the remaining endogenous variable of the steady-state, the price level p. In steady-state, the demand for money and the supply of money must change at the same pace. Assuming that the demand for money is of unit elasticity with respect to the price level, then the nominal demand for money grows at the rate of inflation. For the steady-state to be maintained, the money supply has to grow as well.

Thus the demand-side serves to determine r and p. This means that shifts in the functions on the demand side require changes in r and p for the steady state to be restored. In terms of equation (11) a fall in the investment function would require a sufficient fall in the interest rate to stimulate investment back to the previous level, to regain the steady state. With relatively small effects of interest rates on investment such a change in interest rates may, in some relevant sense, need to be large.

In the short-run, the demand-side of the economy is much more important than in the steady-state. The level of aggregate demand in nominal terms facing firms forms the basis of their price and output decisions. Those decisions are summarised in the p-curve, which is essentially a curve along which the economy moves (when the p-curve has been modified for any lags between costs and price). The w-curve is a steady-state relationship (based on $\dot{w} = \dot{p}$), whereas in the short-term the rate of change of wages depends on unemployment and the real wage.

Attempts by workers to increase real wages and by firms to increase profits can be represented by upward shifts in the w-curve and downward shifts in the p-curve respectively. The initial manifestation of such attempts would be increases in wage and price inflation. If, for example, firms seeks to increase profits, then prices rise faster than otherwise, which is followed by workers seeking to maintain real wages generating faster wage increases. Eventually the higher rates of inflation run into the barrier created by a declining real money supply, lower output and higher interest rates. The steady-state level of output would be lower and the economy would move down to fluctuating around that level. The lower steady-state output could involve higher rates of inflation if the banks were prepared to extend loans to help finance higher nominal expenditure or if government responds to generally lower levels of output by seeking to boost demand. By such routes the initial rise in inflation following attempts to raise real wages or profits becomes built into the system.

Once the rate of inflation has been established in a particular range within the economic system, it is seen to be rather difficult to reduce it by the deflation of demand leading to lower levels of economic activity. From the price change equation given in the previous chapter (p.99) (and an analogous version with cost lags appears as equation (14) below) it can be seen that the effect of a fall in output on price change depends on the sign of $(e_c + e_m)$, where e_c is the elasticity of marginal cost and e_m of the mark-up with respect to output. When firms operate over the range where unit costs are declining then e_c is negative. Unless the value of e_m is sufficiently positive to offset that, then $e_c + e_m$ would be negative such that declining output leads to faster price increases. When output has reached a lower level so that the rate of change is zero, then there is no effect of price increases (relative to cost increases). Total profits and their share in income are likely to fall with declining output. Falling output leads to falling real wages and higher unemployment. The rate of change of wages depends on the balance between them, with the lower real wage pushing up wage increases whilst higher unemployment restrains them.

The way in which we have discussed the supply side has tended to play down what happens to profits, and we must now pay them some regard. An increase in the target real wage is often predicted to lead to an increase in the real wage and a fall in output. The combination of those effects would be a fall in profits. When profits form a major source of finance for investment and influence the demand for investment, it could be anticipated that investment would decline following the shift in the target real wage. The initial impact of an increase in the target real wage would be an increase in wage inflation, followed by an increase in price inflation. When profits and investment are felt to be substantially threatened by increased demands for real wages, firms and their allies can be expected to press for counter-measures. A first step may be the creation of the association of wage increases with inflation, and of the notion that wage rises are a major proximate cause of price inflation. Inflation can then be presented as a major problem. Policies can then be directed against real wages as an apparent means of reducing inflation. In the British context these policies have taken two main forms. During much of the 'sixties and 'seventies, incomes policies have been tried. The evidence suggests that, even when combined with price control, periods of incomes policies have seen a reduction in the rate of increase of real wages.[13] However, in subsequent periods, the real wages appear to have risen faster and to catch up some of the losses during the incomes policy periods. The second approach has been the use of deflation of demand, which has been used particularly by the Thatcher government in Britain. Further periods of high levels of unemployment serve to weaken the trade union movement and to damp down the claims for real wages. Thus high levels of unemployment serve a dual purpose of having a short-run effect on wage inflation, and a long-run effect on real wage claims. However, such policies are not without their problems for firms. Low levels of demand are not conducive to investment, thereby undermining the growth of the economy. Deflation may initially have a more devastating effect on price increases than on wage increases, thereby hitting profit margins in the short term. A deflationary policy introduced through control of money supply may tend to injure firms in the short term. Interest rates rise so transferring profits from firms to banks. Control of the money supply leads to control over bank lending, and thereby hits those who make use of bank lending, i.e. firms rather than households.

In some respects the conclusions of this steady-state analysis look similar to the conclusions from a (neo-classical) monetarist analysis with output and employment determined by supply-side considerations to which the demand side adjusts and with the rate of increase of the money supply equal to the rate of inflation. But there are numerous important differences. First, our analysis deals with the steady-state around which the economy is believed to fluctuate, and the steady-state position is not one to which the economy tends. The economy may occasionally attain the steady-state level of output, but only as one level amongst many passed through during a business cycle. Second, aggregate demand is highly relevant in explaining the path of the business cycle, and influences short-term profits, output change etc. and thereby investment. Investment clearly adds to the capital stock and therefore the productive capacity of the economy. Third, unemployment does not represent the voluntary decisions of workers but is required to contain wage claims. Fourth, there is no presumption from the rate of expansion of money supply equal to rate of inflation that the former causes the latter.

Business Cycles

Within the Kaleckian approach, the notion of equilibrium has only a limited use. The economy is seen as fluctuating, changing and growing over time, but not tending towards any position of equilibrium. In the previous sections, we examined the short-term steady-state, which was an artificial construction which allowed an investigation of the relationship between certain exogenous and endogenous variables. In this section, we indicate why it is expected that a capitalist economy will exhibit fluctuations, and explore the nature of those fluctuations. In addition, we would anticipate that there were many exogenous shocks such as changes in foreign prices and external demand, introduction of new technology leading to an investment boom, which would not only change any steady-state position but also trigger off or help to maintain cyclical movements within the economy.

FAST

The first basic cause of cyclical movements comes from the investment function and in particular the accelerator component. If the economy were on a steady growth path, then net investment would be sufficient to meet growing capacity requirements, i.e. $I_t = \triangle K_t = v(Y_t - Y_{t-1})$, so that $I_t/Y_t = v.g/(1-g)$ where $g = (Y_t - Y_{t-1})/Y_{t-1}$ is the growth of output. The depreciation element would be $D_t = \delta K_t$ and hence $D_t/Y_t = \delta.v$. Thus the ratio of gross investment to output would be $v(\delta + g/(1-g))$. A rise in output greater than the steady growth rate would generate a rise in investment. The rise in output has two effects on investment. The first effect operates through the simple accelerator mechanism with the larger change in output raising investment. The second effect arises from increases in profits and profitability which the rise in output generates, and which encourage investment. When finance is available, the rise in the demand for investment leads to a rise in effective demand and then provided there is some output response, to a rise in output. That rise in output feeds back to generate further increases in investment. These upward movements in output and investment reinforce one another. But once the upward movement is broken then the downward movements in output and investment are again

reinforcing. The reasons why the upward and downward movements are broken are discussed below.

The second basic cause of cyclical movement arises from the
interactions of the price change mechanism and the wage change
mechanism. Each of those mechanisms incorporates some elements
of price inflexibility. The wage change equation implies that real
wages are slow to change in that workers attempt to protect their
real wages. In the price equation, the real wage changes with
changes in the degree of monopoly and in real costs, and the extent
to which those factors vary with the level of output may be rather
limited.[14] These elements of relative price inflexibility mean that
changes on the demand side are not met by sufficient changes in
relative prices to maintain a constant level of output. Kalecki (1971)
(p. 169) put this point as follows:

. . . the assumption that q [related to the degree of monopoly] is a
parameter which under conditions described *may* be constant is incompatible with the approach considering q to be just the instrument of securing –
through price flexibility in relation to demand – the full utilisation of
resources. (Business cycles appear in such an approach as merely 'lapses
from full employment', resulting from the imperfection of the instrument).
However, we consider such an approach as utterly unrealistic, since in
laisser faire capitalist economy used to achieve a more or less full utilisation
of resources only at the top of the boom, and frequently not even then. Nor
did these full-employment booms fill a major part of the cycle.

It should be noted, however, from Figure 6.1 that there is some
flexibility of the ratio of w:p from both the wages side and the prices
side.[15]

In this discussion of the business cycle we concentrate on the
private sector. Governments may seek to reduce the cyclical
fluctuations but the effect of those activities require a much larger
study. Further whilst there may have been some reduction in the
amplitude of the business cycle in the post-war world, business
cycles remain and appear to conform to the pattern suggested
here.

Below we suggest that fluctuations within the economy and
economic growth are intimately linked, with investment playing a
crucial role in both. However, for ease of exposition, we discuss the
business cycle as though the underlying growth of output was zero.
Thus, for example, when we talk of output declining, this should be
interpreted as output declining relative to capacity which is likely to
be growing as investment occurs.

Upward movements in output are first slowed and then reversed by four forces. First, firms may have increasing problems in financing the increasing levels of investment. *Ex ante* savings are likely to lag behind *ex ante* investment demand. Increase in the money supply and trade credit are needed to bridge the gap between savings and investment if the investment is to proceed. In the early stages of an upswing, banks may be eager to extend loans, particularly if they find themselves with plenty of free reserves. But as the upswing goes on, increases in the money supply would follow on previous increases and may eventually be met by a reluctance by bankers to extend further loans. This reluctance may arise because the volume of credit money has reached close to the maximum in light of the amount of high powered money in existence and the required reserve ratio. The reluctance may be reflected in rationing of loans and higher interest rates. These serve to dampen down the effective demand for investment. Similarly, firms may be reluctant to extend further trade credit to their customers.

Second, the level of capacity utilisation rises. This may reinforce the demand for investment arising from the accelerator mechanism. A major effect arises from a change in the balance between output rises and price rises arising from an increase in aggregate (nominal) demand, as the expansion continues. The division of aggregate demand into output and prices depends on the reactions of the firms as described by the price equation. For simplicity we take the price equation (10) where last period's input affect this period's output price. In rate of change form this equation becomes:

$$\dot{p} = \alpha\,\dot{w}_{-1} + (1 - \alpha)\,\dot{n}_{-1} + (e_c + e_m)\dot{Q}, \qquad (13)$$

where e_c is the elasticity of unit costs and e_m elasticity of the mark-up with respect to output, and $\alpha = aw_{-1}/(aw_{-1} + bn_{-1})$. The value of α will vary as w and n fluctuate, but we can say little about these variations. In the early stages of an upswing, $e_c + e_m$ may be negative (reflecting declining unit costs), whereas as firms approach full capacity $e_c + e_m$ becomes zero and then positive. For a relative expansion in aggregate demand of k, $\dot{p} + \dot{Q} = k$, so that the increase in demand is divided between price change and output change. Substituting that relationship into equation (13) yields:

$$\dot{Q}(1 + e_c + e_m) = k - \alpha\,\dot{w}_{-1} - (1 - \alpha)\,\dot{n}_{-1}$$

indicating that for given expansion of aggregate demand and cost increases, the growth of output declines as $e_c + e_m$ rises (as it is expected to do as the level of output rises).

A further manipulation of equation (13) leads to

$$\dot{p} - \dot{w} = (\dot{w}_{-1} - \dot{w}) + (1 - \alpha)(\dot{n}_{-1} - \dot{n}) + (1 - \alpha)(\dot{n} - \dot{w})$$
$$+ (e_c + e_m)\dot{Q} \qquad (14)$$

In the early stages of an expansion, the final term on the right-hand side is, as indicated above, expected to be negative. The first term is also likely to be negative (if the pace of wage inflation begins to rise) or zero. We can say little about the effect of expansion on the other terms. Thus $\dot{p} - \dot{w}$ may well be negative, so that the real wage rises, in the early phase of the expansion. In latter stages, the final term becomes zero or positive, which slows down (and then reverses) the growth of real wages.

Third, the decline in the growth of real wages in the context of rising output indicates a shift in the distribution of income towards profits and away from wages. The shift towards profits discourages consumption and expenditure and for a particular level of income depresses aggregate demand. Thus previous increases in output do not lead to a comparable increase in aggregate demand because of the changes in the distribution of income.

Fourth, inflationary pressures build up. In the labour market in the early stages of the cycle, the rise in real wages restrains money wage claims. But in the later stages, the rise in real wages slows down which may help boost wage claims. Unemployment lags behind output, so that in the later stages of the cycle unemployment declines following the rise in output in the earlier stages. The fall in unemployment may place less restraint on wage increases. The increase in wage inflation feeds through into price inflation, which is itself rising as capacity utilisation rises as indicated above. Thus price inflation rises, which feeds back into the wage inflation side. The general rise in the pace of inflation may cause responses by the government to try to restrain inflation, including reduction in aggregate demand. On the foreign trade side, when domestic inflation outstrips foreign inflation, the demand for imports rises and for exports falls. The money supply may fall in real terms as the pace of inflation picks up. Nominal interest rates rise (relative to real rates) and this may discourage borrowing (and thereby expenditure). For borrowing at high nominal interest rates may lock firms into high real interest charges if the borrowing is at fixed interest charges and the nominal interest rates and inflation are expected to decline in the near future. The effect of each of these is to reduce the level of aggregate demand, helping to bring the upswing to an end.

As the rate of growth of output slows, investment falters. The fall in investment leads to further falls in the rate of growth and output, and the reinforcing movements of output and investment contribute to the downward phase of the business cycle. Monetary restraint can prevent aggregate demand being translated into effective demand, but monetary expansion generally only takes place in response to an increase in aggregate demand. Lower interest rates may encourage aggregate demand and thereby lead to monetary expansion. But in a private enterprise economy, the monetary expansion requires the confidence of both bankers and firms that increases in bank loans to finance increased demand will not involve high rates of default. The reduction of inflationary pressures during the downswing may operate weakly through two channels to restore demand. Interest rates in nominal terms tend to fall as the rate of inflation falls, leading to some incentive for firms and households to borrow, particularly if the nominal rates are fixed and are believed to be low relative to what they will be in the future. The real value of the money supply will rise if the rate of inflation is below the rate of increase of the money supply, and this may have some stimulating effect on demand.

A major factor in bringing the downward spiral to an end is likely to be when the accelerator component of investment reaches its lower limit. In other words, that part of gross investment which relies on changes in output reaches zero. Other parts of investment are related to long-term growth and other factors and these continue. Investment ceases to fall, and then output ceases to fall, and following previous declines in output that represents a rise in the growth of output. This leads to a revival in the accelerator component of investment, and the level of aggregate demand begins to move upwards.

The move towards profits and away from wages which takes place during the upswing is reversed during the downswing, and this helps to limit the fall in aggregate demand since the shift towards wages encourages consumer expenditure (for any particular level of income).

The foreign sector may also operate in a manner which tends to damp down the domestic business cycle. During high levels of demand, domestic prices may tend to rise (relative to foreign prices), thereby discouraging exports and encouraging imports which reduce the demand for domestic output. Conversely during the recession period, the foreign sector may serve to lift demand for domestic output.

This line of argument indicates that the business cycle is a regular feature of a capitalist economy, but the cycle itself may not be completely regular. It has been argued by monetarists and others that the private sector will operate in a way which irons out any regular components of a business cycle. Their actions would, it is argued, include building up stocks during periods of low demand and destocking during periods of high demand, thereby reducing the fluctuations of output. However we would argue that although cycles occur regularly they are not of a sufficiently predictable form for this anticipation of the cycle effect to have much impact. Further there are limits (holding costs etc.) which limit economic agents' ability and willingness to permit their inventories to fluctuate counter-cyclically. Also, investment is a major cause of fluctuations, and the demand for investment goods is often demand for specific goods made to the purchaser's specification, again limiting possibilities of stocking ahead of demand.

Overlaying these regular cycles, there are numerous factors which affect the course of particular cycles. The discovery, for example, of a major technological breakthrough would lead to an investment boom, which could set off or reinforce a general boom. The nature of the breakthrough would then influence the response of output and employment. Other factors of particular importance would be changes in overseas trade and prices, and changes in government policy on taxation and public expenditure.

A number of predictions about cyclical movements of economic variables and associations between them can be derived from the above analysis. First, investment demand is a major engine of fluctuations within the economy, and so it would be expected that investment varies proportionately more than, say, consumption expenditure during the course of the business cycle. Second, the share of profits in income moves with or a little ahead of the general business cycle. Third, in the early stages of an upswing, real wages rise but may decline (relative to trend) in the latter stages. In the early stages of the downswing the real wage may rise and then decline in the latter stages of the downswing. Fourth, the relationship between the real wage and employment can be derived as follows. From equation (10) above, it can be seen that the relationship between the real wage and output depends on the extent to which firms base their prices on past costs and the nature of the

$m(Q)c(Q)$ term. In the case of no cost lags, the relationship is illustrated by the p-curve in Figure 6.1. This indicates a positive association between w/p and Q when output is in the AB range and a negative or no association in the BCD range. Thus the overall association between w/p and Q depends on the range over which output varies. The real wage-employment relationship would be expected to be weaker because of lags between output and employment. Thus we could expect the correlation between w/p and employment to be zero or positive, which would broadly conform with the evidence.[16] These predictions relate to a private enterprise economy, and the actual movements in the economy will be influenced by government policy (particularly important here would be prices and incomes policies) and movements in 'exogenous' variables such as foreign prices. Sherman (1976), (1979) uses an approach similar to that above, and derives comparable predictions which he shows conform with the American business cycle experience in the post-war period.

During the course of the business cycle, aggregate demand expands and contracts, and as it does so we would anticipate that money is created and destroyed (or created at a slower pace). The creation of money permits effective demand expansion, followed by expansion of nominal income. Friedman and Schwartz (1963) found evidence for changes in money supply preceding changes in nominal income, which they claimed as support for the importance of money and monetary policy. Tobin (1970b) argued that such findings are consistent with the proposition that fluctuations in aggregate demand lead to change in the money supply and thereby in nominal income. The analysis above indicates why aggregate demand fluctuates, whereas the Friedman and Schwartz view is incomplete in the sense that the causes of money supply fluctuations are left to be explained.[17] The Friedman and Schwartz approach views fluctuations in nominal income arising from fluctuations in money supply, and hence to remove the former it is merely necessary to remove the latter. Our analysis indicates that control over fluctuations in the money supply may be difficult and also that the key cause of fluctuations of output is the nature of the economic system.

The short-term aggregate demand positions have consequences for the long-term supply-side situation. Net investment adds to the capital stock, and thereby shifts the p-curve through effects on real costs as indicated above (p.127). Investment demand influences and is influenced (via output changes, profitability, etc.) by aggregate demand. The target real wage is likely to be conditioned by workers' experience, part of which is the path followed by the economy. Periods of depression, for example, by the experience of lower real wages can lead to the lowering of the target real wage.

A consideration of the cyclical nature of the Kaleckian approach is important for five reasons. First, it serves as a reminder that cyclical movements are an inherent part of the approach, and that whilst steady-state analysis may be a useful analytical tool it does have shortcomings. In contrast, Keynesian and monetarist models focus on equilibrium and its stability, and tend to overlook cyclical behaviour.

Second, it is clear that each upward movement in output initially generates its own momentum but carries with it the seeds of its own destruction. For output to continue to rise, investment must continue to expand, and that requires that the rate of increase of output rises; eventually those increases are not any longer sustainable. The build up of price and wage inflation eventually runs into the barrier created by the money supply. The shift towards profits during the upswing dampens down aggregate demand.

Third, when the economy is inherent cyclical then full employment can at best be attained only around the top of the cycle, so that the average level of employment will be less than full employment. In Kalecki's words 'the reserve of capital equipment and the reserve army of unemployed are typical features of capitalist economy at least throughout a considerable part of the cycle' (Kalecki, 1965).

Fourth, there is an intimate relationship between cycles and the long-run trend. Kalecki (1971) argued that 'the long-run trend is but a slowly changing component of a chain of short-period situations; it has not independent entity. . . .' What happens in the short term (though influenced by what is expected to happen in the longer term) determines what happens in the longer term, and this particularly applies to investment. This can be contrasted with the usual neo-classical approach where what happens in the short run does not change the long-run equilibrium position. The long-run analysis focuses on dynamic equilibrium, in which the conditions for constant growth rates of the variables involved are explored. Thus for the simple neo-classical growth model (Solow, 1956) the condition is derived for equilibrium that $a/v = n+m$ where a is the propensity to save, v the capital-output ratio, n the growth rate of the labour force and m the rate of technical progress. Dynamic equilibrium is brought about by adjustment of v. But the important aspect is that the long-run growth is predetermined by $n+m$, and the economy homes in on that growth rate.[18]

 Fifth, the cyclical nature of the economy places a different perspective on the discussion of public macro-economic policy. The standard targets and instruments approach (Tinbergen, 1952; discussed in, e.g., Peston, 1974) views the economy through equilibrium spectacles. The approach can be summarised as follows. With a linear model, the targets of government policy (represented by vector y) are determined by the instruments of government policy (represented by vector x) and exogenous variables (vector z) by the system of equations $y = A.x+B.z$. In order to achieve specified targets y^*, it is required to set instruments at levels x^* where $x^* = A^{-1}(y^*-B.z.)$. The inversion of the matrix A requires that it is a square matrix, which would arise if the number of instruments and the number of targets are equal. Whilst numerous queries can be raised against the targets-instruments approach, our point here is not to repeat those queries but rather to question whether an equilibrium approach to macro-economic policy can be much use when applied to an economy which is inherently cyclical.

Economic consequences of State activities
A full discussion of the economic activities of the State in a capitalist economy would take us far and wide and well beyond the scope of this book.[19] The purpose of the brief discussion here is to look at the way in which specified government activities impinge on the relationships and equations discussed above. In this way we hope to provide some insights into why certain policies are favoured by particular groups in society.

 The treatment of State activities in conventional macro-economics generally follows two related routes. First, the effects of changes in the levels of taxation, government expenditure or the money supply on output, interest rates, etc. are analysed within the framework of the *IS-LM* approach by appropriate shifts of the equations. Second, macro-economic policy is often discussed within the context of the targets and instruments approach. The derivation of the targets of government macro-economic policy is left as an open question but with the implication that in some way the targets represent the wishes of the electorate. The instruments are then calculated to try to achieve the set targets.

 Our discussion follows the conventional approach in that the effects of changes in specified variables are examined, although a broader set of variables under the control of government is examined, and the focus is on a different set of variables influenced by those changes. But in place of the second part of the conventional approach, we would stress that State activities are strongly influenced by interest groups, and that the general interests of capitalists in maintaining profits modified by the pressures exerted by workers and their organisations are of key significance.[20] This does not exclude mistakes being made so that certain State activities may be thought to be in the interests of capitalists but may in fact operate to their disadvantage. Further, they may be conflicts between the short-term interest and long-term interests, and between interests of a particular firm and firms in general.

We begin with an examination of the price equation in general form $p = g(f)m(Q)c(Q)$, where a major determinant of the mark-up function $m(Q)$ is the degree of monopoly.

The influence of government activities may be felt on this equation through a variety of routes. First, the composition of State expenditure can influence the degree of monopoly and thereby the mark-up of price over costs. The example which comes readily to mind here is expenditure on defence equipment. If, as is often argued, it is the case that suppliers of defence equipment form a tight oligopolistic industry, then the degree of monopoly would be relatively high. Consequently, a switch of expenditure towards defence equipment would change the composition of demand and effectively raise the degree of monopoly.[21]

Second, the range of activities undertaken by the State may influence the degree of monopoly in individual sectors. The effective degree of monopoly is likely to change when an industry is taken into public ownership and the use to which profits are put is likely to change as well. In this discussion, the term industry is used broadly to include provision of education, health services, etc. Under public ownership, an industry could be instructed to follow marginal cost pricing (when under our definition the effective degree of monopoly would be zero). Where a zero price is charged at the point of use (as, for example, with much of education), in the national accounts at least the value of education is aligned with the cost of provision. There are further reactions to these initial changes in the degree of monopoly. The real wage is affected, particularly when 'free' provision is involved. When the industry taken into public ownership produces inputs for other industries, the degree of monopoly in the input-using industries may be enhanced, and some or all of the profits received by the industry prior to nationalisation may be effectively shifted into the input-using industries.[22] Thus there may be some reallocation of profits between industrial sectors, and between private profits and public sector profits. The latter may in turn influence factors such as the level of savings in the economy.

Third, governments often have legislation on the statute book to inhibit or prohibit monopoly, collusion, restrictive trade practices, etc. Although there are good grounds for doubting the seriousness of government intentions in this direction,[23] nevertheless, in principle, governments could operate to reduce the degree of monopoly by measures such as effective prohibition of collusion, price leadership, parallel pricing, etc., and by the dissolution of existing monopolies and oligopolies (i.e. trust-busting).

Fourth, governments can levy taxes on profits and on prices. With the short-run profit maximising oligopolist, a profits tax would be predicted to have no effect on price or output, but would affect post-tax profits, and thereby savings, investment and future capacity. There are two reasons for thinking that the tax does not fall entirely on profits. First, firms may work towards adjusting the degree of monopoly upwards to offset the profits tax. In the case where the degree of monopoly is effectively determined by barriers to entry where potential entrants respond to post-tax profits, then the existing firms could raise pre-tax profits completely to offset the profits tax without inducing entry into the industry.[24] Second, firms may effectively regard profits tax as a cost which is subject to a mark-up.

Fifth, governments can intervene to reorganise sectors of the economy. This has ranged in the United Kingdom from the nationalisation of the health service and of public utilities through government-sponsored reorganisation of the textile, shipbuilding and aircraft industries under private ownership. Reorganisations may be undertaken in the belief that productive efficiency will be increased, reflecting the view that unfettered private enterprise does not always generate efficient industrial structures. The reorganisations may involve changes in the degree of monopoly. When the number of firms is reduced and the industry remains in private ownership then the degree of monopoly would be anticipated to rise.

The wage equation in steady-state modified to take account of government expenditure and taxation was given above as equation

(10). From that it can be seen that when workers seek to maintain their real wages in the face of increased taxation, rises in t_1 and t_2 lead to attempts to increase the real wage in the labour market. The success of that attempt will, as usual, depend on the reactions of the firms. Further, an increase in government expenditure which is appreciated by the workers leads to a fall in the market real wage as the effective target real wage pursued through the market is reduced.

In seeking to determine the effect of the public provision of services such as education and health care on wage and price determination we can proceed down two paths. The introduction of, say, a health service free at the point of provision could be seen as an increase in government expenditure with a reduction in the price level facing the workers (since health care is now priced at zero). On the other side, taxation would be increased to finance the health service. The alternative is to treat a 'free' health service as a subsidy (so that t_2 declines) and again it is financed by taxation (so that t_1 and t_2 rise on that count). The second alternative appears slightly more convenient when a change of regime is analysed.

The effect of government activity in terms of expenditure and taxation on the wage equation is basically the balance between the burden of taxation on wages (direct and indirect) and the perceived benefits of public expenditure.

On the demand-side the analysis of government activity does not depart substantially from the traditional Keynesian approach. The main difference is the need to distinguish taxes on wages from those on profits. The form of profits which influences savings and investment will presumably be post-tax profits, and similarly for the influence of wages on savings. The effect of government expenditure, when only demand-side considerations are taken into account, would be rather similar to that derived from the standard Keynesian analysis. The differences which arise are three-fold. First, as indicated in the immediately preceding discussion, taxation and government expenditure affects the supply-side and thereby influences the level of output and the real wage. Second the levels of output and unemployment determined on the supply-side may be regarded as unacceptable, for there is no strong reason for thinking that the level of unemployment will, in any sense, be that of full employment. Thus the pressure on governments in a post-Keynesian era will often be towards expansion of demand, which in the short run will generate expansion of output. But in the longer term inflation gradually builds up and becomes built into the wage and price determination process. Third, there will be periods when investment falters. This may be a cyclical phenomenon arising from accelerator-type factors, or from a decline in confidence in the future. It may arise from a decline in investment opportunities, from, say, the exhaustion of investment opportunities associated with a technological break-through, or in the profitability of investment (from, say, rising capital intensity of production). A decline in investment is presented in Figure 6.3 as leading to a shift in the *IS* curve from IS_1 to IS_2. We take the case where originally the position of the *LM* curve at LM_1 generated a level of output Q_1 which was consistent with equilibrium on the supply-side. For the system to move back to equilibrium output Q_1 with the *IS* curve at IS_2 requires that the *LM* curve shifts to LM_2. In turn such a shift requires that the nominal money supply increases or the price level falls. In a situation where investment is contracting it is not likely that the money supply will be expanding (perhaps more accurately not expanding faster than the rate of inflation). It is more likely that the

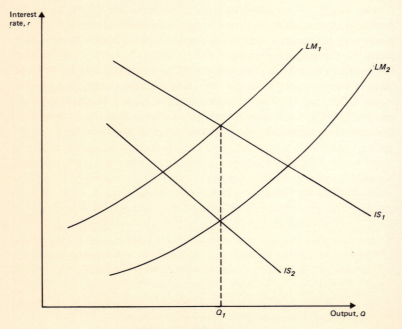

Fig. 6.3: *IS-LM* Curves.

money supply will be contracting. The reduction in the price level which would be required to shift the *LM* curve will require a prolonged period of deflation in order that the general levels of prices and wages are reduced. Thus severe problems of adjustment are revealed. The long periods of depression which such an adjustment would entail can be circumvented by appropriate changes in government expenditure designed to fill the gap left by the fall in investment.

Unemployment in the Kaleckian approach serves to discipline the workers. Thus attempts by government to maintain high levels of employment will undermine the disciplining role of unemployment, leading to real wages rising (relative to productivity) and eating into profits. Thus there arise pressure on the government to restrict real wages (e.g. through the use of incomes policies) and to forego full employment. Kalecki (1971) argued that 'the assumption that a government will maintain full employment in a capitalist economy if it only knows how to do it is fallacious'. He gave three basic reasons why there would be opposition from 'industrial leaders' to full employment achieved by government spending. These were '(i) the dislike of government interference in the problem of employment as such; (ii) the dislike of the direction of government spending (public investment and subsidising consumption); (iii) dislike of the social and political changes resulting from the *maintenance* of full employment.' In the present context we have focused essentially on this third reason. For, as Kalecki argued, 'lasting full employment is not at all to [business leaders'] liking. The workers would "get out of hand" and the "captains of industry" would be anxious to "teach them a lesson".'

Notes

1 For further discussion see Chick (1973).
2 For example, Baran and Sweezy (1967) who argued that there is a 'tendency for the surplus to rise' over time. This can be roughly translated into the terms of equation (1) and (2) as a tendency for d to rise. In order to avoid a fall in income, expenditure made out of the surplus can be raised directly by, for example, sales promotion. In the terminology of the last chapter (p.95) fixed costs F are increased. In the present context, that is effectively equivalent to a rise in the marginal propensity to consume out of profits. Expenditure out of the surplus can be raised indirectly through the taxation of profits and using the proceeds to finance government expenditure.
3 The effect of a change in d on profits is given by $d\pi/dd = s_w(Z+s_wIM)/k^2$

where $k = (s_w + d(s_p - s_w))$, on wages by $dW/dd = -s_p(Z + s_w IM)/k^2$ and on income by $dY/dd = -(s_p - s_w)(Z + s_w IM)/k^2$.

4 For $Y = (Z - ds_p IM)/ds_p$ and $dY/dd = -Z/(d^2 sp)$.

5 For further discussion of the model used in this section see Sawyer (1982a).

6 This corresponds to a fixed factor proportion production function, which is aligned to the assumption made below that changes in the relative prices of inputs do not lead directly to changes in input use.

7 It is difficult to say precisely what the shape of the p-curve under short-term steady-state conditions would be like in that steady-state is not generally observed. But, we argue below, that during cyclical fluctuations the economy moves along a path which is closely related to the steady-state p-curve. In the first phase of an upswing in demand and output, measured labour productivity expands rapidly, whilst in the second phase the expansion in productivity slackens to a rate close to the average trend rate of increase of productivity. This would suggest that the $c(Q)$ function declines substantially with respect to output at low levels of output and then flattens out for the middle range of output levels. The combination of such a $c(Q)$ function and a degree of monopoly and profits mark-up which rises with output would suggest a p-curve similar to that illustrated in Figure 6.1. For evidence for the United States see Sherman (1976) especially Table 4.2. For the United Kingdom for manufacturing industries, calculations from the Economic Trends Annual Supplement for the three cyclical upswings between 1963 and 1975 indicate that in the first phase output per head rose at an average rate of 2.51 per cent per quarter, whilst in the second phase the rate dropped to 1.10 per cent per quarter. Over the whole period, labour productivity rose at an average rate of 0.84 per cent per quarter.

8 With an unchanged degree of monopoly, then for any particular level of output profits in total would remain unchanged, but with increased capital equipment the rate of profit would decline.

9 In the more general case when the target real wage is a function of U and the degree of monopoly is a function of output, then the factors held constant would be the target real wage function and the degree of monopoly function.

10 Much of the discussion of Tylecote (1981), in attempting to explain differences in the inflationary experience of developed countries, could be interpreted within this framework.

11 This would depend, in part, on the form of firm behaviour being assumed. A sales-maximising firm subject to a profit (to shareholders) constraint would count interest charges as cost.

12 For discussion of the length of the production process see Coutts, Godley and Nordhaus (1978), Chapter 4.

13 See Henry and Ormerod (1978), Tarling and Wilkinson (1977).

14 In manufacturing industry in Britain, the ratio of a crude measure of profits to sales on an annual basis fluctuated between 0.194 and 0.217 during the period 1970 to 1978. The lowest ratio was reached in 1975, and apart from that year the lowest ratio was 0.201. The calculations are made from the Census of Production figures. The measure of profits

is crude in that certain costs and depreciation are not deducted.

15 Indeed if there were no flexibility in the real wage then the *p*-curve and the *w*-curve would not intersect.

16 'Several economists, including Kuh (1966), Bodkin (1969), Modigliani (1977) have noted that the contemporary correlation between real wages and employment is usually not statistically significant, and even when it is, is often positive' (Neftçi, 1978). Neftçi's own work shows a positive relationship between current employment and current real wages, but an overall negative relationship between employment and real wages when lagged real wages are included in the regression. The significance of Neftçi's work for our conclusions is not straightforward. First, he tests for *causation* between employment and real wages, whereas our analysis points to an *association* between employment and real wages. Second, he removes the systematic cyclical elements in employment and real wages, whereas in our approach those cyclical elements are crucial in generating the association between employment and real wages.

17 Friedman and Schwartz often seek to explain sharp changes in the money supply in terms of mistakes made by the monetary authorities. But the regular fluctuations of the money supply remain to be explained.

18 For a critique of the neo-classical approach to growth see Himmelweit (1979).

19 See, for example, Aaronovitch and Smith (1981), Part Two; Baran and Sweezy (1967), Chapter 6; Gough (1979); Milliband (1969).

20 The incursion of State activity into the social welfare area is often seen as an advance for the working class. But it is not without advantage to the Establishment. George (1973) describes the introduction of national insurance benefits in the United Kingdom as follows:

> The motives behind the provision of insurance benefits 'can hardly be described as philanthropic. National insurance was the Liberal response to the threat of socialism'. In the first place it was felt that the National Insurance Act would help undermine the growth of a revolutionary Marxist movement in the country. Contented workers are not a real threat to the social system even if they do not accept it fully. Britain was copying the example of Bismarck's Germany which was the first European country to introduce insurance schemes 'out of fear that the prevailing social order might be overthrown by revolutionary agitation of the working class' (Quotes are from Gilbert (1966) and Rhys (1962) respectively).

Similarly, 'in the mid nineteenth century education came to be seen as the most effective antidote to the ideas of the "agitators" who were spreading subversion in the rapidly growing poor urban population' (Aaronovitch and Smith, 1981). Further the extension of education has often been a response to the perceived deficiencies of trained manpower required by the productive system.

21 See, for example, Baran and Sweezy (1967), Chapter 7.

22 An illustration may help. A vertically integrated monopolist who maximised profits would set price $p = (e/(e-1))$ times marginal cost, where e is the price elasticity of final demand. Now compare that

situation with one where the final elasticity of demand is the same but there is a number of firms involved in the chain of production. The total profits gained by these firms will be less than or equal to those gained by the profit maximising monopolist. The division of profits between the firms involved would in this case depend upon the elasticity of demand at each stage in the chain. In the more general case, the division of profits would depend on the degree of monopoly at each stage. Now consider what would happen if the first firm in the chain were nationalised and reduced its mark-up and profits. The maximum profits for firms in the chain remain unchanged, and the chance is created for the remaining private firms in the chain to increase their profits.

23 Aaronovitch and Sawyer (1975), Conclusion, and Sawyer (1981a), Chapter 16.

24 This assumes that the demand conditions in the industry permit the level of profits to be raised by a sufficient amount to offset the profits tax.

7 Empirical Support for the Kaleckian Approach

In this chapter we argue that there is a substantial amount of empirical support for the Kaleckian approach, which is sufficient for it to be taken seriously. The evidence here relates to the 'building blocks' of the Kaleckian approach, which can usually be compared with those of the conventional approaches. We are not able at this stage to present evidence for a complete model for a variety of reasons. First, the econometric estimation would present considerable problems, not least the discovery of appropriate lag structures in a model which is inherently cyclical. Second, some crucial variables like the degree of monopoly present formidable measurement problems. Third, the alternative approach has been presented to give some insights into the workings of the macro-economy without providing a complete description. Some important features of the real world such as the foreign exchange and financial markets have not received much attention and would require further work before a complete model was available. However getting some of the building blocks right should set us well on the way since, barring logical mistakes, difficulties could only arise from placing emphasis on the trivial and overlooking factors of importance.

A complete consideration of the relevant evidence would take us well beyond the space available. Consequently, we summarise extensively and draw heavily on surveys of empirical work. The symbols used in this chapter have the meaning attached to them throughout the book and listed at the beginning.

Investment
The investment function in many theoretical macro-models is of the form $I = I(r)$. The neo-classical approach focused on the cost of capital services relative to output price as the determinant of the desired capital stock. The approach outlined in Chapter 5 suggested

many other factors such as changes in output (actual or expected), capacity utilisation and profitability would be relevant.

Jorgenson (1971) concludes his survey on investment by saying that 'real output emerges as the most important single determinant of investment expenditure . . . [and a] second important determinant of investment in the availability of finance.'

Eisner and Nadiri (1968) conclude that 'our results indicate . . . (that) the role of relative prices, the critical element of the neo-classical approach, is not confirmed. . . . The elasticity of capital stock with respect to output is reasonably high, in a number of instances approaching unity. This is consistent with flexible accelerator models.'

The results of Panič and Vernon (1975) in their disaggregated study of UK business investment 'also shows that, once the British data are disaggregated, both profitability and confidence become, as one could expect, very important in explaining investment behaviour in industry.' They also conclude that 'by far the biggest proportion of new investment will take place only when demand has increased or promises to increase in the near future to such an extent to cause serious pressure on existing capacity', and also that 'the conditions which prevail during a recession make it difficult for [firms] . . . to [invest] either from their own funds (which most of them prefer) or by borrowing.'

Junankar (1972) concluded that 'most studies that include profits or some other variable for liquidity suggest that it is a statistically significant variable. . . . Current opinion thus suggests that profits, independently of output, are important in determining *short-run* investment.' He also expresses the opinion that 'demand factors as represented by the accelerator are more important than relative prices in determining investment.'

Wage determination

The conventional approach to wage determination discussed in Chapter 4 is based on the rate of change of real wages being a function of the excess demand for labour. When excess demand for labour is zero, real wage changes will be zero and the level of unemployment will be at the 'natural' level, at which unemployment is essentially voluntary. Two methods of measuring excess demand for labour have been proposed. The first is that unemployment is inversely related to the excess demand for labour which leads to the expectations-augmented Phillips' curve, i.e. $\dot{w}$ =

$f(U)+\dot{p}^e$. The second is to postulate that the excess demand for labour is a negative function of the real wage so that $\dot{w} = g(w/p)+\dot{p}^e$.

The alternative approach outlined in Chapter 5 focused on the demands of workers, the determination with which those demands were pursued and the factors which govern their achievement or otherwise. Variants on that approach have often been labelled the real wage model or real wage resistance hypothesis. However, as Henry (1981) notes, 'there are substantial differences between . . . authors about the underlying theory and econometric specification . . . that the description "real wage model" must be treated with caution.' A formulation for this approach put forward above was

$$\dot{w} = a_1+a_2\dot{p}^e+a_3lnU+a_4(ln(w/p)-lnT)+a_5P/P_{min}.$$

We can immediately note that there is a considerable overlap of symbols between the equations representing the two approaches, although the variables behind the symbols may be measured in different ways and have different implications (which is especially so for unemployment). However, this does lead to difficulties in empirically discriminating between the two approaches,[1] although some differences may arise from the precise specification of the variables involved.[2]

The approach to wage determination explored in Chapter 5 has many implications, of which we focus on three. First the money wage objective of the workers in a particular time period is heavily influenced by notions of a 'just wage' and of fairness. These notions may arise from ideas of the 'correct' real wage (partly based on previous experience) and from comparisons with other groups of workers. At the macro-level we have stressed the real wage comparisons, but the differentials comparisons may influence the general rate of inflation and at specific times when traditional differentials have been disturbed contribute substantially to upswings in wage inflation. Second, the militancy and 'pushfulness' of trade unions are probable influences on the rate of wage change. Hines (1964), Godfrey and Taylor (1973) are among the authors who have tried to model such influences. Purdy and Zis (1974) discuss the conceptual and measurement problems involved in this area. The problems surrounding the measurement of militancy, however, make the econometric testing of this approach particularly difficult. Third, the proponents of many of the variants of the alternative approach have argued that unemployment (at least over the range regarded as tolerable in the first three decades of the post-war world) may have little effect on the rate of wage changes.[3]

Johnston and Timbrell (1974) test a bargaining theory (based on Johnston, 1972) in which wage changes are determined by, *inter alia*, number of settlements in the period, expected price inflation, movements in the retention ratio (of net of tax to gross earnings) and 'catch up' variables which measure the extent to which recent real wage changes have deviated from a postulated constant rate of increase of 2 or 3 per cent (with a number of alternatives tried).

They conclude, based on econometric estimation for the UK, that:

(i) Movements in the retention ratio (or alternatively in a 'catch-up' variable) have had a significant effect on wage rate movements in recent years.
(ii) Price expectations also have an effect on wage rate bargaining and this effect has been fairly steady and persistent throughout the whole sample period, 1952–71. . . .

They conclude that 'it has not been possible to find a conventional Phillips Curve for either the short or long sample period, which does not have perverse signs on the excess demand variable.'

Henry, Sawyer and Smith (1976) make an evaluation of models of wage inflation for the United Kingdom. They conclude that 'the results on the modified Sargan model [i.e. equation above with $a_5 = 0$, and post-tax net earnings used for w/p] give it impressive support.'

Artis and Miller (1979) survey a number of UK studies on inflation. They conclude that

The overall performance of augmented Phillips Curve estimates is thus clearly less than resoundingly successful in respect of the principal requirements of the hypothesis. A proponent might argue his case on the need for very careful and detailed specification, whilst appealing to the ample scope for error afforded by the undoubtedly difficult problem presented by the range of available data. . . . A less sympathetic observer would be more inclined to argue from the lack of robustness of the approach to differences in specification that the hypothesis itself is not empirically sustained by recent UK experience.

For the real wage hypothesis, they argue that its 'distinguishing characteristic . . . is that the coefficient on the lagged real wage term should be significantly negative, a prediction which is borne out with the exception of the equation due to Apps in the equation results noted in the table.'[4] But they argue that 'the structural stability of equations in the "real wage" vein has been little investigated, but, where it has, it has usually been found wanting. However, a significant difference is made to this conclusion when real wages are taken after tax."[5]

Henry (1981) compares a real wage model based on a formulation similar to that given above (with real post-tax earnings appearing on the right-hand side instead of w/p and with $a_5 = 0$), and an excess demand model based on Parkin, Sumner and Ward (1976) in which the demand and supply of labour are explicitly modelled. He concludes that:

(a) there are deficiencies in the theory of the structural version by Parkin, Sumner and Ward of the excess supply model, and where these are corrected and the model applied, as it should be, to earnings movements, there seems little empirical support for it. This is of importance, since their study is one of the most comprehensive excess supply models applied to UK data.
(b) As for real wage models, the results here (estimated by single equation methods show that the [real net earnings] model is to be preferred on empirical grounds over the real wage model. [For the variant of real wage equation given above which was used] with certain exceptions . . . the equation stands up reasonably well [over the period 1963–78], and compares with the original result which was obtained over the period 1948–74 [in Henry, Sawyer and Smith (1976)].

There has been much less interest in the real wage hypothesis in the United States as least as far as macro-econometric estimation is concerned. Mitchell (1978) undertook a disaggregated study which included 'relative wage status' of one industry vis-à-vis others as an explanatory variable in wage change equations. He finds that 'both the union and non-union sectors exhibit some sensitivity to business conditions, as represented by the unemployment rate. Even in the non-union sector however the magnitude of the sensitivity is not large.' The relative wage status of an industry plays a significant role in determination of wage changes in many industries.

From their analysis of Australian wages awards, Trivedi and Rayner (1978) conclude that 'the major determinations [sic] of changes in award wages appear to be past growth in real wages, the change in wage drift and average productivity.'

It may be queried why the major survey of inflation by Laidler and Parkin (1975) has been ignored. They concluded that 'the weight of the available evidence leads us tentatively to accept some variant of the expectations excess demand view of wage inflation and to reject the sociological and other push hypotheses.' Our reasons for rejecting their conclusion include the following. First, much of the evidence cited above post-dates their survey. Second, they appear to take any evidence of the effect of demand conditions on wage and price inflation as evidence for the effects of *excess* demand. Excess demand only has a meaning in competitive markets, whereas the approach outlined in Chapter 5 indicates that demand factors may influence wage and price changes in oligopolistic environments. Third, they appear willing to explain the influence of any variable on wage inflation in terms of expectations or excess demand. One example of a number is

> it may be the case that strikes are another possible proxy variable for labour-market demand pressures. . . . (I)t might be argued that strikes are the outcome of mismatched expectations about inflation rates held by employers and workers. It is entirely plausible that such mismatching increases as the rate of inflation increases and hence produces a positive correlation between strikes and wage change entirely independently of push or militancy.

No evidence for these suppositions is produced, and we argue below that some research on strikes supports our alternative approach. They also translate demand pressure into excess demand. It would appear that there is virtually no evidence which could be produced which would in the eyes of Laidler and Parkin contradict the expectations-excess demand approach. However, the papers cited in note 2 seek to discriminate between that approach and a real wage resistance/collective bargaining approach and find in favour of the latter. We discuss Laidler and Parkin (1975) below in note 10.

Some indirect support for our approach to wage bargaining comes from work on the determinants of strike activity. Daniel (1976) concludes that 'our finding [is] that strikes and other disruptions to work tended generally to be responsive to below average offers, and associated with, if anything, below average settlements, rather than productive of above average increases.' Knight and Wilson (1980) find that 'employee pressure leading to strike incidence appears to derive its greatest impetus from slow advance in real pay rather than from deterioration in inter-industry differentials although in a few high paying, highly unionized, industries, both are important.'

Daniel (1976) investigates the process of wage determination in industry. He argues that if, as [our results] indicate, neither the trend in product demand, nor the establishment's cash flow situation had any general influence on the level of settlement agreed, then this would suggest that 'social' or 'institutional' factors had more influence on the outcome of negotiations than did 'economic' ones. [The social and institutional factors include] the increases in cost of living and the acceptance by management of the principle that workers should be compensated for increases in the cost of living; and the principle of comparability of increases with those doing similar kind of work.[6]

Prices and price changes

In the macro-economic sphere discussion on price changes has concentrated on whether demand influences have an effect on the rate of change of prices. Whilst that question is clearly of importance, it has obscured the basic distinction between theories based on price-makers and theories based on price-takers.[7] It was argued in Chapter 5 that the price-makers approach differs from the price-takers approach in the way in which demand influences were modelled. In Chapter 5, price was viewed as a mark-up over costs with theories varying in their determinants of the mark-up and how the mark-up would vary over the trade-cycle. Markets in which the competitive forces of demand and supply are active and in which excess demand influences price changes are seen as of limited importance within capitalist economies. Our brief survey here focuses on the price-maker/price-taker distinction, with little regard being paid to the question of the direction of the influence of the level of demand on price change.

Most discussion on pricing within the sphere of industrial economics and theories of the firm debates the determinants of the make-up of prices over costs, which are relevant (e.g. marginal or average), and the extent to which prices are rigid (particularly downwards). It is generally accepted that firms are price-makers, and the question of price-makers or price-takers is rarely raised.[8] Silberston (1970) concluded a survey of empirical studies on pricing by saying that

full cost can be given a mark of beta query plus, but no more than this, since there are so many marginalist and behavioural qualifications. It seems clear that the *procedure* of calculating prices very often starts with an average-cost type of calculation, but the qualifications that arise are concerned with the next stages of the process, including the exact method by which full costs are calculated.

Skinner (1970) opens his article with the statement that 'there seems to be little doubt that "cost-plus" pricing is fairly widely used in British industry.' Hay and Morris (1979) argue that 'the empirical evidence . . . reviewed shows that despite much diversity in pricing and widespread adherence to simple rule of thumb, prices and margins do respond to cost and demand changes in a manner consistent with that model [of simple monopoly pricing].' Thus the debate revolves around whether the mark-up of price over costs varies with the level of demand, and not whether *excess* demand affects price changes.[9]

Coutts, Godley and Nordhaus (1978) conclude that their estimates 'indicate that there is no general or economically significant tendency for prices to change relative to normal costs over the course of the business cycle. If there is an indication of any affect at all it probably is, that, given costs, final prices *decrease* with increases in demand.' Sawyer (1981b), in estimating price change equation rather like that derived in Chapter 5 (p.99) arrives at a similar result, and concludes that

(i)n our estimation . . . in at most 21 industries (out of 40 examined) did the output function (and by implication demand) play statistically a significant role. But the number of industries in which output increases tended to raise prices was less than the number where output increases tended to lower prices, and the net impact of output changes on price was rather small.

The only way in which those findings can be reconciled with the neo-classical approach is to argue that markets clear instantaneously (which in the context of quarterly models means the prices fully adjust within a quarter) so that price always equals marginal cost. Thereby the rate of change of prices is equal to the rate of change of marginal costs. It is further required that marginal costs are constant with respect to output, so that the rate of price change equals rate of change of input prices.[10]

Unemployment
In the neo-classical monetarist approach, unemployment diverges from the 'natural' rate of unemployment only to the extent to which perceived real wages are incorrectly set, and the presumption is that unemployment will tend quickly toward the 'natural' rate. We have already indicated (p.4) that the unemployment at 'natural' rate is seen as essentially voluntary, and 'remaining unemployed is regarded as simply another occupation, say, the null occupation

(leisure), that the individual may choose' (Lippman and McCall, 1976). The search unemployment approach is concerned with the way in which workers respond to a situation where there is a dispersion of wages and wage offers. The worker is perceived as receiving wage offers and deciding whether to accept the wage offer or to remain unemployed in the hope that a better wage offer will be received in the future. Models of search unemployment postulate different ways in which unemployed workers arrive at some kind of reservation wage, and investigate alternative rules for the sampling of wage offers.[11] The implicit assumption is that there are plenty of offers, and the search by the unemployed is for an acceptable wage rather than for a job. The search unemployment approach postulates utility maximising individuals, and implicit in that is an unchanging utility function. In other words, demoralisation and frustration generated by unemployment are excluded by assumption.[12] Thus the long-term unemployed person who through demoralisation or belief in the lack of job opportunities had effectively given up looking for work would be classified as having a 'taste' for unemployment in the search approach.

The search unemployment approach is frequently used to show why the 'natural' rate of unemployment is not zero, and in some ways is merely a sophisticated version of frictional unemployment. It does not, as it stands, tell us anything directly about the average length of unemployment, since that would depend on the sampling rules, how the reservation wage is set and the distribution of wage offers. However, the implication of this approach is that the duration of unemployment is relatively short, and that unemployment is concentrated on certain groups or regions only to the extent that people in those groups or regions have a 'taste' for unemployment or searching. It also indicates that changes in costs (to the individual) of unemployment lead to changes in the amount of unemployment, as the individual exercises choice of being unemployed or employed in the light of the relative costs and benefits. This has led particularly to the suggestion that changes in the average level of unemployment parallel changes in the 'natural' rate of unemployment, which has been caused by changes in unemployment benefits and the level of public assistance.[13]

The alternative approach developed in Chapters 5 and 6 stressed the role of unemployment in restraining wage claims. It emphasised that unemployment would tend to a level which ensured consistency between the claims of labour and the claims of capital, and, in general, that the level of employment is not expected to be that of full employment. Some of the unemployed may be involved in search unemployment in the sense that they are looking for higher wage offers rather than searching for jobs, but this is expected to be a relatively minor part of total unemployment.

It would be consistent with the Kaleckian approach to argue that oligopolistic competition generates conditions of 'unequal development'.[14] Regions and areas which are relatively prosperous and dynamic attract new firms through the expansion of local demand, lowering of costs through economies of agglomeration, availability of finance generated by local savings, etc. The reverse picture would apply in the relatively unprosperous regions and areas. The prosperous areas would offer relatively high levels of employment and earnings while the less prosperous would suffer low levels of employment and earnings. It would also be consistent with the Kaleckian approach to postulate that the concept of the 'dual labour market' had some validity.[15] Space limitations precludes further elaboration except to make the important point that in the Kaleckian approach the level and the distribution of unemployment are largely determined by the operation of the economic system, and do not result from the choice by workers between unemployment and employment in any meaningful sense.

Arising out of the search unemployment approach is the dynamic view that the unemployed are not a constant population but one constantly changing with substantial inflows and outflows into the unemployed pool. Then 'the proponents of the dynamic view interpret a large part of unemployment as an indication of "normal turnover" as people search for new jobs' (Clark and Summers, 1979). Figures indicating an average duration of unemployment of six to eight weeks have been cited in support of this dynamic view. However such figures relate to the average completed duration of all spells of unemployment over a given period (Akerloff and Main, 1980), and the use of other concepts of average duration of unemployment give different impressions. Essentially each of these concepts relates to a weighted or unweighted average of a particular population, and the choice of concept effects substantially the order of magnitude of the figures produced.[16] Akerloff and Main (1980) compare a figure of 7.2 weeks for the United States in 1977 for the average completed duration of all spells of unemployment over a given period, with 13.1 weeks as the average duration of interrupted spells of unemployment (i.e. length of unemployment to date) of those currently unemployed. Further, on a comparable basis Aker-loff (1979) indicates that the average duration of completed spells of those currently unemployed is 28.6 weeks.

For Britain, the average duration of interrupted spells of unemployment has gradually risen since the mid-'sixties and has been over 16 weeks for men and 10 weeks for women since 1976 (Knight, 1981). Main (1981) uses a weighted average unemployment spell where the spells of unemployment are weighted by the eventual length of unemployment. Such a weighted average figure of x weeks indicates that the 'average' or typical week of unemployment is experienced by someone who will be unemployed for x weeks. On this weighted average basis, Main gives figures of 50 to 60 weeks for males in the UK in the early 'sixties rising to 80 weeks in the late 'seventies.

Unemployment as officially recorded can end either in withdrawal from the labour force or in finding work. Clark and Summers (1979) indicate that in the United States, in 1974, the mean duration of unemployment was 1.91 months, but when those withdrawing from the labour force were excluded the mean duration rises to over 4 months.

A person who has been unemployed faces a higher probability of unemployment than someone who has not been unemployed. This means that average duration of a single spell of unemployment is a misleading guide to how much unemployment an individual suffers in, say, a year; and that unemployment is more concentrated than an analysis of spells of unemployment would indicate. The work of Akerloff and Main (1980).

strongly suggest that statistics on average unemployment durations of completed spells seriously underestimate the unemployment experience of all groups of persons considered . . .: persons with single spells because on average single spells are longer than multiple spells; and persons with multiple spells, because the unemployment experience of these persons includes the multiplicity of spells.

Creedy and Disney (1981) found that their

analysis of the pattern of movements over the three year period . . . showed that past experience [of unemployment] is important. In particular, those individuals who are fully employed in one year are more likely to experience some sickness or unemployment (or to leave the labour market) if they have previously experienced sickness or unemployment, than if they were previously employed.

For example, for individuals employed in 1972, the probability of being employed in 1973 was 0.83 if they had been employed in 1971, but the probability fell to 0.51 if they had been unemployed for more than 2 months in 1971.

There is also a need to look at features of the distribution of unemployment other than the mean. Disney (1979) finds, for example, in the United Kingdom for a sample of 48-year-old men that 3 per cent of the sample accounted for 80 per cent of weeks of unemployment in 1971, and for 60 per cent over the period 1971–73. Clark and Summers (1979) also find unemployment experience heavily concentrated. In 1974, those unemployed for more than 2 months accounted for 69 per cent of total unemployment experience. Over the period 1965–68, Clark and Summers report that almost 40 per cent of unemployment can be traced to persons who are out of work for a year or more. They describe their central thesis as that 'most unemployment, even in tight labour markets, is characterized by relatively few persons who are out of work for a large part of the time. We find that "normal turnover", broadly defined, can account for only a small part of measured unemployment.'

The final feature is that unemployment is not a welcomed experience. Nickell (1980) argues that 'there is little evidence to suggest that being prone to unemployment is very much a matter of personal choice. . . . Becoming unemployed is not a very pleasant experience for most people and remaining unemployed for a long period of time is even less pleasant, for reasons which are not entirely related to loss of income.' The estimates of Brenner (1976), which were used by Rowthorn and Ward (1979) in their cost-benefit analysis of steel factory closures, indicate the effects of a rise of 1 million in the numbers of unemployed over a five-year period to include 50,000 more deaths, 60,000 additional cases of mental illness and 14,000 more people receiving prison sentences. Whilst not all of those effects would fall on the unemployed, a substantial proportion could be expected to.[17]

Savings propensities
In this section we first look at corporate savings and then at personal savings. Some relevant figures for British corporations operating in manufacturing, distribution and service industries are given in Table 7.1. It can easily be seen that the proportion of gross post-tax profits which is retained by corporations has exceeded 60 per cent in

Table 7.1: Savings and sources of funds for UK corporations

	1969	1970	1971	1972	1973	1974	1975	1976	1977
Savings ratio[1]	64.9	62.9	68.8	81.6	83.1	81.0	83.5	86.3	n.a.
Sources of funds[2]									
Issue of shares	4.1	1.4	3.5	3.0	0.4	0.9	8.8	6.3	4.5
Issue of loan capital	4.6	5.7	13.2	4.7	5.5	1.0	4.1	3.0	5.1
Increase in amount owing to bank	12.5	12.9	-3.7	5.3	13.9	19.1	-1.1	9.0	6.1
Increase in short-term loans	—	7.3	1.4	2.9	2.5	3.9	2.8	0.6	0.6
Increase in trade and other creditors	27.0	23.4	4.5	17.9	30.7	27.8	23.7	25.7	17.6
Retained earnings	44.8	41.5	73.1	62.0	44.4	45.6	59.3	52.5	63.8
Other	7.0	7.9	8.0	4.0	2.7	1.6	2.4	3.0	2.2

Source: Calculated from *Business Monitor*.
Notes: (1) Retained earnings as a percentage of gross post-tax profits minus interest payments.
(2) Percentages of total use of funds minus dividends, interest payments and taxation and minus expenditure on acquiring subsidiaries financed by share issue. This equals expenditure on fixed assets, current assets and on acquiring subsidiaries financed by cash.

every year since 1969, and 80 per cent in recent years. These gross savings (retained earnings) finance replacement investment and stock appreciation as well as net investment. The major, but not dominating, role of retained earnings in the finance of corporations is also illustrated in this table. However, that role may be overstated by these figures in that retained earnings include depreciation provision, and investment is measured gross rather than net of depreciation. Using figures given for industrial and commercial companies in the UK, national income statistics reveals that, for example, retained earnings minus capital consumption as a proportion of net investment are usually less than ten percentage points below retained earnings as a proportion of gross investment.[18]

There are few studies on personal savings out of different types of income, and the types of income which are identified vary among the studies. Further, statistics on savings by source of income are not directly available, and the method adopted has basically been to regress aggregate personal savings on income from different sources, e.g. $S_t = a + bW_t + cP_t$, where S is savings at time t, W wages and P distributed profits.

Burmeister and Taubman (1969) conclude, for Canadian data, that 'we have found S_w [propensity to save out of labour income] is less than S_r [propensity to save out of non-labour income] even if only personal savings is considered. The difference is not significant in any one equation, but the difference persists in all forms. If allowance is made for corporate savings, S_r will become larger.' In particular, they tested to see whether recipients of non-labour income compensated for higher corporate savings by making lower personal savings, and found that if anything the reverse was true.

Taylor (1971) reported a propensity to save out of labour income which was above that out of property income. But, as is often the case, the standard error on the savings propensity out of property income was large relative to the coefficient, and the difference in the savings propensities was not statistically significant.[19] There were some rather odd features of Taylor's results, such as high savings propensities out of labour income (0.499 in one equation); and very high propensities out of transfer income (0.893 in one equation). Finally, property income included the imputed rent from owner occupation, which is also added to consumption, so that for a substantial proportion of property income, a propensity to consume of unity is built into the statistics, and the propensity to save out of property income is thereby lowered.

Arestis and Driver (1980), using British data, work with consumer expenditure rather than savings. The propensity to consume out of wages and salaries is generally found to be somewhat above the propensity to consume from self-employment and unearned income. Murfin (1980) finds a much more substantial difference between propensity to consume out of wage income compared with that out of non-wage income. He reports short-run propensities to consume of 0.287 and 0.078 respectively, and long-run propensities of 0.837 and 0.228.

We would conclude, albeit tentatively in view of the sparse evidence, that the propensity to save out of wage income is less than the overall propensity to save out of non-wage income (when personal and corporate savings are considered).

Conclusion

A full consideration of the evidence on macro-economic relationships would take us far and wide. In this chapter, we have sought merely to establish the case that there is a substantial body of evidence which is favourable to the Kaleckian approach and which provides sufficient reason for further work within that broad approach. Although, because of the dominance of the Keynesian-monetarist orthodoxy little directly relevant empirical work has been undertaken on some parts of the Kaleckian approach, nevertheless there is significant support for it.

Notes

1 Horsman (1979) and Parkin (1977) argue that the evidence produced by Henry, Sawyer and Smith (1976) in favour of the target real wage equation quoted in the text is also evidence in favour of the excess demand approach. Horsman argued that the statistical insignificance of unemployment in the expectations-augmented Phillips' curves estimated by Henry, Sawyer and Smith (1976) and the negative relationship between $\dot{w}$ and w/p indicates that unemployment is a poor measure of excess demand, and that excess demand is a negative function of the real wage. It can be noted that Sargan (1964) derived an equation similar to that given in the text from both a collective bargaining approach and an excess demand approach.

2 Kahn (1980) argues that an equation of the form $\dot{w} = f(U) + b\dot{p}^e$ can be derived from a collective bargaining and an excess demand approach, but different prediction concerning cyclical movements in the real wage can be derived. On this basis, for American data, he concludes in favour of the collective bargaining approach. Henry (1981) puts forward a similar argument (pp.30–1) and concludes on the basis of British data

that 'the argument that the real wage effect merely echoes an excess supply mechanism at work in determining wage inflation, . . . is simply not supported by the evidence of the time-series behaviour of unemployment and real wages.'

3 Indeed it can be argued that a rise in unemployment may quicken the pace of wage inflation. If the rise in unemployment is paralleled by falls in overtime worked, average production levels, then actual earnings fall, which tends to push up wage inflation. There may be other associated changes, e.g. if the rise in unemployment has been generated by a tax increase, then real post-tax wages will tend to fall.

4 In the table of Artis and Miller there are five equations reported which include the lagged real wage term, all of which have a negative coefficient, of which four are statistically significant.

5 Artis and Miller also conclude that

It is apparent in other ways also that estimates of the real wage hypothesis are as yet unsatisfactory. The approach probably requires modelling the process of generating the real wage target in more sophisticated ways, more decisive tests of the relative significance of taxes and prices, and some attempt to assess the importance of the 'social wage' as a potentially offsetting factor.

6 A study by Walker reported by Routh (1980), pp.210–11 comes to a similar conclusion.

7 Note the statement by Laidler and Parkin (1975) that 'the United States literature abounds with arbitrarily mis-specified price equations in which *levels* of prices rather than rate of change of prices are regressed on the level of excess demand.' This statement may be correct that many price equations are mis-specified, but not for the reasons given. First, note that the level of output or demand rather than the level of excess demand is often used. Second, price-making models postulate that price level (relative to costs) is related to the level of demand (p.98 above).

8 See, for example, Devine *et al.* (1979), Chapter 6; Hay and Morris (1979), Chapter 4; Hague (1971); Silberston (1970).

9 The profit-maximisation approach is often contrasted with the full-cost pricing model. Parkin (1977, p.351) argued that empirical 'work in Britain and North America had not favoured the mark-up hypothesis. The evidence there suggested that factors such as demand pressures systematically entered into the determination of the mark-up.' For a direct test of the excess demand approach *see* Sawyer (1982c).

10 Note the extraordinary explanation offered by Laidler and Parkin (1975). 'Also relevant to the interpretation of all empirical work on price determination is the fact that actual unit cost changes fall during booms and rise in recessions. . . . There is a fundamental difficulty here in identifying the separate effects of actual cost changes, "normal" cost changes and excess demand.' We take the first sentence to mean that actual unit costs decline with output. That can only be reconciled with perfect competition (and hence the excess demand approach) if the range of output over which firms operate combines declining average costs with constant or increasing marginal costs. For with declining

marginal costs perfect competition with price=marginal cost is unstable.

11 For surveys on search unemployment see Lippman and McCall (1976) and Hey (1979), Chapters 13, 14 and 26.

12 The reaction of some to unemployment was described in the following terms:

first there is shock, which is followed by an active hunt for a job, during which the individual is still optimistic and unresigned; he still maintains an unbroken attitude. Second, when all efforts fail, the individual becomes pessimistic, anxious and suffers active distress; this is the most crucial state of all. And, third, the individual becomes fatalistic and adapts himself to his new state but with a narrower scope. He now has a broken attitude (Eisenberg and Lazarsfeld, 1938, quoted in Sinfield, 1981a).

13 For proponents of the view that higher unemployment benefits have generated higher levels of unemployment see, for example, Maki and Spindler (1975); Grubel and Maki (1976); and Grubel and Walker (1978). Authors who think that any effect of unemployment benefits is small or negligible include Atkinson (1981); Nickell (1979); Sawyer (1979b), (1981c).

14 See, for example, Myrdal (1957); Seers and Vaitsos (1980); Holland (1976); Kaldor (1978).

15 See, for example, Bosanquet and Doeringer (1973).

16 For further discussion on the relationship between different measures of average length of unemployment spells see Akerloff (1979), Akerloff and Main (1980).

17 See Knight (1981) for details of the duration of unemployment and composition of the unemployed in the United Kingdom. See, for example, Hill (1978); Metcalf and Nickell (1978); and Sinfield (1981b) for further discussion of unemployment in UK.

18 The source is National Income Accounts Tables 5.4 and 5.6. Calculations were made for the period 1970–79. In three of those years retained earnings were larger than gross investment (including increase in stocks and work-in-progress) and companies were net acquirers of financial assets.

19 For example, a coefficient for savings propensity out of property income of 0.277 with a standard error of 0.322.

8 Concluding Remarks

The main thrust of this book has been a comparison on a theoretical plane of the Keynesian, monetarist and Kaleckian approaches to macro-economics. The argument in the previous chapter was that the Kaleckian approach is more in tune with empirical evidence than the Keynesian and monetarist approaches, particularly over central issues such as the nature of unemployment and the causes of inflation. Indeed it can be argued that many features of the Kaleckian approach, such as cost-based pricing, differential savings out of wages and profits, the accelerator component of investment, are well-established parts of many macro-econometric models of the economy.[1,2] This highlights a curious contrast between the theoretical macro-economic models (such as those discussed in Chapter 3 and more sophisticated ones in the same mould), which underlie much policy discussion and the macro-econometric models which are designed mainly for forecasting and policy simulation purposes. The equations entered into macro-econometric models are often chosen on the basis of statistical criteria from a selection of possible equations, and there may not be a coherence between the various equations entering the overall model. For example, some equations in the model may rely on one type of economic behaviour whilst others may be drawn from another type. On other occasions a list of possible variables which have been postulated as influencing the variable of interest is drawn up, even though a variety of theories is drawn up. Econometric estimation is then undertaken to determine which variables on the list are indeed empirically relevant.[3] We have sought to provide an analysis which accords with significant aspects of the real world in its assumptions, which provides predictions which are consistent with the evidence, and at the same time provides a coherent and internally consistent approach to macro-economics. The central notion is that the modern capitalist economy is oligopolistic and that macro-economic theory must take this fact on board. Thus an industry is typically dominated by a few firms, and at the economy level a significant proportion of decisions on investment, pricing, etc. is in the hands of relatively few firms and within those firms decisions are in the hands of a small number of individuals.[4] Further, the pursuit of profits is a major objective of firms, which feeds into explanations of pricing behaviour, investment and savings as well as the relations between firms and government. The labour market is characterised by collective bargaining and attempts by workers to defend and increase their real wages. The pursuit of profits by firms and of real wages by workers is the central conflict in the economy. This central conflict can be 'resolved' by levels of output and unemployment which lead to the profit and real wage demands being compatible.[5]

An upsurge in the demands for profits or wages (or equivalently a deterioration in opportunities for wages or profits) will, in the first instance, appear as an upswing in inflation. After that initial rise, the higher rate of inflation may increase as wages and prices respond to each other. The ultimate pace of inflation will depend on the response of government and the banking system in terms of expansion of aggregate demand and the money supply.

Within the Kaleckian approach, unemployment of significant proportions becomes the norm rather than the exception. This arises from a number of considerations. First, unemployment serves to damp down the real wage claims of workers, whilst excess capacity serves to hold down profits so that the central conflict referred to above is 'resolved'. The unemployment and excess capacity 'needed' for this purpose may be substantial. Second, there may be a tendency towards a lack of effective demand (sufficient to maintain full employment) when investment expenditure falls short of full employment savings. Third, in a cyclical economy full employment occurs, at most, at the top of the trade cycle, leaving significant unemployment for the other times.

It is often said that there were two major advances in economic theory during the 'thirties, which were the theories on imperfect competition (Chamberlin, 1933; Robinson, 1933) and the principle of effective demand (Keynes, 1936). The theories of imperfect competition indicated reasons why individual firms would usually operate with excess capacity, whilst Keynes addressed himself directly to the causes of unemployment and excess capacity. In general, there has been little attempt to integrate these two advances. Indeed the broad trends within economic theory appear to have been to try to forget both concepts. The work of Kalecki (1971) involved an economy of imperfect competition (of the oligopoly variety) and the principle of effective demand from the outset.[6] We have sought to argue in this book that an approach to macro-economics which starts from the insights of Kalecki offers a more adequate macro-economics than that offered by the Keynesians and monetarists.

Notes

1 A leading American macro-econometric model builder, Klein, acknowledged the influence of Kalecki's ideas on such models when he wrote 'whilst it should not be said that all the basic ingredients of modern econometric systems stemmed from Kalecki's model, it can be said that all the components of Kalecki's model are finding their way into strategic places in modern econometric models. His theories of the early 1930's are seen to be intellectual *tours de force* in the light of modern developments' (Klein, 1964).

2 For summaries of UK econometric models see Ormerod (1979); Laury *et al.* (1978); Cuthbertson (1979).

3 I have argued elsewhere (Sawyer, 1982b) that a similar and inconsistent approach to econometric estimation has been followed in industrial economics.

4 For example, in 1977 the largest 100 private firms accounted for 42 per cent of net output, 46 per cent of sales and 49 per cent of capital expenditure in the UK private enterprise manufacturing sector. Within those largest firms, crucial decisions over investment, location, etc. are likely to be in the hands of relatively few directors.

5 In a broader political context the 'resolution' of this conflict may be attempted by shifting power from one side to the other. On the right of politics this would involve breaking the power of trade unions, whilst on the left this would be attempted through reduction of the power of large firms (particularly multinational firms) and the enhancement of the power of workers (e.g. through extension of industrial democracy).

6 We would argue that the resurgence of monetarism, particularly on the theoretical plane, and the conclusion of the 'impossibility' of unemployment owed much to the reliance of Keynesians on the perfect competition model. Within that model, a lack of effective demand leads to unemployment only whilst prices fail to adjust. This price inflexibility seems a thin reed on which to rest the explanation of unemployment, particularly a long period of unemployment as experienced in the inter-war period. 'It is difficult to conceive how production in general can be limited by demand with unutilised capacity at the disposal of the representative firm as well as unemployed labour—unless conditions of some kind of oligopoly prevails' (Kaldor, 1978, p.xxi, fn. 1).

Bibliography

Aaronovitch, S. and Sawyer, M. (1975), *Big Business* (Macmillan, 1975).

Aaronovitch, S. and Smith, R. (with Gardiner, J. and Moore, R.) (1981), *The Political Economy of British Capitalism* (McGraw-Hill, 1981).

Akerloff, G. (1979), 'The Case against Conservative Macro-Economics: An Inaugural Lecture', *Economica*, Vol. 46.

Akerloff, G. A. and Main, B. G. M. (1980), 'Unemployment Spells and Unemployment Experience', *American Economic Review*, Vol. 70.

Ando, A. and Modigliani, F. (1963), 'The Life Cycle Hypothesis of Saving: Aggregate Implications and Tests', *American Economic Review*, Vol. 53.

Ando, A. and Modigliani, F. (1965), 'The Relative Stability of Monetary Velocity and the Investment Multiplier', *American Economic Review*, Vol. 55.

Arestis, P. and Driver, C. (1980), 'Consumption out of Different Types of Income in the UK', *Bulletin of Economic Research*, Vol. 32.

Arrow, K. (1959), 'Towards a Theory of Price Adjustment' in Abramovitz, M. (ed.), *The Allocation of Economic Resources* (Stanford University Press, 1959).

Artis, M. and Miller, M. (1979), 'Inflation, Real Wages and the Terms of Trade' in Bowers, J. K. (ed.), *Inflation, Development and Integration —Essays in Honour of A. J. Brown* (Leeds University Press, Leeds, 1979).

Artis, M. and Nobay, A. (eds.) (1978), *Studies in Contemporary Economic Analysis, Vol. 1* (Croom Helm, 1978).

Asimakopulos, A. (1975), 'A Kaleckian Theory of Income Distribution', *Canadian Journal of Economics*, Vol. 8.

Asimakopulos, A. (1977), 'Profits and Investment: A Kaleckian Approach' in G. C. Harcourt (ed.), *The Micro-Economic Foundations of Macro-Economics* (Macmillan, 1977).

Atkinson, A. B. (1975), *The Economics of Inequality* (Oxford University Press, 1975).

Atkinson, A. B. (1981), 'Unemployment Benefits and Incentives' in J. Creedy, (ed.), *The Economics of Unemployment in Britain* (Butterworth, 1981).

Austin, M. (1979), 'Investment' in D. Gowland (ed.), *Modern Economic Analysis* (Butterworth, 1979).

Bain, G. S. and Price, R. (1980), *Profiles of Union Growth* (Basil Black-well, 1980).

Bain, J. S. (1956), *Barriers to New Competition* (Harvard University Press, 1956).

Baran, P. and Sweezy, P. (1967), *Monopoly Capital* (Penguin, Harmonds-worth, 1967).

Barro, R. (1974), 'Are Government Bonds Net Worth?', *Journal of Political Economy*, Vol. 82.

Barro, R. and Grossman, H. (1971), 'A General Disequilibrium Model of Income and Employment', *American Economic Review*, Vol. 61.

Barro, R. and Grossman, H. (1976), *Money, Employment and Inflation* (Cambridge University Press, 1976).

Baumol, W. J. (1952), 'The Transactions Demand for Cash: An Inventory Theoretic Approach', *Quarterly Journal of Economics*, Vol. 66.

Baumol, W. J. (1959), *Business Behaviour, Value and Growth* (Macmillan, 1959).

Blinder, A. and Solow, R. (1973), 'Does Fiscal Policy Matter?', *Journal of Public Economics*, Vol. 2.

Bodkin, R. G. (1969), 'Real Wages and Cyclical Variation in Employment: A Re-examination of the Evidence', *Canadian Journal of Economics*, Vol. 2.

Bosanquet, N. and Doeringer, P. B. (1973), 'Is there a Dual Labour Market in Great Britain?', *Economic Journal*, Vol. 83.

Branson, W. H. (1979), *Macro-Economic Theory and Policy* (Harper and Row, 1979).

Brenner, H. (1976), 'Estimating the Social Costs of National Economic Policy', *Achieving the Goals of the Employment Act, 1946, Vol. 1, Paper 5* (US Congress Joint Economic Committee).

Buiter, W. H. (1980), 'The Macro-Economics of Dr. Pangloss: A Critical Survey of the New Classical Macro-Economics', *Economic Journal*, Vol. 90.

Burkitt, B. and Bowers, D. (1979), *Trade Unions and the Economy* (Macmillan, 1979).

Burmeister, E. and Taubman, P. (1969), 'Labour and Non-Labour Income Saving Propensities', *Canadian Journal of Economics*, Vol. 2.

Burrows, P. (1979), 'The Government Budget Constraint and the Mon-etarist–Keynesian Debate' in S. T. Cook and P. M. Jackson (eds.), *Current Issues in Fiscal Policy* (Martin Robertson, 1979).

Chamberlin, E. H. (1933), *The Theory of Monopolistic Competition* (Har-vard University Press, 1933).

Chick, V. (1973), 'Financial Counterparts of Savings and Investment and Inconsistency in Some Simple Macro Models', *Welfwirtschaftliches Archiv*, Vol. 109.

Chick, V. (1978), 'The Nature of the Keynesian Revolution: A Reassess-ment', *Australian Economic Papers*, Vol. 17.

Clark, R. and Summers, L. (1979), 'Labor Market Dynamics and Unem-ployment: A Reconsideration', *Brookings Papers on Economic Activity*, Vol. 10.

Clower, R. W. (1965), 'The Keynesian Counter-Revolution: A Theoretical

Appraisal' in Hahn and Brechling (1965) (partially reprinted in Clower, 1969).

Clower, R. W. (ed.) (1969), *Monetary Theory* (Penguin, Harmondsworth, 1969).

Committee to Review the Functioning of Financial Institutions (1980), *Report* (HMSO, Cmnd. 7937).

Corry, B. A. and Laidler, D. E. W. (1967), 'The Phillips Relation: A Theoretical Explanation', *Economica*, Vol. 34.

Coutts, K., Godley, W. and Nordhaus, W. (1978), *Industrial Pricing in the United Kingdom* (Cambridge University Press, 1978).

Cowling, K. (1981), 'Oligopoly, Distribution and the Rate of Profit', *European Economic Review*, Vol. 15.

Cowling, K. (1982), *Monopoly Capitalism* (Macmillan, 1981).

Cowling, K. and Waterson, M. (1976), 'Price Cost Margins and Industrial Structure', *Economica*, Vol. 43.

Creedy, J. and Disney, R. (1981), 'Changes in Labour Market States in Great Britain', *Scottish Journal of Political Economy*, Vol. 28.

Cripps, F. and Godley, W. (1976), 'A Formal Analysis of the Cambridge Economic Policy Group Model', *Economica*, Vol. 43.

Currie, D. (1978), 'Macro-Economic Policy and Government Financing: A Survey of Recent Developments' in Artis and Nobay (1978).

Currie, D. and Smith, R. (1981), *Socialist Economic Review, Vol. 1* (Merlin Press, 1981).

Cuthbertson, K. (1979), *Macro-Economic Policy* (Macmillan, 1979).

Daniel, W. W. (1976), *Wage Determination in Industry*, P. E. P. Broadsheet, No. 563.

Davidson, J. E. H., Hendry, D. F., Srba, F. and Yeo, S. (1978), 'Econometric Modelling of the Aggregate Time-Series Relationship between Consumers' Expenditure and Income in the United Kingdom', *Economic Journal*, Vol. 88.

Davidson, P. (1965), 'Keynes' Finance Motive', *Oxford Economic Papers*, Vol. 17.

Davidson, P. (1978), *Money and the Real World* (Macmillan, 1978).

Deacon, A. (1981), 'Unemployment and Policies in Britain since 1945' in Showler and Sinfield (1981).

de Cecco, M. (1977), 'The Last of the Romans' in Skidelsky (1977).

DePrano, M. and Mayer, T. (1965), 'Tests of the Relative Importance of Autonomous Expenditure and Money', *American Economic Review*, Vol. 55.

Desai, M. (1975), 'The Phillips Curve: A Revisionist Interpretation', *Economica*, Vol. 42.

Devine, P., Lee, N., Jones, R. and Tyson, W. (1979), *An Introduction to Industrial Economics*, Third Edition (Allen and Unwin, 1979).

Dillard, D. (1948), *The Economics of John Maynard Keynes: The Theory of a Monetary Economy*, (Crosby Lockwood, 1948).

Disney, R. (1979), 'Recurrent Spells and the Concentration of Unemployment in Great Britain', *Economic Journal*, Vol. 89.

Dornbusch, R. and Fischer, S. (1981), *Macro-Economics*, Second Edition (MacGraw-Hill, 1981).

Drazen, A. (1980), 'Recent Developments in Macro-Economic Disequilibrium Theory', *Econometrica*, Vol. 48.

Eichner, A. A. (ed.) (1979), *A Guide to Post-Keynesian Economics* (Macmillan, 1979).

Eichner, A. S. and Kregel, J. A. (1976), 'An Essay on Post-Keynesian Theory: A New Paradigm in Economics', *Journal of Economic Literature*, Vol. 13.

Eisenberg, P. and Lazarsfeld, P. (1938), 'The Psychological Effects of Unemployment', *Psychological Bulletin*, Vol. 35.

Eisner, R. and Nadiri, M. I. (1968), 'Investment Behaviour and Neo-Classical Theory', *Review of Economics and Statistics*, Vol. 50 (reprinted in Helliwell, 1976).

Eltis, W. (1976), 'The Failure of the Keynesian Conventional Wisdom', *Lloyds Bank Review*, No. 122.

Eshag, F. (1977), 'Kalecki's Political Economy: A Comparison with Keynes', *Oxford Bulletin of Economics and Statistics*, Vol. 39.

Fallick, J. L. and Elliot, R. F. (eds.) (1981), *Incomes Policy, Inflation and Relative Pay* (Allen and Unwin, 1981).

Feige, E. L. and Pearce, D. K. (1977), 'The Substitutability of Money and Near-Moneys: A Survey of the Time-Series Evidence', *Journal of Economic Literature*, Vol. 15.

Feiwell, G. (1975), *The Intellectual Capital of Michal Kalecki* (University of Tennessee Press, 1975).

Ferber, R. (ed.) (1967), *Determinants of Investment Behaviour* (National Bureau of Economic Research, New York, 1967).

Ferguson, C. E. (1969), *The Neo-Classical Theory of Production and Distribution* (Cambridge University Press, 1969).

Fiegehen, G., Lansley, P. S. and Smith, A. D. (1977), *Poverty and Progress in Britain, 1953–73* (Cambridge University Press, 1977).

Friedman, M. (1953), *Essays in Positive Economics* (University of Chicago Press, 1953).

Friedman, M. (1956), 'The Quantity Theory of Money—A Restatement' in M. Friedman (ed.), *Studies in the Quantity Theory of Money* (University of Chicago Press, 1956).

Friedman, M. (1957), *A Theory of the Consumption Function* (Princeton University Press, Princeton, New Jersey, 1957).

Friedman, M. (1968), 'The Role of Monetary Policy', *American Economic Review*, Vol. 58.

Friedman, M. (1969), *The Optimum Quantity of Money and Other Essays* (Aldine, Chicago, 1969).

Friedman, M. (1974), 'A Theoretical Framework for Monetary Analysis', in Gordon (1974).

Friedman, M. and Meiselman, D. (1963), 'The Relative Stability of Monetary Velocity and Investment Multiplier in the US 1897–1958', in *Stabilization Policies* (Commission on Money and Credit, Washington, D.C., 1964).

Friedman, M. and Schwartz, A. J. (1963), *A Monetary History of the United States, 1867–1960* (National Bureau of Economic Research, Princeton University Press, Princeton, New Jersey, 1963).

Garegnani, P. (1970), 'Heterogenous Capital, the Production Function and the Theory of Distribution', *Review of Economic Studies*, Vol. 37.

Garegnani, P. (1978), 'Notes on Consumption, Investment and Effective Demand: I', *Cambridge Journal of Economics*, Vol. 2.

George, V. (1973), *Social Security and Society* (Routledge and Kegan Paul, 1973).

Gilbert, B. (1966), *The Evolution of National Insurance in Great Britain* (Michael Joseph, 1966).

Godfrey, L. and Taylor, J. (1973), 'Earnings Changes in the U.K., 1954–70: Excess Labour Supply, Expected Inflation and Union Influence', *Bulletin of The Oxford University Institute of Economics and Statistics*, Vol. 35.

Goodhart, C. A. E. (1975), *Money, Information and Uncertainty* (Macmillan, 1975).

Gordon, R. J. (ed.) (1974), *Milton Friedman's Monetary Framework* (University of Chicago Press, Chicago, 1974) (revised version of papers first published in *Journal of Political Economy, Vol. 80*).

Gordon, R. J. (1976), 'Recent Developments in the Theory of Inflation and Unemployment', *Journal of Monetary Economics*, Vol. 2 (reprinted in Korliras and Thorn, 1979).

Gordon, R. J. (1981), *Macro-Economics*, Second Edition (Little, Brown and Company, Boston, 1981).

Gough, I. (1979), *The Political Economy of the Welfare State* (Macmillan, 1979).

Green, F. (1979), 'The Consumption Function: A Study of a Failure in Positive Economics' in Green and Nore (1979).

Green, F. (1981), 'The Effect of Occupational Pension Schemes on Saving in the United Kingdom: A Test of the Life Cycle Hypothesis', *Economic Journal*, Vol. 91.

Green, F. and Nore, P. (eds.) (1979), *Issues in Political Economy: A Critical Approach* (Macmillan, 1979).

Grossman, H. I. (1972), 'A Choice-Theoretic Model of an Income-Investment Accelerator', *American Economic Review*, Vol. 62.

Grubel, H. G. and Walker, M. A. (eds.) (1978), *Unemployment and Insurance: Global Evidence of its Effects on Unemployment* (Fraser Institute, Vancouver, 1978).

Grubel, H. G. and Walker, M. A. (1978), *Unemployment and Insurance: Global Evidence of its Effects on Unemployment* (Fraser Institute, Vancouver, 1978).

Hague, D. C. (1971), *Pricing in Business* (Allen and Unwin, 1971).

Hahn, F. (1971), 'Professor Friedman's View on Money', *Economica*, Vol. 38.

Hahn, F. (1978), 'On Non-Walrasian Equilibria', *Review of Economic Studies*, Vol. 45.

Hahn, F. (1980), 'Monetarism and Economic Theory', *Economica*, Vol. 47.

Hahn, F. and Brechling, F. (eds.) (1965), *The Theory of Interest Rates* (Macmillan, 1965).

Hannah, L. and Kay, J. (1977), *Concentration in Modern Industry: Theory Measurement and the UK Experience* (Macmillan, 1977).

Hansen, A. H. (1953), *A Guide to Keynes* (McGraw-Hill, 1953).

Harcourt, G. C. (1975), 'The Cambridge Controversies: The Afterglow' in Parkin and Nobay, 1975).

Hart, P. E. and Clarke, R. (1980), *Concentration in British Industry, 1935–1975* (Cambridge University Press, 1980).

Hart, P. E., Mill, G. and Whittaker, J. K. (eds.) (1964), *Econometric Analysis for National Economic Planning* (Butterworth, 1964).

Hay, D. and Morris, D. (1979), *Industrial Economics* (Oxford University Press, 1979).

Helliwell, J. F. (ed.) (1976), *Aggregate Investment* (Penguin, 1976).

Henry, S. G. B. (1981), 'Incomes Policy and Aggregate Pay' in Fallick and Elliott (1981).

Henry, S. G. B. and Ormerod, P. (1978), 'Incomes Policy and Wage Inflation 1961–77', *National Institute Economic Review*, No. 85.

Henry, S. G. B., Sawyer, M. and Smith, P. (1976), 'Models of Inflation in the United Kingdom: An Evaluation', *National Institute Economic Review*, No. 77.

Hey, J. D. (1979), *Uncertainty in Micro-Economics* (Martin Robertson, 1979).

Hicks, J. (1975), 'What is Wrong with Monetarism', *Lloyds Bank Review*, No. 118.

Hill, M. J. (1978), Evidence in Royal Commission on the Distribution of Income and Wealth (1978).

Hillier, B. (1977), 'Does Fiscal Policy Matter? The View from the Government Budget Restraint', *Public Finance*, Vol. 32.

Himmelweit, S. (1979), 'Growth and Reproduction' in Green and Nore (1979).

Hines, A. G. (1964), 'Trade Unions and Wage Inflation in the United Kingdom, 1893–1961', *Review of Economic Studies*, Vol. 31.

Hines, A. G. (1971), *On the Reappraisal of Keynesian Economics* (Martin Robertson, 1971).

Hirshleifer, J. (1958), 'On the Theory of Optimal Investment Decision', *Journal of Political Economy*, Vol. 66.

Holland, S. (1976), *Capital Versus the Regions* (Macmillan, 1976).

Holmes, J. and Smyth, D. J. (1970), 'The Relationship between Unemployment and the Excess Demand for Labour: An Examination of the Theory of the Phillips Curve', *Economica*, Vol. 37.

Horsman, A. A. (1979), 'Cripps on Wages and the Quantity Theory—A Monetarist Reply', *Cambridge Journal of Economics*, Vol. 3.

Johnson, H. G. (1973), *The Theory of Income Distribution* (Gray Mills, 1973).

Johnston, J. (1972), 'A Model of Wage Determination under Bilateral Monopoly', *Economic Journal*, Vol. 82 (reprinted in Laidler and Purdy, 1974).

Johnston, J. and Timbrell, M. C. (1974), 'Empirical Tests of a Bargaining Model of Wage Rate Determination', *Manchester School*, Vol. 42 (reprinted in Laidler and Purdy, 1974).

Jorgensen, D. W. (1967), 'The Theory of Investment Behaviour' in Ferber (1967).

Jorgensen, D. W. (1971), 'Econometric Studies of Investment Behaviour: A Survey', *Journal of Economic Literature*, Vol. 9 (reprinted in Korliras and Thorn, 1979).

Junankar, P. N. (1972), *Investment: Theories and Evidence* (Macmillan, 1972).

Kahn, L. H. (1980), 'Bargaining Power, Search Theory and the Phillips Curve', *Cambridge Journal of Economics*, Vol. 4.

Kaldor, N. (1955), 'Alternative Theories of Distribution', *Review of Economic Studies*, Vol. 23 (reprinted in Kaldor, 1960).

Kaldor, N. (1959), 'A Rejoinder to Mr. Atsumi and Professor Tobin', *Review of Economic Studies*, Vol. 27.

Kaldor, N. (1960), *Essays on Value and Distribution* (Duckworth, 1960).

Kaldor, N. (1961), 'Capital Accumulation and Economic Growth' in Lutz (1961) (reprinted in Kaldor, 1978).

Kaldor, N. (1976), 'Inflation and Recession in the World Economy', *Economic Journal*, Vol. 86 (reprinted in Kaldor, 1978).

Kaldor, N. (1978), *Further Essays on Economic Theory* (Duckworth, 1978).

Kaldor, N. and Mirrlees, J. (1962), 'A New Model of Economic Growth', *Review of Economic Studies*, Vol. 29 (reprinted in Kaldor, 1978).

Kaldor, N. and Trevitick, J. (1981), 'A Keynesian Perspective on Money', *Lloyds Bank Review*, No. 139.

Kalecki, M. (1965), *Theory of Economic Dynamics* (Allen and Unwin, 1965).

Kalecki, M. (1971), *Selected Essays on the Dynamics of the Capitalist Economy* (Cambridge University Press, 1971).

Kantor, B. (1979), 'Rational Expectations and Economic Thought', *Journal of Economic Literature*, Vol. 17.

Katouzian, H. (1980), *Ideology and Method in Economics* (Macmillan, 1980).

Keynes, J. M. (1936), *The General Theory of Employment, Interest and Money* (Macmillan, 1936).

Keynes, J. M. (1937a), 'Alternative Theories of the Rate of Interest', *Economic Journal*, Vol. 47.

Keynes, J. M. (1937b), 'The General Theory of Employment', *Quarterly Journal of Economics*, Vol. 51.

Klein, L. (1964), 'The Role of Econometrics in Socialist Economics' in *Problems of Economic Dynamics and Planning: Essays in Honour of Michal Kalecki* (PWN—Polish Scientific Publishers, Warsaw, 1964).

Klein, L. (1975), Foreword to Feiwell (1975).

Knight, K. G. (1981), 'The Composition of Unemployment' in Currie and Smith (1981).

Knight, K. G. and Wilson, R. A. (1980), 'Strike Frequency and Industrial Wage Differentials: An Econometric Study of British Production Industries', *Bulletin of Economic Research*, Vol. 32.

Knowles, K. G. and Winsten, C. B. (1959), 'Can the Level of Unemployment Explain Changes in Wages?', *Bulletin of Oxford University Institute of Economics and Statistics*, Vol. 21.

Korliras, P. G. and Thorn, R. S. (eds.) (1979), *Modern Macro-Economics* (Harper and Row, New York, 1979).

Kuh, E. (1966), 'Unemployment, Production Functions and Effective Demand', *Journal of Political Economy*, Vol. 74.

Laidler, D. E. W. (1973), 'The Influence of Money on Real Income and Inflation: A Simple Model with Some Empirical Tests for the United States, 1953–1972', *Manchester School*, Vol. 41 (reprinted in Laidler, 1975).

Laidler, D. E. W. (1975), *Essays on Money and Inflation* (Manchester University Press, Manchester, 1975).

Laidler, D. E. W. (1977), *The Demand for Money: Theories and Evidence*, Second Edition (Dun-Donnelley, New York, 1977).

Laidler, D. E. W. (1981), 'Monetarism: An Interpretation and An Assessment', *Economic Journal*, Vol. 91.

Laidler, D. E. W. and Parkin, J. M. (1975), 'Inflation: A Survey', *Economic Journal*, Vol. 85 (reprinted in Korliras and Thorn, 1979).

Laidler, D. E. W. and Purdy, D. (eds.) (1974), *Labour Markets and Inflation* (Manchester University Press, 1974).

Laury, J. S. E., Lewis, G. R. and Ormerod, P. A. (1978), 'Properties of Macro-Economic Models of the UK Economy: A Comparative Study', *National Institute Economic Review*, No. 83.

Layard, P. R. G. and Walters, A. A. (1978), *Micro-Economic Theory* (McGraw-Hill, 1978).

Leijonhufvud, A. (1968), *On Keynesian Economics and the Economics of Keynes* (Oxford University Press, 1968).

Leontief, W. (1971), 'Theoretical Assumptions and Non-observed Facts', *American Economic Review*, Vol. 61.

Levačić, R. (1976), *Macro-Economics: The Static and Dynamic Analysis of a Monetary Economy* (Macmillan, 1976).

Lippman, S. A. and McCall, J. J. (1976), 'The Economics of Job Search : A Survey', *Economic Inquiry*, Vol. 14.

Lipsey, R. (1960), 'The Relationship between Unemployment and the Rate of Change of Money Wage Rates in the UK, 1862–1957, A Further Analysis', *Economica*, Vol. 27.

Lipsey, R. (1974), 'The Micro-Theory of the Phillips Curve Reconsidered: A Reply to Holmes and Smyth', *Economica*, Vol. 41.

Lucas, R. E. (1975), 'An Equilibrium Model of the Business Cycle', *Journal of Political Economy*, Vol. 83.

Lucas, R. E. and Rapping, L. A. (1969), 'Real Wages, Employment and Inflation', *Journal of Political Economy*, Vol. 77.

Lutz, F. (ed.) (1961), *The Theory of Capital* (Macmillan, 1961).

Machlup, F. (1967), 'Theories of the Firm: Marginalist, Behavioural, Managerial', *American Economic Review*, Vol. 57.

Main, B. G. M. (1981), 'The Length of Employment and Unemployment in Great Britain', *Scottish Journal of Political Economy*, Vol. 28.

Maki, D. and Spindler, Z. A. (1975), 'The Effect of Unemployment

Compensation on the Rate of Unemployment in Great Britain', *Oxford Economic Papers*, Vol. 31.

Marx, K. (1976), *Capital: Volume 1* (Penguin, 1976).

Mayer, T. (1978), *The Structure of Monetarism* (Norton, New York, 1978).

Mayer, T. (1980), 'Economics as a Hard Science: Realistic Goal or Wishful Thinking?', *Economic Inquiry*, Vol. 18.

McCallum, B. T. (1978), 'Price Level Adjustments and the Rational Expectations Approach to Macro-Economic Stabilization Policy', *Journal of Money, Credit and Banking*, Vol. 10.

McCallum, B. T. (1980), 'The Significance of Rational Expectations Theory', *Challenge*, January/February 1980, Vol. 22.

Meade, J. E. (1972), 'The Theory of Labour-Managed Firms and of Profit-Sharing', *Economic Journal*, Vol. 82.

Metcalf, D. and Nickell, S. (1978), Evidence in Royal Commission on the Distribution of Income and Wealth (1978).

Metcalfe, J. and Peel, D. (1979), 'Inflation and Output Dynamics with a Floating Exchange Rate', *European Economic Review*, Vol. 12.

Milliband, R. (1969), *The State in Capitalist Society* (Weidenfeld and Nicolson, 1969).

Minns, R. (1980), *Pension Funds and British Capitalism* (Heinemann, 1980).

Minsky, H. (1976), *John Maynard Keynes* (Macmillan, 1976).

Mitchell, D. (1978), 'Union Wage Determination: Policy Implications and Outlook', *Brookings Papers on Economic Activity*.

Modigliani, F. (1958), 'New Developments on the Oligopoly Front', *Journal of Political Economy*, Vol. 66.

Modigliani, F. (1975), 'The Life Cycle Hypothesis of Saving Twenty Years Later' in Parkin and Nobay (1975).

Modigliani, F. (1977), 'The Monetarist Controversy or Should We forsake Stabilization Policies?', *American Economic Review*, Vol. 69 (reprinted in Korliras and Thorn, 1979).

Modigliani, F. and Brumberg, F. (1954), 'Utility Analysis and the Consumption Function: An Interpretation of Cross-Section Data' in K. Kurihara (ed.), *Post-Keynesian Economics* (Rutgers University Press, Brunswick, New Jersey, 1954).

Moggeridge, D. (ed.) (1973), *The Collected Writings of John Maynard Keynes, Vol. XIV* (Macmillan, 1973).

Moore, B. J. (1979), 'Monetary Factors' in Eichner (1979).

Morgan, B. (1978), *Monetarists and Keynesians—their Contribution to Monetary Theory* (Macmillan, 1978).

Mueller, W. F. and Hamm, L. G. (1974), 'Trends in Industrial Concentration 1947 to 1970', *Review of Economics and Statistics*, Vol. 56.

Muellbauer, J. and Portes, R. (1978), 'Macro-Economic Models with Quantity Rationing', *Economic Journal*, Vol. 88.

Murfin, A. J. (1980), 'Savings Propensities from Wage and Non-Wage Income', *Warwick Economic Research Papers*, No. 174.

Muth, J. F. (1961), 'Rational Expectations and the Theory of Price Movements', *Econometrica*, Vol. 29.

Myrdal, G. (1957), *Economic Theory and Underdeveloped Regions* (Duckworth, 1957).

Neftçi, S. N. (1978), 'A Time-Series Analysis of the Real Wages–Employment Relationship, *Journal of Political Economy*, Vol. 86.

Nickell, S. J. (1978), *The Investment Decisions of Firms* (Nisbet, Cambridge Economic Handbooks, 1978).

Nickell, S. J. (1979), 'The Effect of Unemployment and Related Benefits on the Duration of Unemployment', *Economic Journal*, Vol. 89.

Nickell, S. J. (1980), 'A Picture of Male Unemployment in Britain', *Economic Journal*, Vol. 90.

Ng, Y-K. (1979), *Welfare Economics: Introduction and Development of Basic Concepts* (Macmillan, 1979).

Ormerod, P. (ed.) (1979), *Economic Modelling, Current Issues and Problems in Macro-Economic Modelling in the UK and the US* (Heinemann, 1979).

Orr, D. (1970), *Cash Management and the Demand for Money* (Praeger, New York, 1970).

Paniç, M. (1976), 'The Inevitable Inflation', *Lloyds Bank Review*, No. 121.

Paniç, M. and Vernon, K. (1975), 'Major Factors behind Investment Decisions in British Manufacturing Industry', *Oxford Bulletin of Economics and Statistics*, Vol. 37.

Parkin, J. M. (1975), 'The Causes of Inflation: Recent Contributions and Current Controversies' in Parkin, M. and Nobay, A. (eds.), *Current Economic Problems* (Cambridge University Press, 1975).

Parkin, J. M. (1977), 'Inflation in the United Kingdom: A Comment on Godley' in L. B. Krause and W. S. Salant (eds.), *Worldwide Inflation* (Brookings Institution, Washington, D.C., 1977).

Parkin, J. M. and Nobay, A. (eds.) (1975), *Contemporary Issues in Economics* (Manchester University Press, 1975).

Parkin, J. M., Sumner, M. T. and Ward, R. (1976), 'The Effects of Excess Demand, Generalised Expectations and Wage–Price Controls on Wage Inflation in the UK', *Journal of Monetary Economics*, Vol. 2.

Pasinetti, L. L. (1974), *Growth and Income Distribution* (Cambridge University Press, 1974).

Peston, M. H. (1974), *Theory of Macro-Economic Policy* (Phillip Allan, Deddington, 1974).

Peston, M. H. (1980), *Whatever Happened to Macro-Economics* (Manchester University Press, 1980).

Phelps, E. S. (1967), 'Phillips Curves, Expectations of Inflation and Optimal Unemployment over Time', *Economica*, Vol. 34.

Phelps, E. S. (ed.) (1970), *Micro-Economic Foundations of Employment and Inflation Theory* (W. W. Norton, 1970).

Phelps Brown, E. H. (1972), 'The Underdevelopment of Economics', *Economic Journal*, Vol. 82.

Phelps Brown, E. H. (1975), 'A Non-Monetarist View of the Pay Explosion', *Three Banks Review*, No. 105.

Phillips, A. W. (1958), 'The Relations between Unemployment and the Rate of Change of Money Wage Rates in the United Kingdom, 1861–1957', *Economica*, Vol. 25.

Prais, S. J. (1976), *The Evolution of Giant Firms in Britain* (Cambridge University Press, 1976).

Purdy, D. L. and Zis, G. (1974), 'On the Concept and Measurement of Union Militancy' in Laidler and Purdy (1974).

Purvis, D. (1980), 'Monetarism—A Review', *Canadian Journal of Economics*, Vol. 13.

Rhys, V. (1962), 'The Sociology of Social Security', *Bulletin of the International Social Security Association*, Nos. 1–2, 1962.

Robinson, J. (1933), *The Economics of Imperfect Competition* (Macmillan, 1933; Second Edition 1969).

Robinson, J. (1972), 'The Second Crisis of Economic Theory', *American Economic Review*, Vol. 62.

Robinson, J. (1975), *Collected Economic Papers, Vol. 3*, Second Edition (Blackwell, 1975).

Robinson, J. (1977), 'Michal Kalecki on the Economics of Capitalism', *Oxford Bulletin of Economics and Statistics*, Vol. 39.

Routh, G. (1959), 'The Relationship between Unemployment and the Rate of Change of Money Wage Rates in the UK 1861–1957: Comment', *Economica*, Vol. 26.

Routh, G. (1975), *The Origin of Economic Ideas* (Macmillan, 1975).

Routh, G. (1980), *Occupation and Pay in Great Britain, 1906–79* (Macmillan, 1980).

Rowthorn, R. (1977), 'Conflict, Inflation and Money', *Cambridge Journal of Economics*, Vol. 1.

Rowthorn, R. and Ward, T. (1979), 'How to Run a Company and Run Down an Economy: The Effects of Closing Down Steel-Making in Corby', *Cambridge Journal of Economics*, Vol. 3.

Royal Commission on the Distribution of Income and Wealth (1978), *Selected Evidence Submitted to the Royal Commission for Report No. 6, Lower Incomes* (H.M.S.O., 1978).

Ruggles, N. (ed.) (1970), *Economics* (Prentice-Hall, Englewood Cliffs, New Jersey, 1970).

Santomero, A. M. and Seater, J. J. (1978), 'The Inflation–Unemployment Trade-Off: A Critique of the Literature', *Journal of Economic Literature*, Vol. 16.

Sargan, J. D. (1964), 'Wages and Prices in the United Kingdom' in Hart, Mills and Whittaker (1964).

Sargent, T. J. (1973), 'Rational Expectations, the Real Rate of Interest and the Natural Rate of Unemployment', *Brooking Papers on Economic Activity*, Vol. 2.

Sargent, T. J. and Wallace, N. (1976), 'Rational Expectations and the Theory of Economic Policy', *Journal of Monetary Economics*, Vol. 2.

Sawyer, M. (1976), 'Income Distribution in OECD Countries', *OECD Economic Outlook: Occasional Studies*, July 1976.

Sawyer, M. (1979a), *Theories of the Firm* (Weidenfeld and Nicholson, 1979).

Sawyer, M. (1979b), 'The Effects of Unemployment Compensation on the Rate of Unemployment in Great Britain: A Comment', *Oxford Economic Papers*, Vol. 31.

Sawyer, M. (1981a), *The Economics of Industries and Firms* (Croom Helm, 1981).

Sawyer, M. (1981b), 'The Influence of Cost and Demand Changes on the Rate of Change of Prices', *Applied Economics*, forthcoming.

Sawyer, M. (1981c), 'Incentives, Taxation, Social Security and the State of British Economy' in Currie and Smith (1981).

Sawyer, M. (1982a), 'Collective Bargaining, Oligopoly and Macro-Economics', *Oxford Economic Papers*, Vol. 34, forthcoming.

Sawyer, M. (1982b), 'On the Specification of Structure–Performance Relationships', *European Economic Review*, forthcoming.

Sawyer, M. (1982c), *Business Pricing and Inflation* (Macmillan, forthcoming).

Seers, D. and Vaitsos, C. (eds.) (1980), *Integration and Economic Development* (St. Martin's Press, New York, 1980).

Shephard, R. W. (1970), *Theory of Cost and Production Functions* (Princeton University Press, 1970).

Shepherd, W. G. (1970), *Market Power and Economic Welfare* (Random House, New York, 1970).

Sherman, H. J. (1976), *Stagnation: A Radical Theory of Unemployment and Inflation* (Harper and Row, 1976).

Sherman, H. J. (1979), 'A Marxist Theory of the Business Cycle', *Review of Radical Political Economics*, Vol. 11.

Showler, B. and Sinfield, A. (eds.) (1981), *The Workless State* (Martin Robertson, 1981).

Silbertson, A. (1970), 'Price Behaviour of Firms', *Economic Journal*, Vol. 80.

Sinfield, A. (1981a), 'Unemployment in an Unequal Society' in Showler and Sinfield (1981).

Sinfield, A. (1981b), *What Unemployment Means* (Martin Robertson, 1981).

Skidelsky, R. (ed.) (1977), *The End of the Keynesian Era* (Macmillan, 1977).

Skinner, R. C. (1970), 'The Determination of Selling Prices', *Journal of Industrial Economics*, Vol. 18.

Solow, R. (1956), 'A Contribution to the Theory of Economic Growth', *Quarterly Journal of Economics*, Vol. 70.

Spence, A. M. (1977), 'Entry, Capacity, Investment and Oligopolistic Pricing', *Bell Journal of Economics*, Vol. 8.

Stein, J. (1976), 'Inside the Monetarist Black Box' in Stein, J. (ed.), *Monetarism* (North-Holland, 1976).

Stigler, G. J. (1962), 'Information in the Labour Market', *Journal of Political Economy*, Vol. 70.

Stonebraker, R. J. (1979), 'Turnover and Mobility amongst the 100 Largest Firms: An Update', *American Economic Review*, Vol. 69.

Sweezy, P. (1939), 'Demand under Conditions of Oligopoly', *Journal of Political Economy*, Vol. 47.

Tarling, R. and Wilkinson, F. (1977), 'The Social Contract: Post-War Incomes Policies and their Inflationary Impact', *Cambridge Journal of Economics*, Vol. 1.

Taylor, J. (1970), 'Hidden Unemployment, Hoarded Labour and the Phillips Curves', *Southern Economic Journal*, Vol. 37.

Taylor, L. D. (1971), 'Savings out of Different Types of Income', *Brookings Papers on Economic Activity*, Vol. 2.

Tinbergen, J. (1952), *On the Theory of Economic Policy* (North-Holland, Amsterdam, 1952).

Tobin, J. (1956), 'The Interest–Elasticity of the Transactions Demand for Cash', *Review of Economics and Statistics*, Vol. 38.

Tobin, J. (1958), 'Liquidity Preference as Behaviour towards Risk', *Review of Economic Studies*, Vol. 25.

Tobin, J. (1959), 'Towards a General Kaldorian Theory of Distribution', *Review of Economic Studies*, Vol. 27.

Tobin, J. (1969), 'A General Equilibrium Approach to Monetary Theory', *Journal of Money, Credit and Banking*, Vol. 1 (reprinted in Tobin, 1972).

Tobin, J. (1970a), 'Macro-Economics' in Ruggles (1970).

Tobin, J. (1970b), 'Money and Income: Post Hoc Ergo Propter Hoc?', *Quarterly Journal of Economics*, Vol. 84 (reprinted in Tobin, 1972).

Tobin, J. (1972), *Essays in Economics Volume 1: Macro-Economics* (North-Holland Publishing, 1972).

Tobin, J. (1974), 'Friedman's Theoretical Framework' in Gordon (1974).

Tobin, J. (1980), 'Are New Classical Models Plausible Enough to Guide Policy?', *Journal of Money, Credit and Banking*, Vol. 12.

Trivedi, P. and Rayner, J. (1978), 'Wage Inertia and Comparison Effects in Australian Award Wage Determination', *Economic Record*, Vol. 54.

Turnovsky, S. J. (1977), *Macro-Economic Analysis and Stabilization Policies* (Cambridge University Press, 1977).

Tylecote, A. (1981), *The Causes of the Present Inflation* (Macmillan, 1981).

Vane, H. R. and Thompson, J. L. (1979), *Monetarism Theory, Evidence and Policy* (Martin Robertson, 1979).

Weisskopf, T. E. (1979), 'Marxian Crisis Theory and the Rate of Profit in the Post-War US Economy', *Cambridge Journal of Economics*, Vol. 3.

White, L. J. (1981), 'What Has Been Happening to Aggregate Concentration in the United States?', *Journal of Industrial Economics*, Vol. 29.

Winch, D. M. (1971), *Analytical Welfare Economics* (Penguin, Harmondsworth, 1971).

Wonnacott, P. (1978), *Macro-Economics* (Irwin, Homeword, Illinois, 1978).

Wood, A. (1978), *A Theory of Pay* (Cambridge University Press, 1978).

Worswick, G. D. N. (1972), 'Is Progress in Economic Science Possible?', *Economic Journal*, Vol. 82.

Index